EGO

Maybe the target nowadays is not to discover what we are but to refuse what we are.

Michel Foucault

EGO
THE GAME OF LIFE

FRANK SCHIRRMACHER
TRANSLATED BY NICK SOMERS

polity

First published in German as *Ego. Das Spiel des Lebens* © Karl Blessing Verlag, a division of Verlagsgruppe Random House GmbH, Munich, Germany, 2013

This English edition © Polity Press, 2015

Polity Press
65 Bridge Street
Cambridge CB2 1UR, UK

Polity Press
350 Main Street
Malden, MA 02148, USA

ISBN-13: 978-0-7456-8686-8

A catalogue record for this book is available from the British Library.

Library of Congress Cataloging-in-Publication Data

Schirrmacher, Frank, author.
  [Ego. English]
  Ego : the game of life / Frank Schirrmacher.
    pages cm
  First published in German as Ego : Das Spiel des Lebens, by Karl Blessing Verlag
in 2013.
  Includes bibliographical references and index.
  ISBN 978-0-7456-8686-8 (hardcover : alk. paper) -- ISBN 0-7456-8686-9
(hardcover : alk. paper) 1. Egoism. 2. Economic man. 3. Philosophical
anthropology. 4. Civilization, Modern--21st century--Psychological aspects. I. Title.
  BJ1474.S35613 2015
  128--dc23
                                                                              2015010069

Typeset in 10.75 on 14 pt Adobe Janson by
Servis Filmsetting Ltd, Stockport, Cheshire
Printed and bound in the UK by Clays Ltd, St Ives plc

For further information on Polity, visit our website:
politybooks.com

Contents

PREFACE

We have become incredibly uncomplicated, but unfortunately we ourselves don't notice it. Why do we do what we do? Why do we love what we love? These questions are so complex that we are usually incapable of answering them ourselves. Nor do we realize that other people have long answered them for us.

Forget for a moment what you know about psychology, brain research or even from your own experience about the puzzle of our existence. Unnoticed by us, economists have made the workings of the mind of the modern individual their affair.

To simplify a hyper-complex world and speed up business transactions, a model has been developed behind the scenes that is changing our lives.

According to this model, life can be made much simpler and more profitable if we assume that people are interested only in themselves and their own personal advantage. This book looks at how this originally harmless model has become a trap, and how well this trap is disguised.

All trappers camouflage their traps. In the forest they can do so with leaves and with metal clamps hidden in the earth: artefacts that are made to appear part of their natural surroundings. Among humans the traps are camouflaged as natural laws – hence the statement: 'People are selfish', genetically and morally. Supported by modern calculating machines, an economic model has turned this thesis into a natural law. And we are beginning to feel it.

Many people in today's world think that they have more liberties and freedom of choice than ever, and that they can ultimately accept or reject theories as they wish.

In reality they have not only unknowingly accepted them; they have long been living and working with them.

We are experiencing a new era of information capitalism. It has started to transform the world into a state of mind. It performs and plans great things. It seeks to read, control and sell thoughts; to predict, price and eliminate risks. Its brain is occupied relentlessly with finding out what people do, say, buy and what new moves they are planning. Wherever they encounter it, they are confronted by a system that always knows better. It deprives them of the right to conceive their surroundings differently from what they are. It claims that whatever they do is for their own advantage.

For information capitalism there is no such thing as irrational behaviour. In its eyes, friendship, loyalty and love all have rational reasons motivated by self-interest – hence the proliferation of 'incentives', rewards ranging from bonuses in Wall Street to virtual medals, awards and 'likes' conferred for the most private matters.

There are open games like chess, and hidden games like poker in which the players can't see each other's cards. The information economy is like a round of poker. Its world is one in which people don't really say and do what they think, but everyone becomes transparent when it is assumed that they are acting egotistically. Hence this huge demand for information, this compulsion to dissimulate, to bluff and to leave false clues. Finance algorithms disguise share transactions to confuse lurking predatory algorithms, or else predatory algorithms feed other economic agents at the speed of light with false information to force up prices. People adopt false identities, create Facebook profiles for their personnel head or bank. Entire states send out false signals so as to confuse markets. It is a society in which people mistrust not only one another but also themselves. It has reached the stage where people accept that their education, experience and career do not mean what they thought they did.

The prospect of obtaining answers to questions that have not yet even been asked, the claim to know more about people than they do themselves, the predictions of what people want before they know it themselves, the offer to be a 'friend', are identical in structure to secret service surveillance algorithms that recognize crimes that the perpetrators themselves are perhaps not yet even aware of. The new economy uses machines and defines human relationships with the aid of mathematics. It loves the 'prisoner's dilemma', a canonical example from game theory in which two people share the same fate but cannot communicate with one another and are offered the opportunity to gain an advantage at the expense of the other. Betrayal is not only foreseen but 'the rationally sanctioned norm'.[1]

It would appear that people who come into contact with this idea change their behaviour. A view of the world which believes that behind every human action is the inevitable logic of self-interest is predestined to produce endless egoism.[2] These days, everyone comes into contact with this world view. In an environment in which information, not only in stock exchanges but also at work, in communication and even in friendships, is organized by logical computing machines calculating according to the laws of personal profit-maximization, social values change at an astonishing speed.

Information capitalism questions people's lives and identities, harnesses the real economy for its purposes and is now in the process of rewriting constitutional and international law.

It is not only individuals who are losing their sovereignty. The sovereign rights of European states and parliaments amputated by the current euro crisis are not examples of professional malpractice but part of the operative logic of information capitalism.

It has undermined human thought with a labyrinth of tunnels and shafts and it processes the raw material it extracts on machines that – depending on the desk they sit on – can wage wars, incite revolutions, create money, control people or send the latest holiday photos. It appears to be in a position to cut off entire nations overnight or under certain circumstances to give an individual who connects into it the power of a state.

People are beginning to go underground with it in closed rooms with artificial light and to take the tunnels dug by it for their own thoughts.

A hidden trap must deceive all of the senses. In his *Encyclopédie*, Diderot recommends disguising the smell of iron, because experienced animals associate it with their destruction. A modern standard work on trapping animals describes in all innocence how this is done: 'Entice the animal into the machine, be it with a bait or through its natural curiosity.' According to Otto Mayr, it is no coincidence that for a long time the English words 'engine' and 'machine' had negative connotations of deviousness, trickery, conspiracy and even intrigue.[3] The information capitalism machine is the computer, but the device itself is innocent. It depends solely on who has it in their hands and for what purpose they use it. Once human self-interest is reduced to a formula, it can be used to calculate the behaviour of an entire society.

It was Diderot who described 'trapping' – not the trap – as a 'science'. The challenge is to capture creatures whom experience has made suspicious. They can be caught only by collecting and falsifying information. The trap must present the bait as easy prey. The bear, fox or wolf must be led to believe that it can gain an unexpected benefit. To do this, it is necessary 'to study with great care the places to where the animals withdraw during the day, the places they spend the nights, and the paths they usually follow'.

The trap is also useless without the trapper's strategy. The most successful trappers are those who think like the creature they are trapping; the most successful avoiders of traps are those who think like the trappers who wish to catch them. That is the 'science'; it is pure mathematics and can be programmed by computers: during the Cold War, when it was invented, it was called 'rational choice theory' and given the harmless-sounding name 'game theory'.

Driven psychologically by the fear that totalitarian systems like the Soviet Union disempowered people by claiming to know what was best for them, economists devised an alternative system in which individuals did only what was best for themselves. It became one of the most important strategic weapons in the Cold War, and through it the West scored a resounding victory in the superpower game.

As it turned out, however, that wasn't the end but only the beginning.

The superpower game was over, and the game could now be turned to individual societies. One of the architects of the great trap later admitted that the rules by which the new Game of Life is played need some getting used to. In order to win, you have to accept the idea that 'the universe has singled you out to be its personal enemy'.[1]

A word in conclusion about the aim of this book. It was inspired by the crisis, not by its social but rather by its economic manifestations. The crisis is just a symptom. It shows the instability not only of markets but also of societies which, like markets and people, are organized like *homo oeconomicus* – in my eyes the first case of a system failure of the information economy.

The crisis we are dealing with today is not just about money, profit, the Lehman Brothers bankruptcy or the crisis in Europe. This, if you will, is just the simple side of the question, which is most easily susceptible to analysis. Who knows, perhaps it will be resolved, and people will go about their daily business again.

The information economy evaluates feelings, trust and social contacts as well as shares or goods, and for the first time in history it has the technical wherewithal to do it with increasing degrees of perfection. It is one thing to take for granted in a business transaction or auction that your counterparts will quite naturally look out for themselves and possibly pull a fast one on you. It is something else for social life itself to become increasingly like a business transaction or auction, a world of self-promotion according to completely transparent economic rules. In this world, mistrust, insinuation, bluff, diversionary tactics, have become the norm, be it only, as is often stated, 'to reassure the market'. But they apply not only to states but to an even greater extent to individuals.

These rules are all written down somewhere. They are assumptions, auxiliary structures, models, attributing not mental but mathematical characteristics. One book starts with the quote 'Populating economic models with "flesh-and-blood human beings" was never the objective of economists', and then goes on to prove precisely the opposite.[5] The models themselves have come alive. They are no longer mere instructions to be followed implicitly like a navigation device. They do much more: it is the models themselves that make individuals into the persons they describe. And they describe them, for all their self-imposed reservations, as egoists.

This book is based on a single thesis. It has been raised again recently by a few renegade economists, who call it 'economic imperialism'. They mean by this that the theoretical models in economics hold sway over practically all other social sciences. (The most imperialistic economic theory was obviously Marxism.)

In our world we experience this imperialism as the economization of everything and everyone. It is no coincidence that bestsellers like *Freakonomics* (or the nudge theories of behavioural economists) are so successful. At their core, these books describe an everyday world that breaks down everything into self-interest anecdotes ('Do you penalise parents for late pick-up from childcare and, if so, what is the response? Parents are even more negligent for low penalties, both because it is worth paying the cost and the low penalty falsely signals how little the moral cost is for transgressing norms').[6] However entertaining they are and however controversial the theories, their success shows that they are self-defence theories in a world which, translated entirely into economics, sees self-interest as the innermost core of rational behaviour.

But there is a high price to pay for this self-defence: many of the amusing suggestions, as Gerd Gigerenzer and Nathan Berg have shown in an eminent study of behaviour economics, conceal a neoclassical – or even a neoliberal – ideology.[7] This applies not only to behaviour economics but also to all automated markets, from financial markets to the new social communication markets.

Economic imperialism forces us – even more so since the financial crisis – not to leave the field to a dominant school of Anglo-Saxon economists in particular. A whole world has seen that some of the models postulated as the truth in recent years have weaknesses. If this book looks at two of the most effective structural theories in information economics, namely rational choice theory and game theory, it does not mean that they are the only ones.[8] They are, however, of outstanding importance to the story that this book relates: how individuals can have the feeling that the entire universe is in a conspiracy against them and how, after the end of the Cold War, a new cold war is opening up in the heart of societies.

PART I

OPTIMIZATION OF THE GAME

1

TRANCE

THE MILITARY SEEKS AN ANSWER TO THE QUESTION OF HOW ONE ACTS EGOTISTICALLY

It starts, like a story from *The Twilight Zone*, with a trance. We are in the first years of the Cold War. Somewhere in America, protected by metre-thick bombproof concrete and steel walls, sit highly trained people. They are members of the United States aerial surveillance units. They are gazing at radar screens.

The soldiers are looking for small blinking dots that appear occasionally on the screen. They register even the slightest movement; every signal could be a Russian aeroplane loaded with an atomic bomb. They have been told repeatedly that no job in the entire American armed forces is more vital.

Then inexplicable things happen. An air force officer, who has survived the Second World War without a scratch, manages to break his leg on the short journey from his screen to the coffee machine. Others nod off for a moment. Some are away answering queries. Then there is the artificial light, the underground doors and passages, the growing bunker mentality, and always the green circles of the radar screen: all this reinforces the sense of being inside a 'hypnotic organism'.

'It's difficult to stay awake,' admits a crew member, 'when you're sitting in a dark room staring at a radar screen day after day, week after week, always looking for a signal that needs a decision.' And that's fatal, because 'a minute asleep could mean a city destroyed', as a concerned visitor to the bunker wrote in 1955.[1]

A team of scientists – economists, psychologists and sociologists – alerted by the military tried to track the absences in the green-lit faces. And they finally realized that it was the computers, these vigilant machines, that were hypnotizing the men operating them.

This presented the researchers with an almost insoluble task: how to train soldiers to resist the hypnotic power of their own tools.

Every thirty seconds the men in the white coats scanned the soldiers' faces with cameras controlled by punched cards. Every twenty minutes they photographed their screens, drew diagrams on their writing pads, in which they made notes every hour on the crew's movements and the spatial distances between them – exactly the stuff of many a Hollywood science fiction or horror movie.

The scientists called these 'psychodrama sessions'. The aim, however, was to describe the soldiers' minds in mathematical terms. Not only were men operating machines, but machines were learning how to operate men.[2] To do this, people had to learn how to become machine-readable. And in this way science fiction became reality, because for the first time machines recorded not only movements or time management but also human 'values' and feelings.[3]

It turned out that many soldiers regarded the radar screens as outsize telescopes or as a 'window' into the world. This looked like a place to start. They had to be taught that what they were seeing on the screen was a game in which the other player, the Soviet Union, would do anything to trick them. It was a question not just of registering a signal but of predicting at any given moment the next movements of the blinking dot, which could be the Soviet adversary.

Since the Russians had the atomic bomb and a single aeroplane had the destructive power of entire squadrons of aircraft, the need for completely new strategic thinking had become vital. In the paranoid atmosphere of the time (when people didn't know what we now know in retrospect), when a surprise attack by the Soviet Union was an ever-present threat, the human relationship to information had to be reduced to a simple code: expect the worst. You don't know, the crews were drilled, what the opponent plans, but you do know that its only aim is to trick you.

The mesmerizing green lights on the monitor didn't display the 'truth' or the world as it was. They showed, as a contemporary report described it, a 'poker face'.[4] The soldier at the radar had to imagine himself and the screen as two poker players. It was a cut-throat game, as poker is often described. By seeing himself as a player in a poker game, the soldier was kept awake, stimulated, with his strategic intelligence honed.

The blinking dot could be a harmless commercial aircraft or a Russian aeroplane with a nuclear payload. The man at the machine had to understand that 'poker face' meant not spatial movements but strategic moves and could just as well be a bluff as the real thing.

So as not to fall into the trap, there was only one reliable assumption, one that worked well in economics, as the economists involved knew only too well: acting 'rationally' can only mean operating in one's own interests. For strategic intelligence this meant that if people acted in a certain way, it had to be assumed that they were hiding something in order to win the Game of Life.

Fifty years later, the anthropologist Caitlin Zaloom, who worked for two years as a stock exchange trader in order to describe the fully automated trading world, made exactly the same observation. The traders have to train their attention completely on numbers, which are no longer something fixed and stable but turn into continuously changing real-time signals.[5] Every transaction is a move in a game; all of the players think only of themselves; there are bluffs and surprise attacks, weapons of mass destruction and tactical, pinpoint weapons. The players are permanently screened, and decisions have to be made so quickly that they can only be done by computers.

Above all, however, it is the game theory models developed during the Cold War that are used by today's hedge funds. Entire investment bank departments use computers and game theory to decipher the intentions of rival traders at breath-taking speed from a huge volume of data so as to adapt their own behaviour accordingly.

This would have come as no surprise to those who designed the mind of the new human. It was probably even their intention. It was not psychologists who devised the new 'rational self-interest' behaviour and conceptual models for the military, but economists, physicists and mathematicians. The economists were familiar with markets in which

everyone sought their own advantage. Their strategies for an egotistical society were never limited solely to the military in the Cold War.
The strategies were said to be universal and applicable wherever decisions were made – in poker, in business, at the stock exchange, in war.[6]

In 1950 the American sociologist David Riesman complained in his
international bestseller *The Lonely Crowd* that in modern society individuals were becoming radar operators of their own life. No longer
guided by their inner self but from outside, they could not help pick-
ing up signals from others and adapting their behaviour accordingly.[7]
Now the criticism was reversed: everything becomes logical when one
recognizes that the world is a poker game and everyone wants to win.

It sounded very convincing. When the first information about this
new theory was leaked, a lot of hype developed around it. In a few years
RAND Corporation, the organization to which the scientists who analysed the radar crews belonged, developed under the cloak of military
secrecy into the most powerful think tank in the United States. It was
not just about the Soviet Union anymore. It was about everything.

The birth of this idea has been described as 'a key transition in
American intellectual history'.[8] It is certainly one of the most underestimated. Only if we accept the premise that individuals always act
out of self-interest can the entire complexity of human behaviour be
translated into the language of mathematics. Formulae can be written,
moves calculated, negotiations and compromises modelled and people
trained to a new 'rationality', which they master automatically as if in a
trance – an operation that is impossible if it is assumed that individuals
have to be understood through their unique personal character.

A decisive factor in the worldwide breakthrough was the fact that
these calculations could now be done at lightning speed and then also
in real time. The first computers offered ingenious tools that were just
waiting to be fed with the formulae for people. Calculating machines
are bad at psychology but very good at computing profit maximization.
Economists began to calculate the most complex decision situations
with the aid of computers. With the financial support of the military,
this was also tried out first of all on the Soviet Union.

Computers analysed the signals on radar screens and, as if in a military stock exchange, became better and better at predicting the Soviet
opponent's next moves. What is he doing? What is he planning? What

is he hiding? But the Russians were just as paranoid. Very soon it became 'What will he do if he knows that I know what he is planning?' The computers educated the people working with them. They demonstrated how people should be thinking in the modern world. They provided constant examples. They merged so much with human thinking that soon no military strategist believed that it was possible to think any other way.

'Learn to act rationally' meant learning to think and act on the assumption that everyone is acting out of self-interest. The operation worked even with behaviour that appeared altruistic. One can puzzle for a long time as to why someone might give a complete stranger 10 euros (or why the Russians would launch a disarmament initiative). Only when it is realized, so the theory says, that even in this case the person is seeking an advantage is it possible to understand it.

Soon, however, this theory was not being restricted solely to armament and war strategies. It was not only a tool. It developed into a stealthy, decades-long training in egoism. The computer showed how astonishingly far it was possible to go when all calculations were based on this motivation. It was an innocent machine. But through the information fed into it, it evolved, as has been aptly pointed out, from a training system into an 'indoctrination system'.[9]

No one suspected in the frosty 1950s that fifty years later, long after the disappearance of the Soviet Union, the idea of human behaviour born then would cause so much fear and terror in the world and would change social relations so fundamentally. What we are dealing with today is not the work of a few egotistical hedge fund managers or greedy investment bankers. They are just a symptom. In the cold years of the arms race – and not in the economic crises of the twenty-first century – a creature was let loose whose career did not really take off until the end of the Cold War.

2

GAME

ECONOMISTS GIVE AN ANSWER

The formula that everyone operates egotistically and tries to outsmart the next person was devised during the Cold War. There was a rationale behind the idea. The formula worked because at the time there were two world powers opposing one another, both with the atomic bomb and both capable of completely annihilating the other.

Economics had a long tradition of the self-serving man, *homo oeconomicus*, a kind of virtual doppelgänger used to explain what makes people tick. He was now hauled out of the basement again, where he had been gathering dust. Previously, *homo oeconomicus* had led something of a remote and purely academic life. There were even formulae for him, some dating from the nineteenth century.

This is not the place to recount the two-hundred-year history of *homo oeconomicus*. It would be incorrect, however, to assume that he was simply let loose on the world from the outset as a profit-seeking monster – even if he infiltrated early modern English literature in particular in that guise.[1] As a being who was no longer to be explained by way of his diffuse passions but rather through his uncompromising interests (possibly including concepts such as freedom), *homo oeconomicus* was always an Enlightenment figure as well, and to a certain extent, as Habermas's student Axel Honneth has shown, he could even be called a founding idea of the 'Left'.[2] He is a textbook figure, and clever economists point out ceaselessly that he should never be more than that: an assumption that enables us not only to better explain people and their preferences but also to design social contracts that have the advantage of not aiming for fine-sounding – although just as insubstantial – values such as beauty, truth and goodness.

And yet this is only one side of the story, and the good side at that. The bad side was summed up in a single sentence in 2008 by Lynn A. Stout, professor of law at Cornell University and an expert in corporate governance and finance market regulation familiar with the financial crises of the last few years: '*Homo oeconomicus* is a sociopath.'[3]

Countless authors, including many economists, have shown recently that the assumptions on which *homo oeconomicus* are based do not take sufficient account of the diversity of the human psyche and human society.[4] This book nevertheless claims that the person we are calling Number 2 here has been brought to life in the last few years and has become something that the responsible side of his creators never wanted.

The reasons for this are by no means of a purely 'economic' nature. They have to do with the fact that modern individuals no longer know exactly what their identity is, or whether they have one, many, or none at all. Contemporary philosophies are of no help to them but have rather confirmed the trend. As a result, there has automatically been less resistance to this simplified model, which until the middle of the last century lived to a certain extent as well from its contrast with the real person.

It was the first great victory of 'economic imperialism', which turned everything into economics; but it was a victory because the opposition dissolved. To that extent, economists cannot be blamed for occupying a space given up by others. Subjectivity or individuality was replaced by preferences (which come from outside and do not therefore need to be explained) and the desire for utility maximization.[5] Nothing else was needed anymore. As Michel Foucault put it, *homo oeconomicus* was not just an economic but also a political being and he had the advantage in the eyes of authority that he was 'eminently governable'.[6]

This on its own would not have been sufficient to bring Number 2 to life. Without the computer, without the electronic spark jumping between machine and man, he would still have remained only a model; a theory with the advantage (unlike Marxism) that it was nothing else but that.

'After the fall' is the way the economist and philosopher John B. Davis, not without pathos, describes this expulsion from a non-committal Garden of Eden.[7] It took place in two stages: initially through the emergence of the first computers in the military and economic landscape of the 1950s, and then (with consequences greater than the invention of the steam engine) through the triumph of the 'democratized' computer in mass markets since the early 1980s. The fusion of science and scientists and indeed entire societies with their technologies, the creation of man–machine composites, whether they are called androids or cyborgs, will be a recurrent subject in this book. A revision of the image of the individual in the light of this fusion took place simultaneously in all disciplines, and ironically this revision often ended up with a model that economists had already categorized and conceived as *homo oeconomicus*. Cognitive sciences, for example, which began to play an important role in the post-war era, were no longer interested in the humanization of the machine but, as Jean-Pierre Dupuy formulated it, in the mechanization of the mind.[8] In the famous words of Martin Heidegger, cybernetics, the first science to merge with the computer, replaced philosophy.

Science not only uses technologies as tools to discover or change something. More than that, it discovers and systematically changes whatever the tools enable it to. The ability to calculate a person's preferences – and soon those of an entire society, as appears likely as we approach the era of big data – is possible in real time only when there are tools available that allow this.[9]

Merely by using a calculator, anyone can intuitively grasp the notion that the brain is like a calculator and that mental processes are thus the calculations of a biological computer – an idea that in the 1950s was still not readily accepted.

This is all that Number 2 had ever claimed for himself. The rational individual is a calculating machine. He can be reduced to what he wants and chooses egotistically, his so-called preferences, and they can be calculated mathematically. The formalization of economics through mathematical formulae after the Second World War (Davis calls it an 'arms race' among economists for prestige and influence) indeed makes it possible for individuals to be seen as nothing more than 'mathematical objects'.[10]

Every economist would admit that assumptions about people are simplifications – so radical are these simplifications, in fact, that, as has been rightly pointed out, 'the individual of mainstream economics is pared down to a point of nothingness, excepting the possession of automaton-like choice'.[11] But what if reality becomes precisely this automaton? What if the world turns increasingly into a great machine that operates in this very manner? The problem is not the simplified models. The problem is that we are witnessing a radical change, in which these models encode reality and become real themselves in this way. And not only that: they decide what is rational and what is not. If this is too abstract, just ask yourself what 'preferences' Google or Facebook decides for you, or – much more dramatically and topical – what stock exchange algorithms describe the trader's preferences. The assumptions made by Number 2 – when reading an e-book, with 'smart' appliances, in finance markets, in political life – are already implanted. They are, as Michael Callon puts it, 'performative'; they create the reality they model.[12]

This imperialist victory has antecedents directly connected with the Cold War.

It is self-evident that everyone wants to win rather than lose in markets, and it is trivial to say that no one should be reproached for wanting to do business. The new idea was that now only self-interested motivation counted and that an entire society was to be modelled in its image. The tacit agreement that people in reality are more diverse, richer, more contradictory and more moral than the theory claimed faded in the 1950s and was soon forgotten by some economists. It was now regarded as quite reasonable and in no way morally objectionable to act as the theory demanded.

In fact, for quite understandable reasons, morality did not play a major role at all. The explanation is obvious: during the Cold War it would have been fatally imprudent in this game to want to be anything other than a winner or to consider anything other than personal advantage. But if this was reasonable in a military setting, it was not limited to that setting. The models were designed for dealing not only with the opponent but also with the relationship of individuals with the world.

Many of the economists working in the 1950s at RAND Corporation or advising the military belonged to the so-called 'neoclassical' school based at the University of Chicago, which for some time had been teaching in economics that people are egotistical and that markets are truth machines. Now they saw the opportunity to turn a mere assertion into a natural law.

They started writing formulae and algorithms, and the formulae in turn could be understood by computers. That alone was new. Previously – contrary to what is thought today – the social sciences frowned on the idea of casting human behaviour into mathematical moulds. But if it was assumed that people sought their own advantage, their behaviour could be described mathematically.

These often ingenious economists became experts not only in automating the military but also in automating markets and the people in these markets. They were pioneers in a world that was still half a century away from one in which every person would be linked to computers and markets. But all their formulae could be understood and processed by computers.

They invented something they called 'game theory'. And with the aid of this invention they introduced this cognitive model into our Game of Life. After the Cold War many of the economists with RAND Corporation won Nobel Prizes for economics. It was the culmination of a massive undertaking that transferred the logic of the Cold War to civil society. In the end, in the first decade of the twenty-first century, the ego model had indeed become a natural law. And no one can doubt that it functioned better than all the vague supra-individual value ideologies with their supposed mandatory ethical roles that give rise to the murderous collectivism (or racism) that had been allowed to evolve in the twentieth century. The entire global organism, wrote the senior leader writer of *The New Yorker* following 9/11, 'is based on a kind of basic faith – the unsentimental expectation that people, both individuals and society as a whole, act more or less through rational self-interest'.[13]

In the era of 'rational machines', however, we are beginning to realize that this rationality comes at a cost. And to date, with few exceptions, the world has been in a trance and is barely aware that these economists have changed the human soul more incisively than any psychology.

They didn't build any weapons, produce any goods or solder any processors, but instead essentially wrote the programs for the three great machines that continue to define our world: the military, the market and the computer. They began where people are most easily seduced: with the opportunity to make a profit – not only in the great game of the Cold War, but also in life.

From the mid-1950s, the military in the Cold War sought with the aid of the computer to create a rational, predictable, indefatigable substitute for man, an 'agent' who was interested only in his own survival and who could assess both the risk of an attack and also the best opportunity for a strike.

And as subsequent years were to prove, these were the same qualities that the new economic markets wanted: a person who sought to make profits, could calculate risks and knew when to strike at an auction.

But the most disruptive factor when calculating the future is people themselves. They are an ever-changing risk. They not only fall asleep sometimes at work, but are also refractory and contradictory, play their cards close to their chests, and have so many useless and unreasonable things in their heads that they upset all calculations.

For centuries, efforts had been made to find out what makes people tick, and all of these efforts – be they by soothsayers, philosophers or psychologists – ultimately failed. So how did economists, of all people, manage to devise a formula for human unpredictability?

Their brilliant idea was no longer to ask *what* makes people tick but *how* they should tick for their formulae to work. And the answer was obvious: all problems with the human uncertainty factor vanish into thin air when it is assumed that human thinking and actions are always motivated by self-interest. This theory had the advantage that it always worked and made everything calculable. Your opposite number is opaque? He becomes as clear as crystal when one assumes that he only wishes to increase his profit. People helping others? They do it because they want to do something good for themselves.

The game theorists did not even have to open up people's craniums to control them. All they had to do was to reduce people to a profit-maximizing formula. They didn't need demagogues, pamphlets or ideologists. The books in which rational egoism was discussed were highly abstract and incomprehensible to many. The new game theory spread into daily life simply by being put into practice. It was possible to calculate anything – not only the best way of intimidating the Russians, but also, for example, the moment to give way when two cars are racing headlong towards each other and the first to cede loses the game. This could be effectively applied to auctions or wage negotiations.

But the new theory, which saw every person as an ego machine seeking to win in the poker game of life, conflicted so much with education and everyday morality that there was intuitive resistance at the beginning, when it was fresh and new.

The 'others', the people outside the think tanks and bunkers in the 1950s, felt that something was going on. It was no coincidence that they were suddenly full of a paranoid fear of being manipulated.

Hollywood depicted nightmare situations, in which aliens reconfigured the human brain, controlled thoughts with ray guns or subjected people to brainwashing – usually Communist. Orwell's *Nineteen Eighty-Four* described a world in which telescreens indoctrinated people and kept them under surveillance. It might still have been read as a parable of totalitarian systems when he wrote the book. But fewer than ten years later, people began to suspect that it was not only the military – foreign or their own – but the market itself that was controlling and manipulating them.

In 1957, the bestseller *The Hidden Persuaders* by the American journalist Vance Packard was published. It spoke of advertising agencies that employed hypnotists, and subliminal advertising messages at a cinema in New Jersey that made the spectators buy ice cream as if in a trance.

Although this could never be proved, the hysteria it produced even years later shows that more and more people were beginning to sense that their rational choices were being taken away from them. Packard had written that a different intelligence was being implanted in them and that they were being indoctrinated to become blind consumers – not only through books, words or arguments, but with the aid of technologies that imposed their own rules. Since then, this fear has been repeatedly voiced in Western industrial societies.

At the time this was all rather crude and ingenuous and argued on the basis of conspiracy theories. It was thought that evil powers manipulated the mind by infiltrating people's brains, turning a few knobs and pressing a red button.

In reality it was much more straightforward: people were simply being duplicated. In the digital age, *homo oeconomicus* is now called an 'economic agent': an agent coded by the computer according to the economists' laws.

First this agent took over strategic decisions in the military, then economic decisions in the markets and ultimately and more and more frequently social decisions in human life. He did not need to be intelligent or intuitive but merely capable of calculating in accordance with the rules of game theory.

But he can do more. He trains people. He apparently has the power to make incisive changes in human value systems. No one expressed this more candidly than the man who was referred to where he worked merely as 'Darth Vader'.

His name was Joseph M. Gregory and he worked for Lehman Brothers. As chief operating officer of the investment bank, he realized that a main qualification for modern managers was their ability to merge with the Death Star machines as they bargained continuously for their own advantage.

Just before the explosion of the real-estate bubble in 2008, Gregory was already being asked by his staff why he hired people at Lehman Brothers who knew nothing about the business. 'It's nothing personal,' he replied, 'it's the power of the machine.'

3

PROPHECY

THE TRUTH IS WHAT WE BELIEVE

The year 1989 meant a lot more than we suspected at the time. As one of the great game theory thinkers described it complacently, humanity had 'larger brains as a result of an arms race within our species aimed at building bigger and better computing machines for the purpose of outwitting each other'.[1] And these machines didn't stop thinking just because the threat for which they had been created appeared to be gone.

In the 1950s there was still a long way to go; the technology was missing. Instead there was abstract mathematics or screwball philosophy, like that of Ayn Rand, the American philosopher, who taught absolute egoism to a young Alan Greenspan. At the time it was something to embrace enthusiastically or simply to ignore.

At all events there was freedom of choice.

Until one day first the pocket calculator and then the personal computer became everyday tools and changed everything. In a world of pencil, paper and slide rules, it is impossible to apply a complex formula to calculate the behaviour of individuals. The computation is too involved and by the time the answer is found the opportunity has long gone. Only when interlinked computers make it possible in real time to calculate every transaction and all human behaviour immediately on the basis of formulae do stock exchanges and ultimately parts of political and social reality change.

From the outset, the egotistical model was the soul of the machine, but in the 1980s it remained initially inconspicuous and unassertive. Because the financial markets were not so well developed and many early programmers believed more in community than egoism, they experimented with cooperative algorithms that would simply bring people together.

In the early 1990s, various surrogates for human beings were programmed in the digital space. Some were selfless and immediately accepted compromises; others developed their own values. It was a time of experimentation and trial.[2]

One survived all others, however. Sketched out first on paper as a model of human behaviour, it was coded in the computer with steely Darwinian survival instincts. No one today can escape this 'economic agent' and no one remains unaffected by him.

It is the indoctrination machine of information capitalism, says the sociologist Michel Callon. The theory is 'based on the idea that agents are self-interested. [...] To predict economic agents' behaviors an economic theory does not have to be true; it simply needs to be believed by everyone.'[3]

We have long entered the era of self-fulfilling prophecies. Perhaps we can live with the fact that social media or search engines know us so precisely that they only give us the information we expect. And perhaps also with the fact that we only talk with people who think like we do.

But how can we remain emotionally intact in a society that assumes that individuals are rational only if they act out of self-interest?

'The most serious offence many of the depth manipulators commit, it seems to me,' wrote Vance Packard clairvoyantly in the 1950s, 'is that they try to invade the privacy of our minds. It is this right to privacy in our minds – privacy to be either rational or irrational – that I believe we must strive to protect.'[4]

What would he have said if he had known that in the twenty-first century a complex and fully automated system would tell us what was rational and what was not?

That just fifty years later, governments and entire states would be desperately attempting to influence the financial decisions and conclusions of an endless array of synthetic computer programs – no doubt long communicating with each other in ways that were incomprehensible and undesired by us – which continuously screened the thoughts of entire populations so as to gain an advantage from government decisions and conclusions?

Or that in current high-level political documents a new American and international *raison d'état* would be demanded in which a connection would be made between the need for behaviour-predicting technologies, truth drugs and torture?

Packard might have said that it was just the beginning. After all, he was the person who predicted the era of the artificial monsters.[5]

4

MONSTERS

EVERYONE ACTS RATIONALLY AND SUDDENLY MONSTERS APPEAR

Monsters are being sighted everywhere. And since the era of alchemy we know that they always turn up when cracks appear between the civilized and the natural worlds. It is from these cracks that they emerge.

Every society attempts to sell its social reality as a law, be it the 'divine' law of Absolutism or the natural law of the Enlightenment. And when the social change can no longer be understood through these laws without making $2 + 2 = 5$, and when individuals who cannot abandon the logical system feel they are going insane, these fears are then represented by monsters.

They come and go. In the early twentieth century they colonized the arts, literature above all. Then, with the triumph of totalitarianism, they infiltrated governments and politics. And now they are appearing in financial markets.

Of the many sightings of the 'Monster that ate Wall Street' mentioned by *Newsweek* on 6 October 2008, I should like to mention just four, reported by the most sober and hence credible observers.

Joseph Stiglitz, winner of the Nobel Prize for Economics, speaks of the 'Frankenstein laboratories of Wall Street': 'In the Middle Ages, alchemists attempted to transform base metals into gold. Modern alchemy entailed the transformation of risky subprime mortgages into

AAA-rated products safe enough to be held by pension funds. [...] Finally, the banks got directly involved in gambling.'[1]

'The international financial markets have become a monster,' was the last sentence on the subject by the President of Germany, Horst Köhler, himself an economist, before his resignation.

The science historian George Dyson, who knows more than anyone about the history of artificial intelligence, described the current crash as the unchaining of an artificial creature: 'Just as we later worried about recombinant DNA, what if these things escaped? What would they do to the world? Could this be the end of the world as we know it if these self-replicating numerical creatures got loose? But, we now live in a world where they *did* get loose – a world increasingly run by self-replicating strings of code.'[2]

And finally, the sociologist Manuel Castells, the spiritual father of the networked society: 'We have created an Automaton, at the core of our economies, decisively conditioning our lives. Humankind's nightmare of seeing our machines taking control of our world seems on the edge of becoming reality – not in the form of robots that eliminate jobs or government computer that police our lives, but as an electronically based system of financial transactions.'[3]

These are extreme words, and after 2008 everyone was asking how economists themselves would deal with the disaster caused by their incorrect forecasts. Total loss of control in a system that until then, under the slogan 'great moderation', had been sold as being as stable as the Vatican and as rational as Mr Spock, is naturally even worse than loss of control in a fragile environment.

Absolutely everything that triggered the crisis, which began with the Lehman Brothers bankruptcy and led to the euro crisis, was conceived as a risk-avoidance strategy. Everything was based on the conviction that the great financial market machine had been fed the best mathematical models of humans and markets so as to prevent any possible 'meltdown' or 'mass destruction' and to keep all monsters at bay. And when everything went belly-up, the American Congress and others began to realize that there are some questions to be answered.[4]

As even self-critical economists have painstakingly discovered, these questions have never been resolved. And there is every indication that after the nanosecond of shock, the system is more closed than ever.[5]

To think that the crisis was merely about a Federal Reserve president by the name of Alan Greenspan or a philosopher called Ayn Rand, who then as now preaches self-interest in books that are more successful than the Bible, would be an underestimation. It is not even about economists like Friedrich Hayek or the head of Lehman Brothers, or about pillorying 'greed' and 'self-interest'. Even ultra-orthodox economists at the University of Chicago, the so-called neoclassicists, and the neoliberals, fall over themselves in their moral condemnation of the protagonists.

It is more a question of whether the doctrine of 'rational self-interest' is in the process of producing pure insanity.

In a fascinating dialogue between Congressman Henry Waxman and the former Federal Reserve president Alan Greenspan before the American Congress, the Democratic member asked: 'Do you feel that your ideology pushed you to make decisions that you wish you had not made?'

'To exist you need an ideology,' replied Greenspan. 'The question is whether it is accurate or not. And what I'm saying to you is, yes, I found a flaw.'

'You found a flaw in the reality?' asked Waxman.

'A flaw in the model that I perceived is the critical functioning structure that defines how the world works, so to speak.'[6]

Barely anybody realized that Greenspan was talking about a monster. He was not just speaking of a few mistakes in the interest policy and regulation. As the American journalist Scott Patterson pointed out, in one minute of absolute clarity the man questioned the rationality of the system which claimed that self-interest by 'economic agents (traders, lenders, home owners, consumers, etc.) would create the best of all possible worlds'. Moreover, he recanted, at least in this blackest moment of his career, his belief that it was possible to build an 'efficient market machine' if the computer calculations were based solely on the self-interest of the individual.[7]

You don't have to be a mathematician to understand this. Anyone can see that the market and ego models become permanent self-contradictions, demanding 'rational' behaviour from humans but objectively absurd.

What, for example, is the difference between the advice to crawl under a table in the event of a nuclear attack, as cinema-goers in the 1950s were told, and the advice to provide for one's old age on the markets that are destroying these old age provisions?

This brings us back to the 1950s, when an objectively irrational situation – how is it possible to behave rationally in the face of the objective insanity of a nuclear attack? – led to a new type of mass production.

5

SCREENPLAY

'I HOPE IT WORKS' – CRISIS AS FILM

A system error on the scale we have today should give rise to a major revision.

'The whole intellectual edifice [...] collapsed,' Alan Greenspan announced to the US Congress.[1] But Charles Ferguson's film *Inside Job* showed how untouched those involved were. No self-criticism, no doubts. It was the most brilliant documentation of the crash; Ferguson won an Oscar; and the world contented itself with the fact that, for the sake of its own self-respect, society had called things by their name. Documentaries are one thing; more interesting, however, is the film running in the mind of the public. Composed of everything talked about in newspapers, on the Internet, on talk shows, in parliaments and court cases, this narrative has all the ingredients of a horror or disaster movie.

Moreover, it was just like the disaster movies that were made in the 1950s in Hollywood and Japan against the background of the fear of the bomb and depended, as if this were the only possible focus of the imagination, on monsters. It is the exact replica of the story of irresponsible scientists creating monsters.

All of the roles in the disaster movie on the current financial crisis have been filled, and the narrators of the plot – the traders, bankers and politicians who spoke on dictating machines to American journalists – have not forgotten their own role as protagonists.

Let's look at the screenplay as presented by the main actors themselves.

FIRST: THE MONSTER

It doesn't matter whether it is about an artefact, the thing – the computer, the 'system' – or people themselves. Both alternatives are offered; both stem originally from the nineteenth century, when Mary Shelley wrote *Frankenstein*, who was also repeatedly mistaken for his monster.

Some thus describe the monster as the result of formulae, electricity, hardware and software that had got out of human control.

For others, the monster is not a computer program run amok but the result of deregulation, greed and self-interest. Greed I: People bought houses they couldn't afford and took out further loans on the houses that didn't belong to them. Greed II: The people who seduced them and gave them the money conducted hugely improper transactions that factored in not only their clients' insolvency but also the foreclosures and public auctions that would delay the complete failure of their bonds.

But Alan Greenspan offered Congress a third explanation. The monster, he said, had evolved from 'the best insights' of mathematicians and Nobel Prize winners and 'major advances in computer and communications technology'.[2]

In the general outrage and excitement, it was overlooked that for the first time a global crisis had been explained by the appearance of a cyborg, a mix of man and machine.

As in the tension-building first act of any monster movie, the monster is initially invisible. At this point he looks like Bernard Madoff. The other manifestation of the creature, the machine, tends to be shown in the form of rows of flickering green numbers racing across the screen. The anthropologist Caitlin Zaloom has noted how the changing digits on the screen create a transmutation.[3]

Numbers, the hardest and most incontestable means of communication, from which natural laws are inferred, no longer served to calculate a market but only to interpret it.

Confusion has arisen on account of a competing term, which – before Fukushima – was current particularly in bank crises: meltdown. Through it the human component of the monster was excised and the matter declared a natural disaster. Meltdown. It sounded physical, but what was meant was a statistical monster: the 'maximum credible accident', which was at the same time the most unlikely.

In the 1990s, two authors, one the co-inventor of portfolio insurance, a method of hedging stocks against market risk, proved that the stock market crash of 1987 didn't happen, because it couldn't happen: 'Even if one were to have lived through the entire 20 billion year life of the universe [...] that such a decline could have happened even once in this period is a virtual impossibility.'[4]

Although it sounds so material, it is in truth a fundamental component of teratology, the study of monsters: a monster is a virtual impossibility, and it is precisely for that reason that it is a monster.

SECOND: MAD SCIENTISTS

As is the case with Dr Frankenstein, it is unclear whether the mad scientists are themselves the monsters. They don't wear white coats but torn jeans and sneakers; they are not busy with test tubes but with electronic sparks and mathematical formulae, and they aren't called Dr Strangelove but quants.

As in the Hollywood fantasy, which places them in underground bunkers, in basements, or at the North Pole, these scientists work in secret. For a long time their very existence was kept hidden, as was the case with PDT, the powerful hedge fund from Morgan Stanley, which was unknown even to the company's own employees.

Scott Patterson later reported how clueless the bankers in their suits and ties were at Morgan Stanley when they accidentally crossed the 'magicians' in the lift.

'"Who the hell are these guys?" When queried, PDTers would respond vaguely, with a shrug. "We do technical stuff, you know, on computers. Quant stuff."'[5]

THIRD: THE MONSTER SLAYERS

The appearance of monsters created a market for dragon-killers, mostly young men with strong male-society fantasies in testosterone-producing environments. They are the action heroes of our mind's-eye film about the economic crisis – or at least that's how they see themselves. The traders are the ones who tell the story from the innards of the great Lehman Brothers and AIG machine. Of all the characters in our film, they are possibly the only ones who might serve as Hollywood heroes and role models – because behind their locked doors they sit before the same computers as we do, and because they simulate modern life as a struggle for survival.

They are to some extent the first non-military examples of a digitized society in which they are completely isolated from the people with whom they 'deal'. They 'deal' on computer interfaces and are driven not by moral but by economic gain. Their task is to do what mercenaries and the Terminator do: they 'absorb risks', and as there is no risk that is not insured or evaluated by their employers (interest rate cuts, hurricanes, exploding nuclear power plants), they fight on all fronts.

Their morality is not clear: these well-trained he-men are quite happy to change sides.

One of the favourite combat tricks is 'tobashi', from the Japanese word 'tobasu', meaning 'fly away'. According to the tobashi scheme, the losses incurred by a client or a state are made to 'fly away' or become invisible with the aid of financial products. In 2008 these traders were involved in an operation in which Goldman Sachs made Greece's debts disappear before the eyes of the world with the aid of derivatives.

This trick earned the investment bank around $300 million and Greece a 1 per cent reduction in interest on loan payments. As the Goldman Sachs people knew better than anyone what they had done, they used their knowledge shortly afterwards to attack Greece again.[6]

In the mirror world of his computer screen, this type of trader encountered himself as the hero of a disaster movie.

There are basically two types of monsters: those who come of their own accord and those who are introduced from the outside. Just as Ellen Ripley analysed, killed and resurrected the monster in Ridley Scott's *Alien*, computer traders interpret, assume and absorb invisible risks occurring in modern institutions. Caitlin Zaloom compares the moment in which her trader colleagues expose themselves to the greatest risk with the moment when extreme mountain climbers draw close to their 'true selves'.[7]

At the same time, it is unclear whether in doing so they are hatching the monster or killing it; some do one, some do the other. At all events, they do it for their own gain, just like the superhero, except that their reward is no longer moral but economic; and if they lose, they die.

'You can't make that money back. It's gone,' says Zaloom's trader. 'And believe me, it is a lot like having a death. You go through that.'[8]

It is from this environment that the monster-slayer traders came. In 2008 they could almost have destroyed the investment bank system by successfully betting against it. By short selling they injected the antidote into the investment banks and thus brought about their downfall – and their own rise to astronomical wealth.

One of the success stories was Steve Eisman. 'It was like feeding the monster,' he later admitted. 'We fed the monster until it blew up.'[9]

THE SCREENPLAY

These are the protagonists. The screenplay for our film has consisted so far of countless commentaries, analyses and evocations of crisis and society.

And although journalists act as if it is the most normal thing in the world, experts, Nobel Prize winners, politicians and the media themselves sometimes offer completely contradictory assessments of a comparatively straightforward technical process. Their dialogue sounds like fragmentary radio communication, which in disaster movies inevitably leads to false conclusions being drawn.

'... we have no choice, over ...'

'... the euro is failing, Europe is failing, copy ...'

These radio messages are sent in a context defined by politicians.

'... the most serious crisis since the Great Depression ...'

'... the entire system on the verge of collapse ...'

'... Armageddon ...'

After the German Federal Chancellor dramatically (and almost unprecedentedly) summoned a meeting of senior editors at the height of the Lehman Brothers crisis to warn them against panicking, German and European politics was spinning out of control – as if nervous air traffic controllers (politicians) were attempting to communicate with equally nervous pilots (the markets) over crackling background noise. And for that reason, it was dangerous for this communication to be further disturbed by federal constitutional courts, plebiscites or, above all, 'misleading comments' about the possibility that the entire system was about to crash.

Others also contributed to the background noise: parliamentarians who drew red lines one day, only to cross them the next; media, like the television reporters who spoke about the Brussels summits as if reading from a script, journalists, experts, talking heads, who every other day came up with new and contradictory interpretations.

There cannot be many people in Europe who have been able to remain impervious to these commentaries and the media chaos of the last few years, quite simply because it was talked about and broadcast over and over again, as if the fact of repetition alone would make the situation clearer. This hasn't happened, not because the situation is so complex, but simply because of the background noise, in the literal sense of the word. And, obviously, when it comes to life-and-death situations, the pilot and air traffic controller can't sit down together to discuss matters from a different perspective. Instead they repeat the same information until their opposite number says 'copy', that is, understood.

This is the difference between what is known as 'information' and what we call 'knowledge'. Just as a film screenplay differs from reality, a player's 'moves' are not communication, and the trader's 'information' is not the same as 'knowledge' of the market.

This handling of information is in line with the notion of 'information theory' coming from the early days of computers: information signals don't have to have meaning but need only be sent, again and again ...

Anyone who read market communications in real time in 2012, the countless commentaries and analyses, often with no overlap, cross-references or conclusions, could see the extent to which they had become the script of our daily life. Everything was reduced to yes/no, in/out (Greece, for example), and in the end it all sounded like the parodic predictions of neuroscientist Ralph Gerard:

> A stranger is at a party of people who know one another well. One says, '72,' and everyone laughs. Another says, '39,' and the party roars. The stranger asks what is going on. His neighbor said, 'We have many jokes and we have told them so often that now we just use a number.' The guest thought he'd try it, and after a few words said, '63.' The response was feeble. 'What's the matter, isn't this a joke?' 'Oh, yes, that is one of our very best jokes, but you did not tell it well.'[10]

This is precisely how the European public throws numbers at the monster's head in an attempt to tame it. All of these numbers are just interpretations of whether a society, a state, the eurozone, will survive or not. It is almost impossible to establish a connection between these numbers and the citizens' own identity. They only have to be mentioned for people to laugh, either because they reckon they are insufficient or because they believe that they would just further nourish the monster.

Scientists meanwhile offer fundamentally contradictory antidotes, and while some laugh out loud at '63', others find it a cheap copy. We are talking about a crisis not just in a financial system but in a cognitive system that can no longer distinguish between information and knowledge, because everything has become 'moves' (or screenplay scenarios).

In the mid-1960s, Susan Sontag wrote an analysis of American Cold War science fiction, horror and disaster movies. She noted that the fear of monsters was driven not only by fear of the bomb but also by a feeling of depersonalization – as if people feared that they would lose their personality forever, as in *Invasion of the Body Snatchers*, *The Creeping Unknown*, *Attack of the Puppet People* or *The Brain Eaters*. These alien invaders commit a crime which is worse than murder. 'They do not simply kill the person; they obliterate him.'[11] It was the premonition of a world in which the ego would become a 'black box', defined solely by preferences and – no understatement here – the preference to end all preferences: survival.

Only through dissimulation, tricks, gambling with human irrationality and with the aid of the white magic of science can the individual hero (albeit together with the military) save the world.

In her essay, Sontag also identified the sentence in the banal dialogue that always occurs in the struggle against the monster when the hero, the army or the politicians hedge their defence strategy. Like the 'amen' in church, it crops up every time:

'I hope it works!'

In the early 1950s, a journalist dazzled by the new intellectual weapon 'game theory' visited the Pentagon. He was writing a book entitled *Strategies for Poker, Business and War* because he had heard that the army had found the philosopher's stone for such strategies, a conceptual system for the nuclear age, at least as important as the bomb itself: 'In the spartan surroundings of a Pentagon office a young scientist attached to the Air Force said: "We hope it will work, just as we hoped in 1942 that the atomic bomb would work."'[12]

It did work. It was the philosopher's stone. According to the alchemists, those who possessed it could turn lead into gold. But it has risks and side-effects as well. Without anyone really wanting or even suspecting it, the monsters had returned to our world.

6

REASON

WE BECOME THE MANAGERS OF OUR OWN SELVES

There are always two of us. Wherever we are, there are always two of us. You can be the most solitary person in the world and there are two of you. You can barricade the doors, close the windows, but Number 2 will always find a way in. Number 2 follows us like a shadow and blocks the sun. Number 2 *is* the sun and says: 'Look how brightly I shine.' Number 2 makes decisions for us, makes deals, looks into the future, praises us, gives us presents, punishes us. And above all Number 2 bets on us and increasingly puts our existence at risk. He is unfortunately starting to turn into a monster.

He is a hominid, a human-like creature. Number 2 was not born a monster but as *homo oeconomicus*, a hypothetical simulation, a theoretical mathematical creature that likes to play murderous games. He is easy to calculate but rather difficult to live with.

He has been called 'double', 'dummy', 'economic agent', 'duplicate' or 'counterfeit' man. In this book we shall call him 'Number 2', because at some point he started to think and act for Number 1, the real person.

In the version that we have to deal with today, he is the purely economic agent, who seeks advantage in markets rationally and consistently in accordance with his rules. A small hedonistic machine that is concerned only with fulfilling his consumer wishes ('preferences') and interested in altruism only when it indirectly serves his own purposes. This creature, created by economists, has crystal-clear and calculable preferences – mistrust and self-interest. He is driven by the desire for profit, and his 'truth' begins and ends with the cost. Number 2 has an insatiable thirst for information that he can use to his advantage in the Game of Life.

Until the end of the Cold War, almost everyone who was not intent on waging or avoiding a nuclear war could ignore Number 2. As a result we all lived for decades with him, not paying attention to him or even noticing that he was there. How could we? As long as his formula concerned pre-digital markets and old-fashioned worlds, his scope for action was limited, and real people, particularly back then in Germany, didn't need to bother about him.

The economists amused themselves by giving the name 'game theory' to the rules governing Number 2. This theory, as the American journalist Fred Kaplan puts it, 'said that it was irrational behavior for one to take a leap, do what is best for both parties and trust that one's opponent might do the same. In this sense, game theory was the perfect intellectual rationale for the Cold War.'[1]

The polymath John von Neumann and his colleague Oskar Morgenstern published their work *Theory of Games and Economic Behavior* in 1944, essentially a continuation of a manuscript written in 1928. Initially this economic theory was ignored. Neumann, who was also involved in the development of the atomic bomb and the computer, immediately recognized the opportunity to test out his theses in the military.[2]

Within a few years, under the auspices of RAND Corporation, the theory had developed into a universal tool for all kinds of decision and negotiation problems, at the centre of which was Number 2, a creature who was rational because he always sought only his own advantage.

If game theory was Number 2's tool, 'rational choice theory', developed in 1951 and closely linked with game theory, was his philosophy of life. For all the limitations and relativizations of Number 2's ego trip that were formulated over the years, at heart he adhered to the formula the RAND protagonists had set out in the late 1950s: 'Whenever we speak of rational behavior, we always mean rational behavior directed primarily to selfish ends.'[3]

The 'games' in game theory were pure mathematics and after 1953 were regarded as military secrets, locked every evening in safes by researchers with top-secret clearance.[4] These researchers basically treated the world conflict as an economic 'optimization problem', which could be solved only by a pathologically rational being, the creature we are calling Number 2.

As Sylvia Nasar wrote in her biography of the 'beautiful mind' John Nash,

> RAND was full of men and women committed to the idea that systematic thought and quantification were the key to the most complex problems. Facts, preferably detached from emotion, convention, and preconception, reigned supreme. If reducing complex political and military choices, including the problem of nuclear war, to mathematical formulae could produce light, why then the same approach must be good for more mundane matters. RAND scientists tried to tell their wives that the decision whether to buy or not to buy a washing machine was an 'optimization problem'.[5]

In both their social behaviour and their hyper-rationality, these RAND mathematicians resembled the future 'quants', the mathematicians and physicists who calculated the financial killer products in the investment banks.

The questions they asked were how to find the best strategy against an opponent with the same threat potential as them, when to shoot in a duel, how to find out if the opponent even had a bullet.

It was known that many of the scientists at RAND in Santa Monica on the Pacific coast had worked on the development of the atomic bomb, radar and long-range missiles. Although the public was not informed of the strategic parallels and intersections – even RAND's published information seemed to follow game theory precepts, that is, some was only published so that the opponent would think that RAND thought ... – we can still remember the evening news programmes reporting on increasingly complex and ultimately incomprehensible diplomatic disarmament initiatives, threats or arms build-ups.

'It made sense for both sides,' wrote Kaplan, 'to stop building [atomic bombs], but neither could have the confidence to agree to a treaty to stop building arms, suspecting that the other might cheat, build more and go on to win.'[6]

Perhaps the cleverest and most paranoid mind in this game was the American mathematician John Nash, whom the world got to know in 2001 as the hero of the Oscar-winning drama *A Beautiful Mind*. He proved with apparently irrefutable logic that the Game of Life could be played rationally only if every player was driven by absolute self-interest and a deep-seated mistrust of the other side.

Nash devised the theory of 'non-cooperative' games, in which players could not communicate with their opponents and did not trust them and in which both sides anticipated their opponent's most probable strategies.

The 'most probable' or, in the words of game theoreticians, the 'most rational' moves are always self-interested ones.

It was an intuition of a very special kind. The players had to identify with the self-interest of their opponents in order to make best use of their own self-interest. In the sober language of the theory, the idea was to make the best strategic move with account taken of the opponent's best move and thus to establish a kind of balance.

This was the celebrated Nash equilibrium, and it is nothing other than a global mathematical formula for systematic and successful self-interest. As a mathematical formula it is complicated. But you don't have to learn it. You will find it today in the stock exchange algorithms of hedge funds, on auction platforms, in the most powerful advertising algorithms in the world, and probably also in social networks. It is the great ego machine in the heart of our systems.

Science historian Philip Mirowski summarizes the formula that governs our world:

> We are all little Hobbesian agents, and we are all trying to do each other in, and in equilibrium we agree on how we'll all go about doing it. [...] [The Nash equilibrium] portrays each of us as though we were some kind of algorithmic computers trying our damnedest to outwit each other. [...] This vision of everyone as driven to falling back on their own wits, cynically manipulating others, lacking even a trace of communal intelligence or transpersonal commitment, seems very

much the image of the agent in neoliberalism too. In a phrase, everyone is reduced to the status of an entrepreneur of the self. [7]

The more successful the proposals of the defence experts in their think tanks and the more efficient the functioning of 'mutual deter rence' and 'massive retaliation', two of the guiding principles of the Cold War, the more this logic became persuasive as a good recipe for all types of interpersonal relations.

And the more the Soviet Union faded into the background, the more the original military concept was applied to the world of economics.

The models have nothing to do with the humanistic lip service, particularly in Europe, paid to the image of the cooperative, solidary person as the focus of civic understanding.

A better strategy for modern society was to assume that individual players evaluated their opponents and sought at all times to maximize their own advantages. 'If I think that he thinks that I think ...', and so on. The game does exactly what Vance Packard once described as a dangerous mark of modern society: each person tries permanently to get inside the head of the next person to win the game or, what amounts to the same thing, to do business. Every soldier does this, every stock exchange trader, every Facebook algorithm – our entire world has become a world of getting inside people's heads.

A series of strange events led authors like Douglas Rushkoff and Philip Mirowski to suspect that some of the most important pioneers of the new rationality had signs of high-grade mental disorders like paranoia and schizophrenia. In Nash's case, this was so marked that, as Mirowski writes, the Nobel Prize committee, bizarrely, had to work hard to prevent Nash from appearing in public.[8] An anecdote going the rounds about Nash, in this case in the version by Rushkoff, gives an idea of the difference between playing game theory with people and with machines:

The Rand scientists believed that mutual distrust should rule the day. Each prisoner must assume the other will betray him, and then avoid the ten-year sentence by becoming a betrayer himself. They tested their ideas on Rand's own secretaries, creating all sorts of different scenarios in which the women could cooperate with or betray one another.

In every single experiment, however, instead of making choices in the self-interested way that Rand expected, the secretaries chose to cooperate. This didn't deter John Nash [...] from continuing to develop game scenarios for the government based on presumptions of fear and self-interest. An undiagnosed paranoid schizophrenic, Nash blamed the failed experiments on the secretaries themselves. They were unfit subjects, incapable of following the simple "ground rules" that they should strategize selfishly.[9]

Today the Nash equilibrium is coded into many algorithms used for transactions on financial markets and elsewhere in the brave new world as a compromise reached by two players who suspect the worst of one another but cannot communicate (the fellow players on the stock exchange are unknown).

It was Nash who made these strategies applicable not just to the military but to all forms of social interaction. Above all, claimed his admirers, it was now possible to predict the result of practically any strategy, any auction, any stock exchange transaction. One enthusiastic admirer was the American micro-economist Hal Varian.[10] Today Varian is chief economist at Google and was instrumental in programming game theory models for Google AdWords, a powerful auction algorithm.

What we know today as 'information economics' is not a modern invention but the product of a global conflict that had the world powers locked in mind games. Human and artificial brains ran through millions of conceivable scenarios to manipulate, fool, confuse, motivate, deter and paralyse the enemy. Today its models predict the behaviour of self-interested players.

This might be harmless with AdWords, but it becomes dangerous in the case of stock exchange or behaviour predictions as used by security authorities, social networks or data-protection organizations. Do they say anything about real people? Do they confirm self-interest as the motive of everyone, or are they something even more dangerous: a self-fulfilling prophecy?

One of the most important and thoughtful game theoreticians, the Israeli economist Ariel Rubinstein, has consistently disagreed with this theory: 'I have absolutely no idea how Varian reached the conclusion about the predictive ability of Nash equilibrium,' he wrote, warning that no one should confuse Number 2 with reality or believe that game theory could provide guidelines for action in real life. It did not describe reality but was merely a way, in certain situations, of analysing and was not 'useful' in any pragmatic sense for daily life.[11]

Contradiction is human but pointless. Number 2 is much too efficient. And he can be 'computed'. From the outset he has had a psychological function that should not be underestimated. He strengthens self-belief. Modernism – with Sigmund Freud and the rest, and with the growing moral self-contradictions of the capitalist system – has dissolved the 'ego'. The inevitability with which the idea that being rational means operating in one's own self-interest became a universal law made Number 2 into a welcome alternative – first in the military, and then since the 1990s for its successors, the masters of the universe on Wall Street.

It was left to a gifted science fiction writer to mark the moment at which the small and dangerous thinking machines moved out of the military sphere and into civil society.

Philip K. Dick (1928–82), whose 1955 novel *Solar Lottery* describes a state based on the rules of game theory, wrote in the preface:

> I became interested in the Theory of Games, first in an intellectual manner (like chess) and then with a growing uneasy conviction that Minimax was playing an expanding role in our national life. Although specialists in related fields (mathematics, statistics, sociology, economics) are aware of its existence, the Games Theory has been little publicized. [...] Both the US and the Soviet Union employ Minimax strategy as I sit here. While I was writing SOLAR LOTTERY, Von Neumann, the co-inventor of the Games Theory, was named to the Atomic Energy Commission, bearing out my belief that Minimax is gaining on us all the time.[12]

As Dick rightly recognized, game theory was directed initially at the economy of war in the age of the bomb. Nikita Khrushchev had even gone as far as saying that one plant was churning out atom bombs 'like sausages'.[13] But from the outset it was also about the economy itself and the programming of *homo oeconomicus*.

The lack of concern about the way this political physics formula –
which was at least as important as the formula for the bomb – migrated
so easily from the military to the economic sphere is remarkable.[14]

One explanation was the ultimately unprovable claim that game
theory had prevented a nuclear war, and that anyone who won this
murderous game could win any game.

Philip Mirowski gave another reason in his outstanding standard
work *Machine Dreams*, published in 2004. Many of the publicly accessible papers on game theory were sometimes misleading. It was possible
for authors to publish texts containing the opposite of what they wrote
in the secret military papers. Robert Aumann, Nobel Prize winner for
economics, later reported that before 1989 just a fraction of the models
were known and that they were mostly passed on even among scientists
only by word of mouth.[15] Particularly in the initial stages, however,
when it was a matter of budgets and grants, enough was leaked to make
the strategy sound mysterious and hip.

This is also understandable: as a conceptual model with limited
effectiveness, Number 2 certainly had something to offer. As a tool,
game theory can solve distribution problems – at least when they
concern student dormitories or kidney transplants, to name but two
famous examples.

The problem is that the theory not only describes but also forces
action; it is not only descriptive but also normative; it doesn't just pos-
tulate self-interest but creates it. The rationality it proclaims does not
come of its own accord. If there is no other way, it forces players to be
rational. The idea that it can be in a person's own interests to relinquish
a possible benefit (or victory) is not the product of some moral code but
solely of the fear of punishment. Among Number 2's character traits
are not only self-interest and profit-maximization but also pure fear. It
derives from a logic played out again and again during the Cold War:
rational behaviour by the opponent occurs not through rational arguments but through threats and the fear of annihilation.

Mirowski describes this logic quite clearly: 'For instance, defense
experts like Thomas Schelling were telling their clients that it was
"sensible" to risk all of life on earth to gain [...] temporary political
advantage over an opponent, that it was possible to frighten them silly
to make them more "rational".'[16]

Of course, game theory wasn't everything. The history of this new rationality must also consider the behaviourist ideas of B.F. Skinner, which have a greater influence today on the design of platforms like Google and Facebook than game theory: 'Do this' – 'Get this reward.'

Many decades later, this rationality has reached the heart of civil society. Now banks versed in game theory are saying that if they are not 'rescued', their demise will mean the demise of the entire financial system. The message is an astonishing reversal of moral responsibility: rescue us for your own sake.

Now the question of whether a country like Greece should leave the eurozone can no longer be asked without conjecture as to the collapse of the entire system. Now investment banks and hedge funds are recommending to their customers to join in the game and to invest in the crisis in the European continent on the basis purely of game theory rules.[17]

'The disintegration of the social and economic system,' wrote Philip K. Dick portentously,

> had been slow, gradual, and profound. It went so deep that people lost faith in natural law itself. Nothing seemed stable or fixed; the universe was a sliding flux. Nobody knew what came next. Nobody could count on anything. Statistical predictions became popular ... the very concept of cause and effect died out. People lost faith in the belief that they could control their environment; all that remained was probable sequence: good odds in a universe of random choice.[18]

*   *   *

Not only technologies but also theories can be misused. Perhaps no one warned more clearly against the misuse of his own theory than Ariel Rubinstein. In his memoirs he reported bewilderedly how a useful but highly limited and essentially academic conceptual model was changing the world's value system. It had led to the cultivation and exploitation, as if in a greenhouse, of the unquestioned self-interest of the human ego.

The misfortune occurs when the model is confused with reality – like all of the models that caused Alan Greenspan's world view to collapse when they came into contact with reality. 'For years,' writes

Rubinstein, 'I believed that teaching game theory is not helpful and is even harmful because it can potentially encourage selfishness and deviousness.' And even when an experiment with students proved that this was not necessarily the case, he insisted: 'I still believe such an effect exists.'[19]

It turns people into something they are not. And where intuition still exists, they resist the imposition of being forced to act according to Number 2's rules. Once Rubinstein attempted to bargain in the market in the Old Town of Jerusalem using game theory. He became Number 2. He bargained just as the theory dictated and expected his predictions to be correct. The experiment was a complete failure. '"For generations," responded the trader, 'we have bargained in our way, and you come and try to change it?" I parted from him shamefaced.'[20]

Today we are this market trader. Someone appears from nowhere and demands that we act according to new rules. But now we can't send him away. In automated markets he forces us to follow his logic. Even if we don't play along, we are dragged into the game: taxed, quantified, and everything we do is reduced to a universal ego trip.

For a long time now this has applied not only to economic transactions but also to social networks, media and the 'bad karma' of digital insurrection.

The slightly paranoid world of mutual accusations, deception and mistrust has not become any smaller in the last few years but has evolved almost into a kind of growth hormone of the new information economy – and all of its monitoring, tracking and analysis tools.

It is therefore no exaggeration to say, as Manuel Castells does, that something has been 'unchained'.

This occurred because no one paid enough attention on 9 November 1989. Communism had ended, that was true. But what was to become of those Western capitalist theories whose birth and ideology could be explained only through the existence of Communism? Why did the social market economy, in such a short time and against all predictions, come under such pressure from a social model called 'neoliberalism'?

It had been forgotten that the radicalism of Number 2, all the formulae about self-interest and use optimization, and all the claims about the almost divine omniscience of the market that had arisen between

1950 and 1989, had themselves been part of an ideological war and part of an attempt to disprove the Communist doctrine.

Even arch-conservative economists, as S.M. Amadae had shown, were not sure in the 1950s and 1960s that the Moscow model wouldn't function. Those in power in the Soviet Union believed in planning and (at least on paper) that the higher aim not only surpassed individual self-interest but extinguished it. And they had launched the Sputnik into space and had built the bomb. It was by no means certain that the planned economy experiment was doomed to failure or that the Western system would prevail. The thesis that the market is a truth machine that ensures a harmonious balance because participants always act in their own interests had never been 'proved'. Who could really know?

There were also ideological reservations against a Europe that had given birth to two terrible collectivist systems. It was alarming that people in Western Europe were being attracted by 'unscientific' convictions like solidarity, cooperation and selflessness. The RAND economists and their colleagues from Chicago also found that suspicious.

The basic motivation behind the principle of absolute self-interest was always strategic as well, aiming to prove with the full weight of science that people operated quite differently than their ideological opponent claimed.

And then, after decades, the player from Moscow was bankrupt. What a victory, rejoiced the military hyper-poker players when the Wall fell on 9 November 1989; and all with the power of thought. For the first time in history, it appeared, a mathematical conceptual model, first appearing in computers, had become a weapon.

This victory was the main reason that people began to confuse the idea with reality. The Cold War had been won, they said. What greater proof was needed of the validity of the theory?

'With the Soviet Union,' said Barack Obama while still a senator, referring to the irrationality of the new world order in 2004, 'you did get the sense that they were operating on a model that we could comprehend in terms of, they don't want to be blown up, we don't want to be blown up, so you do game theory and calculate ways to contain.'[21]

The game appeared to work so well that people wanted to continue playing. The theory and associated image of humanity began to take on a life of their own. Detached from the conflict of systems and in spite of warnings from some economists, people began to forget why it had been originally devised. They simply continued and began to change their own society with the aid of modern computing machines.

The German public, busy with reunification, had to deal with the legacy of Communism. Strangely, no one asked what remained of the Cold War and whether it lived on in another form. They failed to notice that the weapon of the Cold War was changing into something called 'neoliberalism' and 'the information economy' and that it was targeting the great achievements of the social market economy.

John McDonald, the first reporter in the early 1950s to penetrate into the top-secret office of the game theoreticians, announced joyfully to the world: 'Mathematicians are discovering a perfect, fool-proof system for playing all cut-throat games including poker, business – and war.'[22] The war of nerves with Moscow was over. The date was 9 November 1989. The Cold War moved into business. It packed its bags and decamped to Wall Street.

7

SOCIAL PHYSICS

Mr Pimbley gives a speech and advises physicists to dress up for Wall Street

Revolutions cost heads and haircuts. Shortly after the French Revolution, cheap labour was used to perform simple calculations in the mass-production factories.

Amazingly, they were already being called 'computers'.

They consisted to a large extent of former hairdressers, who had become unemployed on account of the latest trend in revolutionary hairstyles and the regretful absence of heads of their former aristocratic customers.

It is obviously preferable for a hairdresser to do calculations than for an executioner to cut hair. It's all a question of assigning tasks and the people to perform them, but the two are just a hair's breadth apart. We think of life as evolution, forgetting that it is mutation that produces monsters and unpredictable events.

The systems of the 'closed world' of the Cold War were built with enormous outlay of money, material and talent: radar systems, missiles, the first computers and data networks, the mathematical models – and it was all mental theatrics. Fortunately the bomb was never dropped, and direct military conflict by the two sides was also avoided.

The theatres of war during the Cold War were unreal, hermetically sealed rooms. The science historian Paul Edwards describes them in detail in his classic *The Closed World*. Even the disastrous and in no way virtual wars in Korea and Vietnam were part of Number 2's moves and his fundamental question: how can I defeat someone who has an atomic bomb?

Everything was symbolic, every action a move in the game. This is precisely how the Cold War was waged: not with weapons but through psychological intimidation.

This all ended with the demise of the Soviet Union in 1991. All eyes were on the end of Communism, and we were less interested in what was happening with all the energy that had been developed to deal with the direct threat to the system.

The very night that the Berlin Wall fell, brains that had spent their whole lives considering Marxism-Leninism and historical materialism simply shut down. Functionaries from East Germany's ruling Communist Party became real-estate brokers, and political science teachers opened restaurants.

Concentrating on the collapse of the socialist system and their own triumph, many observers failed to recognize that the machinery of Western thought was also regrouping. While philosophers and journalists were busy with hairstyles – and one of the most popular conceptual wigs was called 'globalization' – people were losing their heads: they were no longer needed where the anatomy of society had planned for them to be.

The distribution of intelligence in society shifted beneath the cranium – and as is often the case when shifts of this type take place, there is usually money involved. And despite what the religion of 'the information economy' would have us believe, this rarely happens because there is a new Einstein, or there are better answers and truths. The brains and talents migrate not only to where the financial incentives are better but also to where the social incentives are more prestigious.

The end of the direct nuclear threat had massive consequences in terms of earnings and career planning for physicists. They could no longer rely blindly on having their research subsidized by the military-industrial complex, as had been the case since the 1930s. Military scientific planning, which had produced the atom bomb, game theory, the computer and RAND Corporation, was reformulating its priorities. At the same time, Wall Street had economists but no physicists who knew how to use the mathematical models in the world-conquering computer.

At the annual meeting of the American Physical Society in 1996, one of them, the physicist Joseph M. Pimbley, spoke almost exclusively about the damage to the self-esteem of his entire profession: 'All physicists today must be prepared to decide how to pursue the remainder of their careers.' And he recommended Wall Street with its new challenges and good pay. 'Why all the focus on money?' he asks.

> Should one choose the job or career that provides the highest income? Of course not. But in a free society with free markets, the financial compensation of the profession is a measurement [...] of the value of the profession to the society. Thus, physicists may serve society better when they pursue careers in finance. What an incendiary statement! Do I really believe it? Not really. But I do believe the assertion is worthy of debate.[1]

'If he were young today,' he said to the assembled American physicists, 'Einstein might be working on Wall Street. Unfortunately, he'd be so well compensated and so tired at the end of the day, he would never have gained such fame!'[2]

Pimbley's speech is a fascinating example of a paradigm shift. While Pimbley was selling the social and economic status of a Wall Street career to his young colleagues, the older ones probably recalled the good old days when physicists had the social prestige of investment bankers (which in 1996 was still intact). In the 1950s and 1960s in particular a different 'bonfire of the vanities' was alight, and *Harper's Bazaar* claimed in its society news that no dinner party could be a success unless there was at least one physicist.

In those days, physicists had police escorts to accompany them to private conferences, and important physicists who were also government advisers flew in B52 bombers if the Pan-Am flight was not convenient.[3]

Physicists, and their spiritual brothers, economists, acted as consultants in all matters, occupied key positions earning lots of money and in the late 1950s provided the most deans at American universities. In addition, they had brought about a threefold increase in physics students.[4]

Looking at the lifestyle and astronomical earnings of Wall Street physicists, the male rituals, the rutting calls indicating that a trader has made a killing, or reading recently disclosed emails from investment banks throwing entire economies to the wolves, one might regard this behaviour as a pathological revelation of the 'beast in man'. This is how people are when left to themselves.

But the opposite is the case. This was precisely the behaviour produced synthetically in the 1950s – particularly among American physicists, soldiers and economists. It explains the re-emergence of people and conflicts thought to have been forgotten and locked in the bunkers of the Cold War. In reality, the Cold War is not over; only the theatre of war has changed.

During the Cold War, lives were at stake, but as the nuclear war fortunately did not occur, the same megalomaniacal thirst for numbers and the same unusual behaviour developed in the self-interested logic of the think tanks of the time, as Paul Edwards describes with a series of examples.[5]

No one portrayed this better than the film director Stanley Kubrick, whose *Dr Strangelove* depicted the prevalent psychology more vividly than any history book.

The notorious physicist Herman Kahn, for example, an authentic model for Dr Strangelove and a prominent employee of RAND, travelled the USA in 1959, giving lectures to thousands of enthusiastic listeners about the economics of a thermonuclear war. Today we would describe them without exaggeration as insane – if they did not exactly mirror the present-day risk calculations on Wall Street.

For example, Kahn related to his fascinated and terrified public that in a worst-case scenario a nuclear attack by the Soviet Union would destroy the fifty-three largest cities in the USA. This would be bad, although 60 per cent of American citizens at the time didn't live in cities.

'Can you live with that?' Kahn would ask in his clipped voice. 'The answer is yes. Particularly the kind of tragedy this is, it's easy to take.

It isn't like the Blitz in London, where everybody saw the little girl's hand or something like that, the kind of experience to carry round the rest of his life. People are over-killed in the *target* area. *You* don't get to see the dead, you understand. It's a little bit distant. You hear that New York is destroyed, but you're in Princeton.'

It is difficult to say how much of Kahn's appearance was a game within a game, a bluff aimed at the Soviets indicating a willingness to sacrifice millions of lives. But the point of the game was precisely to let the other side know that it knew that they knew that it was willing to stop at nothing.

And because nothing is as it seems, Kahn doubtless had another reason for his disaster movie. RAND Corporation was looking for new sources of income and offered the American government to develop urban planning and decentralization scenarios based on cybernetic models.[7]

The unique mixture of unlimited money, computer-controlled data calculations, game theory and the atom bomb seems to have generated the same emotional and sexualized power fantasies that were to appear later in Wall Street insider reports.

The RAND people and generals once held a secret meeting to discuss what would happen if the Soviet Union attacked Western Europe solely with conventional weapons. The Strategic Air Command came up with the plan of firing every available atom bomb at targets in Russia and China, which would have killed an estimated 285 million people. 'Gentlemen,' said Kahn to the general laughter of the generals, 'you don't have a war plan, you have a war orgasm.'[8]

It was also Kahn who, in his bestseller *On Thermonuclear War*, thought up a doomsday machine that would automatically blow up everyone in the world in the event of an attack by the Soviet Union. Kahn himself points out that a machine of that nature would be unreliable and was hence rejected by the Cold War generals.

Fifty years later, the American financial journalist Michael Lewis wrote *The Big Short*, a detailed account of the financial crash and its causes subtitled *Inside the Doomsday Machine*.

No one would risk destroying the world if they were destroyed themselves was the logic of the RAND people.

No one would risk destroying themselves if they could plunge the whole world into ruin was the logic fifty years later of the too-big-to-fail strategies of the likes of Lehman Brothers and AIG.

The emotional hype surrounding the American physicists ebbed in the early 1970s until Ronald Reagan became president. The pay was less and the working conditions more difficult. Atom bombs had long lost their fascination, and the entire military-scientific complex was looked on with suspicion following the Vietnam War and the 1968 movement. Even Hermann Kahn would have found it hard to attract an audience.

When the first massive budget cuts hit physics, and the profession of 'nuclear scientist' was no longer a dream job, many recalled their old friends in the economic sciences, particularly the branch that had been involved in the major nuclear projects and its mind games.

It was at this time that physicists first appeared on Wall Street. Although the exodus was interrupted by Reagan and the explosive fascination of his SDI project, the nonmilitary contact between the two spheres, a social science called economics and a natural science called physics, had given birth to something that would change us forever. It was the start of 'social physics'.

The great migration began in the early 1990s. Older physicists left military research for banks and fund management companies. Initially, these 'quants' or 'rocket scientists', as they were called by Wall Street with reference to the Manhattan Project, were nothing more than human computers, strange figures, slightly resented or mocked by the 'real' bankers.

Their social behaviour and clothing were irritating. The physicists' association advised those who wanted to move from the university laboratories to Wall Street to get their hair cut, dress smartly, dry-clean their clothes and play down their own intelligence and tendency to isolate themselves.

But what happened here was far more than a career move: not only were scientists well groomed and dressed, they became a new species.

Financial scientist Jonathan Berk said almost defensively in the mid-1990s that no one was interested in the work.[9] But a few years later, physicists had taken over the lead from the economic scientists in the quantitative analysis departments.

The actual story of the quants begins in the 1970s with the birth of the formula that 'would change the way the financial system worked forever'.[10] The reference is to the Black–Scholes formula, which predicted the volatility of shares under certain ideal conditions. (People use models even to describe models themselves.)

Today even dispassionate observers like the business journalist Scott Patterson compare the story of the Black–Scholes formula, which was later to win a Nobel Prize, to the tale of Einstein's basic formula, the revolution in our notion of physics, which led to the Manhattan Project and the atom bomb.

> Just as Einstein's discovery of relativity theory [...] would lead to a new way of understanding the universe, the Black–Scholes formula dramatically altered the way people would view the vast world of money and investing. It would also give birth to its own destructive forces and pave the way for a series of financial catastrophes, culminating in an earthshaking collapse that erupted in August 2007.[11]

In the 1980s, the formula, which at its core was an option-pricing model, was given its own key on pocket calculators, and suddenly life was much easier. Some authors date the start of the alchemy in finance at April 1973, when Texas Instruments ran an ad for pocket calculators in *The Wall Street Journal* claiming 'you can find the Black–Scholes value using our [...] calculator'.[12] For the inventors of the formula the story ended in a fiasco: the Long Term Capital Management fund constructed using the model went spectacularly bankrupt in 1998.

It was nevertheless a beginning. A series of similar financial products, safeguarded by the mathematics of securitization or hedging, promised a practically no-risk portfolio and used the formula for things that it shouldn't have been used for.

A later analysis of the crisis and its models described it as 'the equivalent to building a building of cement of which you weren't sure of the components'.[13]

In fact, the entire operation on the finance markets launched in the

1990s sounds like a recollection of the Los Alamos project by the great mathematician R.W. Hamming, in which he recognized that

> the computing approach to the bomb design was essential.... But thinking long and hard on this matter over the years showed me that the very nature of science would change as we look more at computer simulations and less at the real world experiments that, traditionally, are regarded as essential.... There was a computation of whether or not the test bomb would ignite the atmosphere. Thus the test risked, on the basis of a computation, all of life in the known universe.[14]

It was Warren Buffet who, before the crisis began, warned of the 'weapons of mass destruction' on Wall Street. Without taking the comparison too far, it is clear that simulations are not parallel universes under laboratory-tested quarantine conditions but rather that they seduce individuals into taking the ultimate risk, whose consequences have to be borne by everyone else.

The comparison of finance technologies with Los Alamos is valid not only for theoretical but also for sociological reasons. The physicists at Los Alamos found themselves in the same position in the 1930s as in 1996, when Pimbley literally counselled 'emigration'. Back then, countless physicists emigrated, by choice or not, to the military-industrial complex, where they remained until the end of the Cold War. Now it was happening again.

Europe somehow failed to note the gigantic plans with which Wall Street welcomed its physicists. 'I've known people who worked on the Manhattan Project,' said a JP Morgan director quoted in *Newsweek*, 'and for those of us on that trip, there was the same kind of feeling of being present at the creation of something incredibly important.'[15]

8

MASSACRE

GREED AND FEAR WILL SUFFICE AS MOTIVATIONS FOR THE GAME OF LIFE

Stock exchanges used to be full of people who could see one another. Full of noise, shouting, screaming, laughing, waving, glances and grimaces. And it all took place in a real world.

In the 1990s these rooms were reduced to computer screens, places for observation, scrutinizing, projection. The traders and their bosses have been sitting ever since in front of these screens, just as the radar crews once did, and like them they look not at a monitor but at a 'poker face'.

The money, the ever-changing figures, are the troops, the soldiers who are deployed, moved or sometimes sacrificed. 'If you've lost money,' explains the trainer in an investment bank as if it were soldiers killed in battle, 'have a funeral for it. You have to have closure. It is gone ... you have to look at the next trade.'[1]

If you look into the offices and on the monitors in the armoured high-security quant code rooms, you will not see something that *could* be a military command centre. It *is* one. The machines, the screens, the instantaneous extraction of oxygen to prevent fire, Number 2, the digital agent, who attacks or defends with the aid of game theory – this is the brain that produced in us a historically unique arms race.

And for those who haven't noticed that the people inside the brain are doing the same thing as in those days, only this time with grandpa and grandma's savings, the traders will tell them.

'Scalp', 'kill', 'blow out', are their favourite verbs. One investment bank programmed its computers so that noises of battle came out of the loudspeakers whenever there was a change in price or interest. During busy market days, the rooms were filled with the sounds of breaking glass and ricocheting bullets.[2]

What the traders see 'no longer has a form'. They are light dots in the shape of figures, 'moments of opportunity to act that pass quickly and [...] occasion the next set of opportunities'.[3] Many of those who stared into the monitors saw no difference between military and financial operations. Both are opportunities to gain a victory or avoid a defeat.

With the increasingly rapid automation of stock exchanges from the 1990s onwards, their workplaces changed into symbolic theatres of war: the rooms where traders bought and sold became simulated battlefields, and the investment banks strategic military commands, which employed their own 'rocket scientists' called quants to produce financial weapons for them.

The quants implemented Number 2 not *in front of* the screen but *inside* the machine. He made his first conquest as a computer program on stock exchanges; he began to act, conclude transactions; he learned to bluff. And as we have seen, he didn't have to adapt much. The environment in which he operated was almost identical to the closed world of the Pentagon.

Number 2 became a synthetic trader fed with game theory formulae and conducting stock exchange business to an ever-increasing degree. For the first time, self-interest was not only a human characteristic but also something executed by machine programs.

American traders used the German word 'spielen' for their actions ('I've always spieled ... on the other house accounts'). As in the military, the testosterone-fuelled attention of the trader mercenaries merged with the cold logical imperturbability of Number 2. He brought a deadly logical weapon that had worked excellently in the anonymous worlds of the Cold War and proceeded strategically in the automated environment of the markets as the military had once hoped that its troops would: threatening, shooting and hitting, before the opponent noticed what was happening ('first-round killing').

This was translated on the stock exchange into making profits before opponents noticed that they would have to pay for it. And if that wasn't possible, tease them until they were incapable of acting. As in the Lehman Brothers crisis, it could lead to 'Armageddon' through 'weapons of mass destruction'. More often, however, business is in the form of conventional warfare, with 'attacks', 'mowing down' and 'massacre'.

> I don't know how to explain it. It's so wild. If a guy sees it who's not in it, all he could say is "They should be locked up!" It's so violent when it takes off. [...] When we were in the Gulf War, it was 300,000, 400,000 contracts a day for six months. [...] You've gotta be in it.... It's all that counts. [...] Losing 400,000 francs didn't paralyze me. [...] What's good about me is that when I get slapped down, I'm already raging to get back in. [...] C'mon, back to the front![4]

*   *   *

The tragedy is that over the years and to some extent with fierce internal disputes among the players, humane variants of game theory have in fact established and confirmed rules for meaningful cooperation and fair distribution. In his fascinating bestseller *Survival of the Nicest*, the physicist Stefan Klein offers a number of encouraging examples in which *homo oeconomicus* is attacked.

The problem is that the society in which we play today has changed massively in the last few years. More and more areas of our lives are being transformed like the stock exchange, and the economic principle and self-interest of Number 2 have become the basis for interpersonal relations. They are often evident where people work with computers and leave decisions to economic agents: on the stock exchange, in search engines, social networks, personnel departments, tax offices or immigration authorities.

There are no replays in the modern anonymous digital life exchanges. The game and its players keep changing. This applies to the military, finance markets and social life today A wrong move, a wrong life decision, a wrong tweet or a wrong assessment of the opponent can put everything at risk, without the chance of a replay, very often without a second chance of any kind.[5]

The solitary person in front of the monitor in his bunker – be it at the stock exchange, in the office or at home – is increasingly trapped in a virtual world of anonymous one-off interactions. We have descended to the purgatory of non-cooperative games and have arrived precisely where game theory began: in the thought machine of the military and semi-military think tanks of the Cold War and its paranoid atmosphere – where the great ego machine was built that is now in the process of radically and rapidly changing our world and its moral and democratic code.

In order to do this, Number 2 had to deliver a sample of his ability. The victory over the Russians was all well and good but it could not really be demonstrated. Besides, the Cold War was still a war, and it was unclear whether Number 2 would be any good as a civilian. Quite a few economists, who with the end of the war of the systems also wanted to end the neoclassical tradition of a reductionist image of humanity, began to discuss the limitations of the model in public.

The breakthrough that opened the eyes of every investment banker in the world came in 1994. Telecommunications frequencies were auctioned in the USA and soon in many other countries. The 'mother of all auctions' brought astounding results. And the reason was quickly recognized: both the Federal Communications Commission and the bidder had engaged game theory experts to advise on the auction.[6] Simultaneous bidding on the basis of the Nash equilibrium, so the propaganda-like thesis went, brought the state more money than it could ever have dreamed of.

But there was more. In 2000, British physicists and economists organized the auction of 3G mobile network licences according to game theory rules and achieved a sensational and unrealistic profit for the British government of £22 billion. For many people, this was the long-awaited proof of the viability of the model: everyone paid more than they had ever wanted for something abstract that in fact had no real 'price'. And yet they paid with the satisfaction (at least for a few months) of having served their own self-interest as well as possible.

The brain behind the scenes was a man who was in the process of making Number 2 and game theory into the new political and social ideology of the twenty-first century. Ken Binmore, born in 1940, was a brilliant British mathematician and economist. He was convinced that what Philip K. Dick had feared was a tempting opportunity for a new rational social contract.

No one has done more, both behind the scenes and openly, for the civilian career of the mega-egoist. And no one celebrated the success of the auction more loudly as proof of an image of the individual:

> We know that individual human beings are sometimes irrational, and so don't always behave with the consistency that our theories require of a player. But experiments in the field and in the laboratory confirm that human beings are sufficiently consistent in some contexts that our theories work like clockwork. How else would it be possible for us to use game theory to design the big telecom auctions that recently amazed the world by generating billions of dollars in revenue apparently from nowhere?[7]

*   *   *

No one can really understand the political evolution of the British Prime Minister Tony Blair or of parts of the German Social Democratic Party under Gerhard Schröder without comprehending Ken Binmore and what he stood for as muse of New Labour and Agenda 2010. As representative of the new thinking, Binmore not only awoke *homo oeconomicus* for use by computers and finance markets but also began to give a fundamentally new structure to the ethics of the Game of Life, the ideas of cooperation and solidarity. If people were afraid of a world governed by Number 2, they had not understood the new world, as the telecom auctions prove: targeted self-interest can serve the wellbeing of everyone. If people were concerned about a world of calculations and strategic predictions on the basis of the self-interest of each player, now, with a computer on every desk, everyone could play: every trader, every individual.

A year after the fall of the Wall, Binmore began, unsuccessfully at first, to operate behind the scenes to ensure that game theoreticians, led by John Nash, were awarded the Nobel Prize.[8] No other father of Number 2 was so brazen and provocative as Binmore when he announced that he was not 'ashamed' to believe in the great egoists as a world model. We shall see Binmore in action later on, when Number 2 has become big and strong in the world of finance, people and genes. But here in the last decade of the twentieth century, we are only interested for the time being in his fatherly pride at the creature he wants to release into the civilian world.

'Greed and fear will suffice as motivation,' he wrote. 'Greed for the fruits of cooperation, and fear of the consequences of not reciprocating the cooperative overtures of others. Mr Hyde may not be an attractive individual, but he can cooperate very effectively with others like himself.'[9]

This means quite simply that Number 2, the economic agent, *homo oeconomicus*, has become as bad as writers have feared for centuries. But it is possible to do business with him.

BLOOD CIRCULATION

We carry a large number of monsters around with us in our heads. At the beginning, in the nineteenth century, it was writers who told of them. At the other end, in 2010, it is a few clever and witty scientists from the International Monetary Fund.

The nineteenth-century chamber of horrors – Frankenstein, Dr Jekyll and Mr Hyde and Dracula – contained monsters with one thing in common: in reality they were all monsters of economics. They were Number 2 in the version of the mechanical era before the invention of the computer.

The novels were written in times of economic crisis, even panic, and they were penned by authors who, to varying degrees, as Jekyll author Robert Louis Stevenson said of himself, had 'bankruptcy at [their] heels'. When Frankenstein's anonymous monster secretly looked after the households of his 'friends', he called himself the 'invisible hand' – a reference to the 'invisible hand of the market', a metaphor used by the Scottish moral philosopher and Enlightenment figure Adam Smith in the eighteenth century to describe the self-regulation of the market.

The dual nature of Dr Jekyll and Mr Hyde is recognized and legitimized by a single institution, which in Stevenson's world was also an object of discussion because of its own duality, namely the Bank of England.

The American literary critic Gail Houston has shown that the terrible Mr Hyde was recognized without ado as the friendly Dr Jekyll as long as the signature under the cheque was the right one.[1]

As surrogates for humankind, Mr Hyde, Number 2 and *homo oeconomicus* don't need a soul, just their legitimation as business partners. In the novel, the bank establishes Mr Hyde's credit-worthiness and thus provides an identity even for the murderous egoist that he is. Houston reinterprets the fiction in the real world of economics: the fact that the Bank of England housed two entities under the same roof, the reserve bank and a private commercial bank – two institutions that on paper knew nothing of one another and were not allowed to communicate, one eternal and representing the interests of the state, the other terrestrial and profit-oriented – gave rise to the fear during a widespread panic that both could be overrun, because there was no one to play the role of the rational outsider.

The next panic arose in the last decade of the nineteenth century, and the plethora of articles critical of banks published at the time, even by conservatives, would have been worthy of the year 2012. They attacked the thesis of a 'circulating' economy, in which it was bankers rather than the manufacturing industry who injected money 'through all the arteries of trade and commerce'. In the light of the degree of indebtedness, sentences like 'money is the life-blood of trade'[2] led to the increasingly panic-laden question of what would happen *post mortem*, for example in the event of a crash.

The Bank of England was the answer to all doubts, as it assimilated in its 'deathless' body 'two-thirds of the blood which flows no longer in the veins of departed banks'.[3]

This situation produced another monster, Bram Stoker's Dracula. His vampire system is constructed like a company, and in the book he wishes explicitly to move to London, the financial centre of the world at the time. He is a Transylvanian investor who travels with trunks full of currency from all over the globe, has a worryingly large amount of property in London financed by loans, and would like to take over the role of the Bank of England. The entire novel, as Houston points out, is full of references to loans, securities, bank accounts, cheques, real estate. On one occasion, when the count is attacked with a knife, no blood flows but a 'stream of gold'. This is what the count wants and what Van Helsing contests: a monopoly on circulation.

Dracula was written by a highly indebted man in a decade in which the business sections of newspapers reported on 'sensational horrors and heart-rending anxieties' hitherto unknown by anyone alive, at a time when a panic was feared that 'risked the supremacy of English credit' and made a mockery of the 'so-called "financial genius" of the banks'.[4]

When the venerable Barings Bank almost went bankrupt in 1890 (it was not until 1995 that it finally occurred), England experienced a series of large-scale bank mergers. In little over a decade the number of private banks shrank from 250 to a dozen.

Neither Mary Shelley nor Robert Louis Stevenson nor Bram Stoker was 'left wing', and those who might have encountered the ghost of Karl Marx circulating in Europe were also disinterested. None of these authors was an opponent of banks as such, let alone the economic system in existence. With a feel for capital and the power of their imagination, they attacked the economic models with which social behaviour was evaluated, regulated and controlled like a natural law. They saw through these models as fictions and 'machines' that not only described markets but also decided on the reputations, lives and fairness of people.

Hence the monsters. They are not only literary symbols of panic and horror. They are anomalies of the system. In the novels they are brought to life by electricity or chemical reagents. Our Number 2 today was brought to life not by writers but by people who saw themselves as realists. They relied on mathematics.

In 1952, only 2 per cent of the articles in the main economics journals in the USA contained mathematical formulae. By the end of the century, when *homo oeconomicus* or Number 2 ruled the world, a powerful economist felt obliged to recall a time when there was economics without mathematics: 'It may be hard for younger economists to imagine, but nearly until midcentury it was not unusual for a theorist using mathematical techniques to begin with a substantial apology, explaining that this approach need not assume that humans are automatons deprived of free will.'[5]

How was this imperialist victory possible? How was it possible that people began to subject themselves increasingly to the human image of Number 2 that they had rejected in real life? They hadn't created a Mr Hyde. Why an abstract creature now? There were not only philosophical reasons – the postmodern deconstruction of the ego had, as we have seen, accepted economics relatively dispassionately. The earthly residuum had disappeared, the alchemy could begin. But this took place in academic circles, and even within the discipline there were so many byways and side roads, not to mention contradictions, that the strategic victory of Number 2 in daily life can be explained only in economic terms: he was incredibly efficient, and his fusion with the computer endowed him overnight with the brawn of a Superman.

In brief, Number 2 was as successful as he was because at least until recently, especially in stock exchanges, he could do something that people, whatever their ideology, could not match: he could make astonishingly accurate predictions. He ticked like a clock showing the future. The mathematics appeared to say that it wasn't a model but a natural law that was at work. Number 2 is nothing other than an ego machine that can be programmed and employed, but that is precisely where people were duped. He was successful, in the Cold War, in auctions and on the stock exchange. There was no need to preach self-interest. All that was needed was to draw people inside the machine and persuade them that what they were seeing was a natural law.

Newton's abstract world view was convincing not because people could see how the earth orbited around the sun but because his model made it possible to accurately predict comets and planetary orbits. The cosmos where Number 2 held sway was no different.

Formulae that predict the results of economic actions and that thus enforce a specific economic action are no longer conjectures about or descriptions of the market; they create markets. As the sociologist Michel Callon rightly points out, the laws that govern celestial bodies don't care whether we believe in them or not.[6] The most successful models were themselves related to the future: 'futures' and the 'levers' transposed from Newton's mechanical age. Derivatives fixed the prices of things that did not even exist yet.

The extent of this operation can also be described in numbers. Throughout the world the speculative value of derivatives rose from zero in 1970 to $1.2 quadrillion in 2010, twenty times more than the gross national product of the entire world. Thus even dumbfounded economics Nobel Prize winners now talk of the 'alchemy' of the market; the old dream of creating gold just through thoughts and contact has come true. As the alchemists taught, 'work' means the work of the mind. Done properly, it promises the wealth of the world.

For this to happen, power had to flow through the electrical veins of the computer, and people had to connect to this circuit with their PCs and mobile phones. The computer became both the marketplace and the home of the economic agent. Only now could the formulae finally function like genetic programming. People might be irrational, but not the 'autonomous agent', who acted for people on finance markets and soon on all other markets as well. As Hugh Kenner puts it superlatively, what happens when the world enters a new era occurred again: 'Systems were elaborated, and the corresponding men excogitated.'[7]

This great social experiment with the people in civilian society began with the automation of floor trading in the stock exchange.

The criticism of the digital economy should not be confused with the scepticism that greeted the automobile and the railways. We are not talking about technology but about the construction of the social machine.

In the stock exchange trading pits, the traders first communed with their pocket calculators and pre-programmed interest and option buttons and then migrated, as the military had done before them, into the interior of the machine itself and inhabited the closed rooms of the terminals.

'*Homo oeconomicus* really does exist,' exclaimed Callon. 'He is formatted, framed and equipped with prostheses which help him in his calculations and which are, for the most part, produced by economics.'[8]

Among all the prostheses, game theory is one of the most popular. Today we learn early on in school of the spectacular failure over the centuries of all attempts to reduce people to a couple of mechanical cogs, hydraulic pumps or physical formulae. Economists also knew that and developed ideas like 'limited rationality' to make clear that humans don't act like Mr Spock.

But Number 2 replied: people can do what they want. Freedom is their characteristic feature and that of their machines. But if they don't act according to game theory, the market and history and reason will probably destroy them.

Even without this threat, the human factor was helpless against reality. Number 2 was built into the survival machine as an economic agent by the computer software. He takes over transactions, controls auctions, prophesies the future and explains the past – no longer by any means just on financial markets but also in social networks, in analytical procedures used for emails and in all other markets that determine the price for a person through the totality of his data and the entire digital communication market.

We shall observe Number 2 at work in a later chapter. At this point in our portrait we are interested only in the agent as an artificial person, and in the full panoply of his preferences and prejudices.

Spurred on by the increased networking of people who cooperate and don't want to buy or sell (above all themselves), Number 2 really started infiltrating successfully into everything. Now, at the dawn of the commercialized Internet, it was the turn of human beings.

Why do the Internet, mobile phones and the powerful companies behind them want to know what we will do and think next? Because our actions and thoughts are moves in the game. We become users, the users consumers and the consumers Number 2: in search of the best prices, contacts, in brief the best information in the new information economy.

And the next metamorphosis is in the offing: the state of the future – a gigantic commercial, really existing Internet – will 'outsource many functions, rely less on law and regulation and more on market incentives, and respond to ever-changing and constantly monitored consumer demand rather than to voter preferences expressed in relatively rare elections'.[9]

In contrast to real life, the human doppelgänger in the digital systems is always in view. Predicting what he will do, buy or think and determining a price for it is an aim that the military, police, financial markets and all areas of digital social communication have in common.

Practically every person, at least in the Western hemisphere, is already part of John Nash's game. Without even noticing it, we take part every day in auctions like the ones organized by Ken Binmore for the government.

A harmless but all the more powerful auction game is Google AdWords. The science philosopher George Dyson considers this algorithm to be the most powerful in the world at present; more complex and capable than all game theory formulae of the Cold War.[10] This software, which links search queries with advertisements and made Google rich, has become a routine job for Number 2.

Every single search query by a person anywhere in the world is in reality an auction controlled by Number 2, in which it is decided which advertisements and what prices appear on the right margin of the screen. The auction is played out using algorithms modelled on game theory that are no longer distinguishable from those used in real-time trading in hedge funds and derivatives.

> Selling ads doesn't generate only profits; it also generates torrents of data about users' tastes and habits, data that Google then sifts and processes in order to predict future consumer behaviour, find ways to improve its products, and sell more ads. This is the heart and soul of Googlenomics. It's a system of constant self-analysis: a data-fuelled feedback loop that defines not only Google's future but the future of anyone who does business online.[11]

And the future of everyone who communicates in modern society. It's true that pocket calculators replaced mental arithmetic. But the ensuing cultural criticism was wrong. By taking away mental arithmetic, it made it as easy to calculate the Black–Scholes formula as it does to work out 1 + 1.

In the mid-1920s, Marcel Mauss already wrote prophetically: '*Homo oeconomicus* is not behind, but lies ahead, as does the man of morality and duty, the man of science and reason. For a very long time man was something different, and he has not been a machine for very long, made complicated by a calculating machine.'[12] Elections, opinion forming, politics, even the constitutional status of Western democracy, are all ready to be transformed into automated markets: from zero to several billion participants. The consistency of individual life is changing, hijacked by Number 2 and robbed of its identity and nature, like a piece of software attacked by a computer virus.

Understanding the crisis of financial markets is not a question of looking into a wallet or at the stock exchange transmissions on television; all you will see there is the transformation of the future into money with the aid of machines. It offers a glimpse of the future of automated markets and of automated society as a whole.

Those who want to see ghosts can take a ride on the ghost train, but when a ghost appears in broad daylight in full view of everyone, things begin to get interesting.

There is little chance that respect for Number 2 will be exchanged for respect for life stories that cannot be reduced to the simple self-interest that is allegedly programmed genetically in us. And there is little hope that the faces of predominantly American experts and mathematical forecasters, for whom the notion 'welfare state' is just an entry on the debit side of their accounts, will register anything other than amusement and mild disdain when confronted by literary monsters.

At the same time, those who have imposed their version of human rationality reduced to formulae on everyone – and as things stand these are the most influential representatives of the economics profession – are producing a bizarre theatre of irrationality.

Influenced by the crisis, the economist Paul De Grauwe published a self-critical essay questioning the rational self-interest of the conventional economic agent.

> Since they all understand the same 'truth', they all act in the same way. Thus modelling the behaviour of just one agent (the 'representative' consumer and the 'representative' producer) is all one has to do to fully describe the intricacies of the world. Rarely has such a ludicrous idea been taken so seriously by so many academics.[13]

This was stating it mildly, because De Grauwe didn't ask any further questions about the role and morality of Number 2. But the very next day, Michael Wickens, another economics professor, published a reply in the same newspaper proving that De Grauwe was completely wrong. And a few weeks later a further article replied to this exchange with the comment: 'Professor Wickens [...] showed that Mr de Grauwe was wrong, which tended to prove that Mr de Grauwe was indeed right.'[14]

The real-life Kafkaesque agents could be smiling too soon. Perhaps literature and art will play a role again sometime in reminding people of human unpredictability. Two authors from the International Monetary Fund wrote a highly critical analysis of the system failure in the light of the disaster in 2010, which in their eyes was a failure by all economic actors. They are scathing about the agents[15] and urgently recommend with only slightly ironic fervour the installation of a new system. As a candidate they proposed a literary figure, Mrs Rose from Faulkner's short story 'A Rose for Emily'. It is a horror story.

10

NERVOUS SYSTEM

FOR THE FIRST TIME IT'S CLEAR: WE DON'T NEED A BODY TO ACT IN THE WORLD, JUST STRONG NERVES

Number 2 is no longer a character on paper. As long as he was just in books, he was eerie enough, recognizable from the Chicago economist Milton Friedman to the outgrowths of Thatcherism merely as an ideology. It was only the electricity of the computer that made him into what he is.

The idea of an electrically powered robot acting and thinking for its owner is as old as the discovery of electricity and as young as advertisements for food processors. Awestruck visitors to Thomas Edison's theatrical demonstrations in Paris in 1881 spoke of a 'ghostly hand' that switched things on and off, made them move or gave an electric shock.

Light, heat, electric shock and the invisible hand: this is the seductive combination that fills heads not only with science but also with magic. Hardly had the telegraph been invented than scientists started attempting to make contact with the beyond. No sooner was the telephone installed in homes than Kafkaesque anonymous powers started calling. Electricity is closely associated with the fear of elemental powers and monsters roused from the depths of the earth or from inside ourselves.

A nineteen-year-old woman wrote the quintessential fantasy text during a night-time thunderstorm on Lake Geneva: 'Perhaps a corpse would be reanimated; galvanism had given a token of such things;

perhaps the component parts of a creature might be manufactured, brought together, and endued with vital warmth.'[1]

In the past, Dr Frankenstein's monster brought to life by lightning and galvanic current also existed only on paper. It had to hibernate in permafrost for almost 150 years before it was given a second chance. The whole world now quotes Frankenstein's monster as if it really existed. It is not the imagination, wishes and passions of people that have changed but the technical possibilities for putting them into practice. Like so much in the nineteenth century, Mary Shelley's *Frankenstein* was a trial run for the imagination. The monster was there. It only needed the spark of life.

We are living in an era of the second wave of thoughts, theories and ideologies that were once tried out under other circumstances and failed. The disasters of finance capitalism, the mechanization of civilization, the dismantling of the human self so as to better exploit it, the economization of social relations – all of these things had already been tried out in the alchemists' laboratories, in the age of Absolutism, in the industrial revolution and in the industrial complexes of the early twentieth century.

The first time it was always physical: transforming lead into gold, turning automatons into people. With great effort, these human visions are always locked up again, banished to caves or the Pole or simply regarded as kids' stuff. There they wait like the Greek Titans underground or like Sauron in Mordor for the day they can return in a new form under better circumstances. There are hundreds of similar stories in fantasy culture, in scenarios featuring the return of the freak animals or the unchaining of the monsters.

This historical reference is important for understanding the dreams we dream today. The story doesn't begin with Apple or Microsoft or with the first calculating machines by the computer pioneer Konrad Zuse. The software that led to these machines has existed for centuries, in the form not of mathematical code but of the economic wish for a universal thought machine, an automaton to control thinking, to resuscitate the inanimate, to communicate with and observe absent beings.

When the first clockwork machines appeared in the eighteenth century, the fantasy of an artificial being was immediately associated with them; then the steam engine was invented, and the search was on for a thinking version; then came electricity, and beings were connected to power sources. None of them worked, but they were all driven by the same desire to create calculable and controllable duplicate human beings, and if not human beings, then at least their brains.

In the absence of the right tool, the computer, many ended up in a dead end or in science fiction novels. But none of the failures could obliterate the overarching vision. It was never just a matter of the automatic filling out of tax returns or of reservation systems or holiday bookings. There was always much more at stake.

First of all the military, then the stockbrokers, then the whole world had the feeling, after their initial contact with the digital world, that they were communicating with a living organism that was so perfect that they could entrust it with decisions about the life and death of the entire planet.

The talk today of an electronic 'nervous system' permeating the entire world is far more than just a semantic construction. It is precisely this nervous system that economists have been dreaming of for two hundred years: the same economic rationality permeates the entire inhabited and uninhabited universe, the same economics of thought, the same calculability of buying and selling, from neurons to pension fund investment decisions.

There are also dead branches in Number 2's family tree. One was the attempt with the aid of electricity to bring him to life as a robot servant or factory worker. But the cul-de-sac in which it ended in the late eighteenth century led to a new realization taken up a hundred years later: the life force is to be found not in electricity but in the electrical exchange of information. The mistake made in Number 2's first attempt was to connect the electrical contacts directly to the creature instead of using them to link creatures with one another.

On 6 November 1780, the doctor Luigi Galvani (1737–98) took a statically charged scalpel and touched the amputated leg of a frog attached to a table with metal clips, causing the leg to twitch. Galvani thought he had discovered the vital spirits. To verify that the electric sparks could really enkindle life, he attached metal rods to the roof of his house connected by wires directly to the nerves of frogs and other animals in his laboratory. When storm clouds gathered over his house and lightning struck, the animals began to convulse. The news that electricity could quicken the dead spread through Europe like wildfire.

Shortly afterwards, Galvani's nephew, the physics professor Giovanni Aldini (1762–1834), experimented in London with the body of a hanged double murderer. The body twitched violently, one eye opened, the facial expression changed, but the man didn't come back to life. Instead one of the doctors present apparently died of shock.

In Paris the Jacobins began to wire the heads of executed victims and observed how their faces twisted into terrible grimaces. Alessandro Volta (1745–1827), Galvani's great adversary, repeated the frog experiment and discovered that the statically charged scalpel didn't bring back the dead but merely completed a trivial electrical circuit. But because he also deduced that every cell is electrically charged, the fantasy of a connection between electricity and life was only reinforced.

All over Europe, living creatures were cut up and electrocuted: cows' heads, chicken legs, worms. Depending on the observer, it was a spiritual, scientific or economic operation, often all three at once. Nothing could be seen in isolation: the bodies of animals and humans were just an economic cycle, an animal economy, and formed the model for the real economy. Physical laws found in them could be transferred directly to society and the economy. Within a few years an extremely fateful connection was made: electricity became the metaphor for vital energy and economic wealth.

Unfortunately, however, artificial life could not be created in this way. The newly discovered laws of energy and electricity were transferred to the laws of economics and human society. But the great dream remained unfulfilled: a creature that followed these laws predictably because it couldn't do otherwise, something that would have made industrialization much more efficient, didn't exist.

But then an adoring admirer of Galvani had a stroke of genius. Why connect electricity to nerves when it can act as a nervous system in its own right? Why bring a whole body to life when only the brain is needed? He came up with the idea of how this might be done – a hundred and fifty years too early, but still with the basic message that applies today: electricity is not the vital energy; life is nothing but an exchange of information.

In 1800, while the guillotine in Paris was providing enough material for gruesome experiments with electricity and human heads, in Spain the doctor and inventor Don Francisco Salvá (1751–1828) was wondering how disembodied living heads could be made to communicate with one another.

Salvá's aim was to resuscitate not dead bodies but bodiless brains. George Dyson wrote:

> He was rumored to have constructed a single-wire telegraph line over twenty-six miles between Aranjuez and Madrid. Salvá experimented both with electrostatic signals and with the transmission of faint pulses of direct current, indicated by the convulsion of frog legs as much as 310 meters apart [...] in 1804 showing how the frogs could be replaced as both transmitters and receivers of signals by electromechanical cells.[2]

With this apparatus, Salvá invented one of the first telegraphs, as he reported to the Academy of Sciences in Barcelona, which one day, he predicted, would also be 'wireless'.

There was one person in Paris who was highly interested in such inventions, at least more so than in the question of where the soul resided. Napoleon, reported Salvá to the Academy, citing two highly reliable sources, was annoyed at the unreliability of purely visual communication. And he recognized not only the military but also the economic advantages of the new technology.

Until the computer monsters of the Cold War, the military and the economists were always the godparents at the cradle of technology seeking to improve thinking and communication.

The frog's nerve cells, the exploitation of the animal economy, were the first sparks in the increasingly powerful metaphor comparing electrical communication with the 'nervous system'. Even the invention of the battery by Volta failed to put an end to the dissection of the body. Researchers now had electricity, but for a long time they couldn't find a receiver that reacted as sensitively to electrical signals as living bodies.[3] They wired the human tongue, and when that proved impractical, the early nineteenth century 'electro-physiological telegraph' used the fingertips of both hands as receivers. Alexander von Humboldt wired his tongue and rectum and reported in a letter of seeing a white light. In the drawings that art professor Samuel Morse made of his invention, only one hand, operating the 'copper tongue', can be seen. In 1870 the first telegraphers felt themselves 'merging with their networks, describing the transmission of signals from their brains, through their fingers, onto their keys, and then on down the line'.[4]

The more it merged, the more rapid, ethereal, error-free, the communication became. This ensemble was also increasingly taken apart. Ultimately there was no need for the tongue any more or the entire hand – the thumbs-up on Facebook is what remains.

On the two hundredth anniversary of Galvani's birth in 1937, in the era of the telegraph and telephone, everyone understood what had been discovered at the time: 'What in Galvani's hands could move a muscle, brought Marconi's voice across oceans.'[5]

This sounds efficient and logical, as the scientific history of a rational species might relate its own progress: from frog to email. But in the background noise of history, from Salvá's terrace and the SOS signal sent by the *Titanic* to stock exchange prices, the radio communication from Apollo 11 and the chatter of our Facebook friends, for the last two hundred and fifty years a different message has been sent, as it said in a telegram in Bram Stoker's *Dracula*: 'messages which will make both your ears tingle'.[6]

It didn't take long after the metal nerve fibres started to spread their tentacles for the world to fall into a hypnotic state. Mesmerism claimed to transfer thoughts in trance, so much so that the American Congress could no longer decide whether to invest money in Morse or in thought transmission.

The answer: the two had to be combined. James Braid invented the term 'hypnotism' in 1842, and in 1882, by which time the telegraph had become established, F.W.H. Myers coined the concept 'telepathy'. Thought reading and communication with absent souls became research projects of serious scientists, who attempted to make contact with the dead.

The professor of English and science historian Laura Otis relates the drama of this trance with a plethora of examples from Samuel Morse to the phonograph on which Bram Stoker recorded the story of Dracula. Using modern means of communication, people attempted not only to speak with one another but also to establish contact with immaterial beings.

Fragments of these developments can be found in the DNA of Number 2. He is technical but also spiritual; he calculates like a machine and sees things in the future like a medium.

In a still fascinating study from the early 1950s, the economist Friedrich Hayek – unaware of cyberneticists' research – compared the market to a communications network resembling the human neural circuits, with neurons in the form of buyers and sellers doing what was 'useful to the system'.

By the end of the twentieth century this system had been perfected: from genes and neurons to automated financial markets, everything operated according to the models of neoclassical and neoliberal economics. And game theory had made it possible to shape even interpersonal communication according to this image.

The first attempt to awaken the dead failed. The second, the awakening of dead models, starting in the 1950s, was a resounding success. But we should have been warned: with everything so well planned, it doesn't take much provocation for monsters to emerge.

11

ANDROID

On his first appearance, Number 2 was literally a machine that looked like a person. He was not yet a calculating machine, but played the flute or piano.

The year was 1738, and a whole procession of artificial creatures were doing the tour of Europe: they travelled from churches to palaces and from palaces to fairs. Thousands of people followed their traces. Empresses and kings admired them, poets and craftsmen celebrated them, civil servants and soldiers capitulated in the face of their perfection. They were the wonders of their age.

Two hundred and fifty years before the queues formed to buy the latest iPhone, the appearance of this mechanical species was perhaps the first case in which the enchantment in the face of a magic technology was no longer separable from the question of who would exploit both – enchantment and technology – for their own purposes.

'You can see,' wrote an enthusiastic eye witness about a popular mechanical duck, 'how it devours its feed, drinks in measure, looks happy after drinking, then arranges its feathers, pauses a moment, and then relieves itself.' Empress Maria Theresa, for example, had a machine that could write.

Pleasure seekers paid 24 sous in the Tuileries to listen to a song by a mechanical flautist, who had an air pump hidden in his instrument. 'At first many people could not believe that the sounds were produced by the flute which the automaton was holding.'[1]

The most popular automatons were those that looked like human beings. For his *Encyclopédie*, Diderot sought a name that would mean more than just 'automaton' and less than 'human'. The human-like machines were known henceforth as 'androids'.

The superstar of the species was the Music Lady, an organist about whom one observer commented: 'She is apparently agitated with an anxiety and diffidence not always felt in real life.'[2]

In France, 'an anatomical man' was built, and silver mines were simulated in which the miners functioned like small automatons.

After the monarchs, craftsmen and farmers had had their say, it was the turn, as with all pioneering technologies, of the thinkers. And despite their differences of opinion, they all compared Jacques Vaucanson (1709–82), the inventor of the duck and flautist, with Prometheus, the loftiest of the Titans, who could ignite the life spark. Jean-Jacques Rousseau, with his philosophy of the 'natural man', did so; likewise La Mettrie, who ten years later published the book *L'Homme Machine*; and Voltaire was particularly enthusiastic. With his eulogies to 'Prometheus II', he fired the imagination of the Prussian king Frederick II, who tried to entice Vaucanson to Berlin. When he failed to do so, 'the meticulous king of small machines', as Michel Foucault called him,[3] had his own automatons built.

People looked with delight at the perfect machines, whose metal surfaces were designed to create a complete illusion, and they didn't know what they were seeing. A few people, reported Vaucanson, complained that the duck had perforated brass feathers rather than real plumage. Vaucanson explained that he wished 'rather to demonstrate the manner of the actions than to shew a machine'.[4]

In fact, the wonderful surfaces, the perfect simulation of living beings, were there for one reason only: to be seen into – some through a door, like the flautist or the dancer, another of Vaucanson's automatons; others, like the duck, through transparency, giving an unhindered view of the inner mechanics.

The public were meant to see the cogs and springs, the entire internal mechanism of the artificial life – apparently to understand how life and movement work. In his memoirs, Vaucanson himself once again urged readers to inspect the machines to see 'that Nature has been justly imitated'.[5] In reality, however, there was something completely different at stake: the inquisitive humans who stared unsuspectingly at the automatons were guinea pigs in a social experiment. Through their inspection they themselves became part of the machine. The machine was wonderful, and it was a threat. Wonderful, because in the eyes of the people at the time, this artificial life breathed the magic of alchemists and the genius of modern engineers; a threat, because they were the agents of a political idea, that of turning people themselves into machines.

The philosopher René Descartes had already intimated that animals were nothing other than automatons and that humans differed from animals only because they had a soul. Joseph Spence, who saw the duck in Paris in 1741, wrote a letter to his mother in which he developed the idea: 'a good artist might make an animal in clockwork, that should do everything the same real animal can do.'[6]

But who is interested in animals? Humans are what counts. The perfect automatons at some point raised questions about the thing with the soul; playfully and perhaps ironically, like the hype that first surrounded Second Life on the Internet, when people believed that avatars could somehow acquire life.

When it was in the mood, a writing machine by the great watchmaker Jaquet-Droz from Neuchâtel, wrote: 'I think therefore I am.' Sometimes it also wrote: 'I don't think, do I exist at all?'

Hobbes, the author of *Leviathan*, declared man to be an automaton, saying 'what is the heart but a spring; and the nerves but so many strings; and the joints but so many wheels?'[7]

It was a world view that was tailor-made for the needs of the modern era, its economic drive towards efficiency and exploitation and its political will to control through a central brain.

And this was the real mission of the automatons: to show how humans would function if they were machines. Access to the androids' innards was access to people's innards, because when people looked into machines, the machines changed what was in their head. The flautist, the drummer, the dancer and even the duck were world-view factories.

People saw how they were meant to see themselves: as a meshing of cogs, elastic springs and hydraulics that were all dependent on the mechanical central unit. The duck functioned like the human body, except without a soul. And soon people in the Paris salons were saying that their 'clockwork' had run down and needed to be wound up. And if the body functioned like that, then why not the state or the economy?

These androids were in fact information-processing systems, and that was precisely what the monarchs and institutions required as an organizational concept. It wasn't long before Frederick II, as Michel Foucault wrote,[8] transformed his army into an 'automaton' with mechanically drilled movements. Napoleon, who loved automatons as much as Frederick, learned quickly and perfected schools, hospitals and the administration to become machines. Above all, however, he perfected the economy.

The Voltaires and La Mettries whom Frederick invited to his Prussian court may be regarded as eighteenth-century McKinseys. La Mettrie's *L'Homme Machine* can be seen as the building instructions for the Prussian army but also as the world view of Frederick's subjects.

Expert opinions came from everywhere, from Immanuel Kant in Königsberg to the French doctor and economist François Quesnay (1694–1774), as to the degree to which the state could be organized like a machine and when the machine would turn the state into a tyrant. But more important was what the historian Simon Schaffer called the birth of 'technico-politics'.[9]

We need only look at the intentions of Quesnay and the miracle engineers who were building automatons in Paris. They dreamed of machines that not only imitated the entire human anatomy, every bone and every ossicle, but could also simulate the muscles and, with the aid of hydraulic systems, the blood circulation. The idea that the human body was a circulatory system was not yet commonly accepted by doctors. They still stuck to Galen's theory that blood originated in the liver and seeped out through the blood vessels.

Quesnay suggested that doctors be cured of these incorrect ideas with the aid of automatons who would show them. They would become a means of visualizing the circulation of the blood, perhaps the first three-dimensional simulation and the first inkling of the virtual Big Bang that the computer pioneers were to engineer two centuries later.

This sounds like a harmless biology lesson. But just as the mechanics of gearwheels were to change the state, combined with hydraulic circulation they were also to change the notion of economics for ever. The automated body became the human body, and the human body became an economic organism. The blood – money or wealth – flowed between landowners, artisans and farmers. The artisans were like veins, the farmers like arteries, and the landowners, who provided the capital, the heart.[10]

Wealth could only come from nature because, according to Quesnay, this was the only place where something could be created from nothing.

Paradigms like this are popular in economics as long as there are automatons that show how they function. After the discovery of electricity, electric current took over the function of blood, later to be superseded by the exchange processes of atomic structures in quantum physics.

We should bear in mind that the concept of 'economics' as we know it today did not exist in the eighteenth century. Economics was an area of medicine, as in 'animal economy'. Diderot's *Encyclopédie*, for example, defined it as a 'mechanism, the totality of functions and movements that maintains the life of animals'. And we know today that the physical and mechanistic foundations of economics had their origins here.

Adam Smith was in close contact with the French, who gave him the idea for the 'circulation' of all business and the 'invisible hand' that regulates markets. And a whole library of books has now demonstrated that the marriage of economics and physics, brokered by watchmakers, engineers and doctors, was to become perhaps the most fateful and dramatic liaison of the following centuries – and something that concerns us more than ever today.

It is a marriage that was not made in heaven but in the mechanical clockwork of an industrialized society.

Economics has been an automaton from the outset. 'Physics and economics,' wrote the science philosopher Nancy Cartwright, 'are both disciplines with imperialist tendencies: they repeatedly aspire to account for almost everything, the first in the natural world, the second in the social.'[11] Where they joined forces, physics (subcategory mechanics) in the eighteenth century created the matrix with which economics overlaid society. Economics, not philosophy and much less the abstract 'Enlightenment', transformed technology into social organization.

To accuse critics of technological innovation of being Luddites is an astoundingly naïve attitude. Criticism of technology is always criticism of the social and cognitive forces that they produce through their use and abuse by economics as an explanatory model. 'The human body,' wrote La Mettrie, 'is a machine which winds up its own springs.'[12]

The fairground attractions wound up with keys and cranks were the forerunners of what we call 'technical determinism' today: the machine determines our future. In the words of the literary scholar Hugh Kenner: 'If a man does nothing with his life but spin threads, then just how is a thread-spinning machine not a purified man?'[13]

It was not just a question in the eighteenth century of inventing automatons but rather of inventing human beings for the machines.

And it was Vaucanson, the father of the duck and dancer, who shortly afterwards designed the first automatic loom, much to the displeasure of the artisans in the factories, and made a comment that still resounds two hundred and fifty years later: his automatic silk machine was a device 'with which a horse, an ox or an ass can make cloth more beautiful and much more perfect than the most able silk workers.... Each machine makes each day as much material as the best worker, when he is not wasting time.'[14]

In France the fashion for toys was coming to an end. The automatons had produced soldiers and subjects. The next step was to produce consumers and markets.

Beforehand, however, a riot by artisans in Lyon – after his comments about replaceable workers, Vaucanson had to flee the city disguised as a monk – made it evident that people had first to be taught to recognize the machine code, even if the machine didn't look like a human or an animal.

But now people in Britain began to become interested in the toy automatons. James Watt's steam engine was financed by venture capitalists, who also generously supported a man significantly named John Merlin.[15]

Merlin bought the French automatons for his mechanical museum in London, which enjoyed an even more glittering reputation than Vaucanson's machines had done during their heyday in France.

With the money from his backers, he staged a permanent exhibition of androids, which quite simply presented the deconstruction of humans into the individual functions that would become so important later on in industrial production processes. The figures performed 'almost every motion and inclination of the human body, viz. the head, the breasts, the neck, the arms, the fingers, the legs, etc., even to the motion of the eyelids, and the lifting up of the hands and fingers to the face'.[16]

Although they didn't realize it, people were in fact looking at algorithms. They were not written in code as they are today and were thus more tangible, but they were the gateway to a world of division of labour and breaking down functions. The dismantling of clockwork mechanisms, explains Otto Mayr, had been regarded since the seventeenth century as an 'illustration for *analysis*'.[17] It was an unconscious process that had more to do with the demand for artificial body parts than with the needs of modern industry, but it executed exactly what modern algorithms do incessantly today: the breakdown of physical and mental work into formulae to measure the physical and hence the economic value of thought.

Around 1790, the chemist and economist Antoine Lavoisier thought up not only reforms for French agriculture but also a calculating method for thinking and writing to measure intellectual work – in other words to penetrate into the mind. 'By evaluating pulse rate and air consumption,' writes Simon Schaffer, 'the prudent academician and his collaborators reckoned they could determine "how many pounds weight correspond to the efforts of a man who recites speech, a musician who plays an instrument."'[18]

This would all soon be used in the era of labour rationalization and Taylorism as a model for the new society in the twentieth century: the conversion of repetitive micro-movements such as the lifting of an arm or the stretching of a finger into physical force and efficiency formulae. But for now workers still consisted of muscles, bones, hands, arms and legs. Throughout the entire industrial revolution and well into the twentieth century, they still sought refuge in the idea that they were selling their physical strength but not their souls.

The poet William Wordsworth was one of the few people who took a different view of the cute androids in Merlin's Haymarket Theatre.

He didn't rejoice. He described what he saw as 'a parliament of monsters'.

The ascendancy of the toy creatures lasted another hundred years in Europe. It ended up, as in a novel, as a fairground sideshow. In the 1930s, a mysterious photo was discovered in a French museum of the most famous example, the lifelike duck, whose wretched state Goethe had already commented on and which Napoleon didn't wish to buy back for that reason. It was thought to show the half-skeletal mechanical animal in Dresden.

By the time the artificial species left the world stage of the imagination, the great nations were populated by machines that could act independently and regulate themselves. They were like a mutation of the fragile automatons; and they were no longer welcomed by an applauding fairground public, but treated with awe and fear.

12

BRAIN

HUMANS BECOME MACHINE-FRIENDLY

The automatons were rusting, and the age of the steam engine was approaching. Machines have the power to produce social norms without having to communicate or justify them. As the history of technology has shown, they can be more effective than legislative apparatus.[1]

Their functionality is their selling point, and they work in people's heads even when they have long been scrapped in the real world. Without ever having seen a steam engine, people still talk about a 'full head of steam', because machines can be understood intuitively.

Likewise, the safety value on a steam engine, known as the 'governor', was sufficient to justify the idea of self-regulating systems and hence liberalism in general.[2]

The governor takes us from Watt's steam engine to the term 'cybernetics' (from *gubernator* or *kybernetes*: helmsman) and the *gouverneurs* of the European Stability Mechanism, self-regulating and hence legally immune.

Sigmund Freud also borrowed metaphors like pressure, energy, force and displacement from the world of machines for his interpretation of the unconscious. Talk of machines – or computers today – is always about social physics as well.

The governor in the steam engine planted the metaphor of

self-regulation in people's heads. But the safety valve was not there to protect people; unattended, machines had the habit of ripping off the arms or legs of the people who had dealings with them. The valve didn't prevent this. It was designed rather to protect the system so that the expensive machine would not fly apart. That was the second political statement by the machine: the functioning of the machine was more important than the functioning of the human being.

When we talk today of digital systems amputating people and the user fusing with the machine, this darkly recalls an era when this happened quite literally and for the first time. The steam engine amputated people so frequently that a large automated market for artificial ribs, hands and legs arose. The spare parts for humans were modelled on the mechanical wonders in Merlin's automaton museum. A complete reversal had taken place: humans themselves were turning into androids to operate the machine. And this was the third political statement: the worker had to literally fuse with the machine.[3]

As we can't build robots, people have to become robots. This is the political code that is also carried by Number 2 in the hypermodern environment of the twenty-first century, because the mathematical modelling of his egoism and the amputation of all emotional personality is nothing other than the transformation of humans into automatons. This is not an exclusively modern fantasy. The Victorians also had this dream: a machine that thinks for humans.

At the same time as Wordsworth was seeing the 'parliament of monsters' in London, a mother was on the way to Merlin's museum with her small boy. Years later the boy would recall Vaucanson's dancer, 'an admirable *danseuse*, with a bird on the fore finger of her right hand, which wagged its tail, flapped its wings, and opened its beak. This lady attitudinized in a most fascinating manner. Her eyes were full of imagination, and irresistible.'[4]

This boy would one day purchase the rundown mechanical dancer to show to his guests. Inspired by Vaucanson, he would also design the first complete digital calculator in 1823 and shortly afterwards a difference engine that could break down not only movements but also thought processes.

This English mathematician, Charles Babbage (1792–1871), the true father of the computer, had thought out everything in his head: the punched cards, the computer-controlled division of labour, the automated factory, and machinery that has been taught arithmetic instead of poetry.[5] And if that were not enough, he also foresaw game theory.

'I selected for my test the contrivance of a machine that should be able to play a game of purely intellectual skill successfully; such as tic-tac-toe, drafts, chess, etc.... I soon arrived at a demonstration that every game of skill is susceptible of being played by an automaton.'[6]

Practically no one who studies Babbage, this nineteenth-century nerd, can escape the eerie shock of recognition. In his head he quite simply developed a steam engine of thought. It was to be what the artificial arms for the worker were on the real steam engine: the prosthesis for the newly emerging class of businessmen and traders who would fuse with the nascent system of capitalism, with its numbers and profits and utility functions.

But it was too early for Number 2. In contrast to the situation a century later, no one wanted to build an atomic bomb and no one needed military chains of command without human beings, and the British government was only interested in the plan in passing. Babbage complained that the world was interested only in his dancer and not in the difference engine. In his apartment he had the dancer in one room and the unfinished calculating machine in another. Hardly any of his visitors were interested in the abstract machine, but everyone wanted to see the simulation of a human automaton. And yet it was the difference engine that would enable the idea of the automaton to find itself. Babbage couldn't know that today, a century and half later, in the age of big data, huge data supermarkets, warehouses and industries would develop for human thought. It was therefore all the more far-sighted of him to call his calculating machine a 'factory'.

To transform movements, forces, the mechanics of the human body, into physical formulae was all well and good; but to reproduce thought itself in mechanical formulae and to make it into a measurable value – that wasn't well and good, it was massive.

In fact, Babbage's contemporaries were interested in a human automaton, but their approach was much more direct. Babbage didn't realize that in London's Victorian salons, later than in other European capitals, in the spirit of Galvani and above all Mesmer and his 'animal magnetism' the same goal was being pursued with other means. 'Mesmeric mania' took hold in 1851, an obsession with using physical energy to turn people into living automatons, as strong as a steam hammer, as clever as Newton and even capable of predicting the future – everything we have today, except that in those days it was achieved not with formulae but with people themselves.[7]

It seems that it is not people's dreams that change but just the tools used to realize them. Séances were all the rage; the mesmerist would stare for hours into his subject's eyes, move his hands close to the other person's body to generate heat fields, until in an atmosphere of semi-obscurity and absolute quiet a state was achieved that military crews in the USA were later to experience as they were stared at by their radar screens: 'trance' or 'coma'.

In these séances, maids in a trance (the subjects were mostly women and generally servants who had no choice) felt that they could lift tons or suddenly showed new cognitive abilities, even giving rise among observers to utopian ideas for reconstructing the education system.[8]

It is interesting to compare what was happening in these dim London salons with what Charles Babbage was doing in his apartment a few streets away. Alison Winter describes it in her fascinating story of Victorian mesmerism:

> Indeed, if one considers that Babbage himself had complained that everyone loved his dancer, while few noticed the difference engine, one might conclude that animal magnetism was compelling because it *combined* the salient features of a dancing automaton and a thinking machine, and did so in the body of a human being. It turned a woman into a machine and showed that the mechanical part of a human being was capable, as the difference engine was, of doing intellectual work 'without the exercise of volition and thought'.[9]

It may be seen as the dress rehearsal for the drama of our information-economy century, in which only the main character, the computer, was still absent because it had not yet been invented. The dreams were the same; just the medium or tool to transport it from the script to reality had not yet been found.

Before Number 2 enters the scene – the duplicated but reduced man who shows the real person how to compute, transact business and calculate the world – attempts were made again and again with Number 1.

William Benjamin Carpenter, one of the most respected physiologists of the nineteenth century, had already conceived the idea of the individual as an automaton, fed from the outside by electro-biological input, a being 'for the time (so to speak) a mere *thinking automaton*, the whole course of whose ideas is determinable by suggestion operating from without'.[10] Evidently, a hundred years before the first simulations by the military, the idea of becoming cleverer, stronger and more awake was already inseparably linked with an indoctrination machine.

As for Babbage, all of the inspired mathematician's ideas also had to wait a century. The world tried first through psychology, beginning with séances and ending with the era of manipulation and the sophisticated tools of indoctrination, mass suggestion and propaganda, in short 'hidden persuaders'.

In the late nineteenth century the idea of 'magnetic fluids' marked the beginning of the American advertising industry. 'Electricity', offered in the form of pills, was scientifically demonstrated by the inventor of Alka-Seltzer, for example, as the panacea for rejuvenating old and tired bodies.

Following the first successful experiments with mass suggestion through a mixture of spiritism and behaviourism, A.J. Walter Thompson, the largest advertising agency in the world, stated in its 1925 annual report that 'advertising is a non-moral force, like electricity, which not only illuminates but electrocutes'.[11]

That was the difference between the twentieth and the twenty-first centuries. Today it is possible to calculate and control the wishes of every individual. The mass psychology in the London salons of the time operated with 'forces', not with individuals.

But there is a difference between manipulating the masses and calculating and anticipating the behaviour of individuals and influencing them with customized advertising messages, for example. There is a difference between manipulating people from outside through suggestion and getting into their heads and finding out what they think, hide and want.

In the first case it is possible to control masses; in the second case it is possible with sufficient data to determine the rules of the game and operate like natural laws. Babbage was already interested in a technology that would permit social life to be reorganized completely rationally with new rules. It was not yet the time for a self-interested doppelgänger, perhaps because it was inconceivable to imagine a machine that forced people not only to work economically but also to think purely rationally.

The feeling that something wasn't quite right was expressed in monsters, from Frankenstein's creature and Mr Hyde to Dracula, who haunted the dreams of the era.

But another literary monster, a more civilized creature, arose at the time, on the right side of the law, but no less freakish. This weird defender of justice and law spied on people, combined clues from an apparently senseless mass of information and was always on the lookout for people who claimed to be something they weren't. Edgar Allan Poe modelled his supersleuth Dupont on him. Sherlock Holmes, whom Conan Doyle housed just a few minutes' walk from Babbage's actual apartment, was, as Hugh Kenner suggests,[12] probably meant to be the personification of Babbage's difference engine. And even Agatha Christie's Hercule Poirot is constructed from Babbage's hyperrational genes.

Combining, decoding, uncovering, identifying and seeing the other person's perspective through observation – as soon as people come anywhere close to digital technology, they apparently want to get immediately inside the head of the next person, be it as a detective or an algorithm. In every person there are doors that lead to the interior, transparent skulls like those of Vaucanson's automatons. And anyone trying to imitate the logic of the great detectives, as Sherlock Holmes decoded his environment or computer inventor Alan Turing cracked codes, will soon realize that it is possible only if the world is expressed as a mathematical state in which everything has its function.

The Victorian factory with its physical discipline, time clocks and force calculations did this extensively for human labour. For thought and control, it worked initially only in books. A novel is also a factory in which everything has its place and time, controlled by the author.

But writing for people was a dead end. It was better to write for machines, with which humans would fuse.

By the 1950s, the texts that organized, described, monitored and motivated humans were being written in machine language.

Hugh Kenner writes of Charles Babbage's legacy: 'The computer simulates thought when thought has been defined in a computer's way; the automaton simulates man when man has been defined in an automaton's way.'[13]

13

GENES

EGOISM CONQUERS THE GENOME

The machine in Vaucanson's time looked like a human. In the twentieth century, humans had to become machines.

Perhaps the seizure of power by Number 2 would have been less comprehensive if it had been limited to economic models. But biology was responsible for turning the human species into a factory for egoism. Biology experts discovered in the late 1970s that game theory was ideal for explaining the Darwinian model of survival, in other words the struggle for advantage, profit maximization and reproductive chances.

In 1976, the British biologist Richard Dawkins first formulated his thesis that living creatures are merely survival machines for the purpose of preserving selfish genes. Dawkins and his followers, convinced that they had found a universal theory for human societies, had first to content themselves with being suppliers to neoliberal economists, particularly in the USA, because neoliberal thinkers in Europe were reluctant to base the self-interested business model on the investment and de-investment strategies of genes.

We mention Dawkins only as the most prominent protagonist. When he wrote his book *The Selfish Gene*, there was already agreement that, in simple terms, the self-organization of markets corresponded to the self-organization of living beings. In the 1950s, cybernetics, economics and biology had already all independently replaced the term 'energy' by 'information', providing the groundwork for the new universal theory in which 'information', from the DNA and computers to financial markets, became the all-powerful principle.[1] Friedrich Hayek, who had already discovered the importance of information for markets back in 1935 and later transferred it to cognition, as always played a brilliant role.[2] But it was Dawkins who popularized it all in a completely new way.

All theories of destiny, whether shaped by genes or a divinity, can normally rely on self-preserving instincts. In the eyes of the public it didn't help either that sociobiologists were endeavouring with game theoreticians to prove that this egoism could have interesting social effects if it were acknowledged that living beings help others if they see an advantage for themselves. The thesis always worked: 'giving to do yourself a favour' and the other grotesquely simplified psychological advertising messages.

This was the biologistic foundation stone of a new morality. Number 2's egoistic gene had found its way into biology. In the USA, for example, Jeffrey Skilling, head of the fraudulent Enron group, was a great admirer of Dawkins's work, describing it as his 'favourite book and main source of inspiration'.[3] He introduced the 'rank and yank' system at Enron: every six months all employees were ranked; the top 5 per cent received lavish bonuses, and the bottom 15 per cent were fired or relocated. According to Skilling this was a 'lesson from nature'.[4]

Europe was immune to this self-interested cocktail only as long as these ideologies remained on paper and were not incorporated in a new and functioning technology. As we saw with Vaucanson's automatons, if a machine is convincing enough, people are willing to make it into a metaphor for their lives.

In this way the machine becomes the trap, the cage, the automaton, from which there is no escape. The all-clear that sounded in the 1970s and 1980s, signifying that there was no danger of Europe developing into a society of biologistic self-interest, was unfortunately premature.

Only in retrospect does it become evident that Dawkins's influential bestseller *The Selfish Gene* was effectively the biological basis for robot- and algorithm-controlled financial markets and societies.

Dawkins describes evolution as a gigantic 'biological computer' in which 'genes [...] control the behaviour of their survival machines, not directly with their fingers on puppet strings, but indirectly like the computer programmer'.[5] And in which profit and loss, the self-interest and cooperativeness of the selfish gene, are calculated in a 'vampire economy' – his favourite example – according to game theory models.

Written around ten years before the computer became a universal tool, it sounds at first like an exciting conceptual experiment that can be rejected or accepted. It appeared light years away from the idea of transforming society, as the theories of 'balance', 'force' or 'self-regulation' embodied in the steam engine and brought forth by the industrial era had once posited.

But then, one day, there was a PC on every desk. And then, over-night, this PC had linked up with all other PCs in the world and adopted game theory models just to automatically negotiate bandwidths, storage allocation and data transmission with other computers. And on the next day financial algorithms were operating like selfish genes. And in this way the rules of the antiquated human society had been changed.

Enter the alchemists, the neoliberal economists, with Ken Binmore at their head. They took over the metaphors of the selfish biological computer from the sociobiologists, as they in turn had borrowed their metaphors from physics in the nineteenth century. The great illusion was no longer to talk of biology but to treat genes like microscopic economic agents (supplemented by a social equivalent, the 'meme' – ideas, concepts, ideologies – which apparently behaved like computer programs). In a world in which there were only four computers, this didn't matter. In a world in which every person communicates with them, it was a revolution – comparable not with Gutenberg but with the birth of the great ideologies of the twentieth century.

14

KINSHIP

EVEN NATURE CALCULATES LIKE A
STOCK EXCHANGE TRADER

We know that the American biotech businessman Craig Venter created the first synthetic living being with a computer in 2010. The software, said Venter in a legendary presentation to the entire Silicon Valley elite, is the genes, the hardware the body.

Venter is one of those scientists who create potential monsters in their laboratories. A living being is a living being because it is software. It can be programmed, albeit only at the bacterial stage. But the modern medicine that is emerging today is turning into an information science based on this algorithmic idea. Stem cell medicine, for example, creates avatars on the computer from which can be devised more efficient, durable and profitable replacement organs that work for us.

There will be no area of human life that will be perceived as it is and not as an 'optimization problem'.[1]

The same thing is happening simultaneously, however, with the social programming of humankind. Number 2 has only two genes: one for self-interest and one for profit (and perhaps a third for fear). If life is software, then software is also life. Who is interested in people made of flesh and blood when what is considered the core of their behaviour can be programmed more cheaply and cleanly as a digital copy?

The prerequisite for the emerging new electrobiologistic universal theory for everything and everyone was the interlinking of genes, computer algorithms and their programmability.

While evolution biologists discovered game theory for calculating Darwinist survival and selection processes, in the 1990s Ken Binmore introduced the 'selfish gene' to game theory. Modern biologists and economists suddenly had a lot to talk about, because once biologists had seen biology as an information science, they were dealing basically with the same things. The explosiveness of this cooperation becomes clear in a harmless-sounding sentence: 'That is not to say that our genes determine what will be regarded as fair in any particular society,' says Binmore, 'only that they will determine or constrain the algorithm that a society uses in deciding what is fair. But such an algorithm cannot operate without some input to chew on.'[2]

Why do we have to have read this? Because after doing so, only dreamers could still insist that they were anything other than robots, when the innermost core of both humans and robots is defined by something that sets algorithms in motion.

Here we have the model, packed in transparent film like a new iPhone. Those who write the algorithms write the new human being. *In information capitalism, we become the sum of our algorithms. That is why it is so profitable to define, analyse and compare them.*

It doesn't matter whether they produce results determined today by Google and tomorrow by even better search engines, or by bank, police or hospital computers. It is as futile to complain about the digital determination that a person is a security or credit risk as it is to rail against the gene for Alzheimer's or lactose intolerance.

The only uncertainty is whether the predisposition will really give rise to the full-blown disease. And just as certain lifestyles are recommended and prescribed for persons with genetic predispositions, we will experience the same thing with social incompatibilities defined by algorithms.

Already today, insurance companies in the UK are reducing premiums if you allow your driving style to be monitored. In *Business Week*, Stephen Baker describes an American company that compares 25-year-old employees with 50-year-old ones on the basis of taxonomies so as to determine how today's 25-year-olds will be when they are 50. And people who control their social communication to increase their credit-worthiness have already begun to take part in the game.

We can see in real time and with the naked eye how neoclassical economics, Darwinism and computer technology are merging to form a new super-theory. Many believe that Marx got stuck in the nineteenth century, but Darwin's dangerous students have managed to make the British fit to play the game in the twenty-first century.

Genes are tiny survival machines in the survival machine that is the individual, which is a tiny survival machine in the survival machine that is the market. This is not a miracle but the result of a simple, almost mindless, process, for which nature thankfully uses the same recipes as the automated financial markets. Nature itself is turning into Number 2, and Number 2 into a law of nature. In the words of the philosopher Daniel Dennett: 'Here, then, is Darwin's dangerous idea: the algorithmic level *is* the level that best accounts for the speed of the antelope, the wings of the eagle, the shape of the orchid, the diversity of the species and all the other occasions for wonder in the world of nature.'[3]

What drives all these calculating machines? Self-maximization of individual survival profit, cooperation only if it serves selfish interests, 'mindless' purposefulness, as the sociobiologist John Maynard Smith observed,[4] and the ability to exploit the weaknesses of the next person.

At this point in our narrative I would like to ask you to turn round and see how a door is slowly opening behind you. It is the door through which Number 2 is attempting to slip into the room. It won't be long before an argument will break out, as in a comedy, as to who is the real Number 1, you or him. But while you are arguing, the decision has long been made elsewhere: you are one and the same.

Like a distant cousin who comes to visit and then never leaves and gradually takes over control of the entire household, Number 2 is turning the 'digital you' into his own monstrous ego. 'I am your kin,' he says. And with its concept of the 'selfish gene', sociobiology says: he has the same genes as you.

'People presumably feel somehow diminished,' writes Binmore, 'at the suggestion that they are "no better" than robots – just as bourgeois Victorians felt their dignity impugned when they learned of their kinship with the apes. [...] The fear that society will fall apart if people learn of their true nature seems to me absurd.'[5]

Few have recognized the merging of biological and economic theories and the emergence of this new ideological machine more clearly than the American biologist Stephen Jay Gould. He attacked Dennett for attempting to explain the wonders of nature exclusively through the calculations of selfish algorithms. Gould appeared to be speaking here in 1997 about biology, but he could just as well have been speaking about the financial markets in 2007, because he simply pointed out that unexpected events can change everything:

> Is the diversity of species no more than a calculational consequence of natural selection? [...] I marvel at the probability that the impact of a meteor wiped out dinosaurs and gave mammals a chance. If this contingent event had not occurred, and imparted a distinctive pattern to the evolution of life, we would not be here to wonder about anything at all![6]

Whether it was a meteor that wiped out the dinosaurs, or the 'black swan', the unexpected event that can destroy financial markets, in a world in which Number 2 has become a natural law they will be the constant companions of this society. The technical term is 'unintended consequences' – and we would do well to remember it when a historical Facebook entry falls into the hands of a loan broker or the stock exchange keeps on producing senseless information.

'The law of unintended consequences,' explains statistics professor Andrew Gelman, 'is what happens when a simple system tries to regulate a complex system.'[7] It is precisely in this way that Number 2 with his economic stubbornness regulates humans made of flesh and blood.

As the first experiments with secretaries at RAND already demonstrated, people do not usually act as the theory predicts they will. For whatever reason, education, morality, convictions, all undermine the self-interest premise. But the more delimited the market in which Number 2 has the say becomes, and the more apparent it is that *everything* is turning into a market and that in the modern information economy everyone markets themselves like a product, everywhere from their CV to the social network, to the point, as Philip Mirowski put it, of having to become the managers of themselves, the higher the price that will have to be paid for resistance.

In life there is no meteor or black swans. The matter is more subtle and therefore more dangerous. When a single wrong signal (an ill-judged tweet, a traitorous sympathy in an email) can be sufficient to destroy a life, and where the digital signals of our life are continuously captured, stored, evaluated or sold, society begins to wage a cold war with itself. It is increasingly obliged to live in two worlds: that of Number 2, and its own – a form of schizophrenia that constantly produces contradictions. The result is that we live in the society that Philip K. Dick predicted: nothing means what it is anymore, and one's own life is reduced to a risk and probability calculation.

15

SCHIZOPHRENIA

THE WORLD IS MUCH MORE SUITED TO EGOTISTICAL AUTOMATONS THAN DREAMY HUMANS

It is astonishing how refractory people are when you want to turn them into egoists. You present them with the ultramodern image of humanity as self-interested, but most won't play along. On the contrary, there is an almost unbridgeable chasm between what they *should be* and what they *are*.

Back in 1955, when game theory – still without computers but designed like an automaton – was fashionable, John W. Campbell warned against applying mathematical rules to society, claiming that people who grew up in a culture of hidden games would have terrible psychological problems.

He meant growing up in a society where nothing is as it seems. Acting contrary to what one thinks, and thinking what one doesn't know, produce enormous contradictions that can be recognized, like a disease, from their symptoms.

Some people are now feeling the great contradiction, which, as John W. Campbell predicted, produces terrible psychological problems when the truth is being told: on the one hand, a world of collective intelligence, networking, transparency, participation and cooperation, ranging from blogs to the Arab Spring; on the other hand, the exact opposite and, more than ever, egotistical shadow networks of a calibre where it is no longer a question of tax evasion but the disappearance of billions and the collapse of states, with considerable personal profit at the same time for the perpetrators.

Or: knowledge economics versus depletion of knowledge institutions. Or: transparency versus installation of opaque boards of governors and irresponsible parliaments. Or: anonymity versus disclosure of the most intimate facts. Or: participation versus discrediting of plebiscites, which, as true polling machines, could upset the 'markets'. Or: absolute creativity and promises of fame for everyone versus inflation of self-exploitation and unpaid micro-labour. Or: 'the end of work' versus creation in threshold countries of sweatshops straight out of a Dickens novel. Or, finally: cooperation versus population explosion of these self-interested economic agents on all digital platforms.

Contradictions such as these are the reason why even enthusiastic pioneers of the network society are alarmed at a 'structural schizophrenia between function and meaning' and why paranoia is threatening to become the essential feature of communication.[1]

Fans of Number 2 don't deny this either. They reply simply that the problems only arise because we are still too much Number 1. Everything is a question of attitude, says Ken Binmore, adding encouragingly that 'for cooperation to work in a society, it is not necessary that its citizens be Dr Jekylls, who treat each other like brothers'.[2]

But the reluctance of humans to play this game was a problem not to be underestimated. People proved to be somewhat too unpredictable for the cut-throat game theory rationality. Too much human and too little automaton contaminated the alchemy formula. There was thus a repeat of what the military had done in the Cold War: to have people act through machines 'which they trust'. At a time when people and markets communicate at lightning speed via the Internet and electronic exchanges, would it not be helpful to allow Number 2 to do the work all on his own?

'In this sense, game theory (and mechanism design) seems much more suitable for automated agents than it is for humans', said Nir Vulkan, one of the pioneers of electronic markets on the eve of the commercialized Internet.[3]

That is the message: we don't need you. Not only because you are too slow and sometimes fall asleep at the screen, but because we have the chance to build better ego machines than you could ever be. There is something better than humans for doing business. All that is required is to persuade people to give automated agents legitimation and authority. The agent is not only coded software but coded ideology.

Number 2 works in digital environments like a company that wants to increase efficiency and competitiveness. Only people can diminish his success. For that reason Number 2 must be unfettered. The 'invisible hand of the market' becomes the hand of Number 2. The success not just of stock exchanges but of *all* marketplaces – from the marriage market to the 'marketplace of ideas', Vulkan prophesied in 1999, will 'in the long run [...] depend on the performance of self-interested agents, the behaviour of which cannot be controlled.'[4]

We now have what Vulkan predicted. Not only a model for humanity but countless self-interested (often brainless) digital agents spreading on digital platforms like protozoa. Not much is needed to program Number 2: self-interest, profit orientation and the ability to trick. Anyone looking for the birth announcement in which all components of human life became information markets will find it in these sentences.

The galvanists' dream and Mary Shelley's great fear have come true in the digital age: the switch with which people turn on their computers and mobile phones ignites the electric spark that brings Number 2 to life.

Naturally his scope for action at the beginning was as limited as that of a baby (Microsoft drew him at the time as a child). He lived in a little stall and had to be fed with promises. He made mistakes and aroused protective instincts.

It was not his intelligence but his scope for action that steadily grew. When powerful economies dematerialized and deindustrialized as the real economy shifted its production to other parts of the world under the siren sound of globalization, an economy of financial markets asserted itself in the most powerful industrial nations, and Number 2 became increasingly omnipresent. That was only logical: deindustrialization and the rise of the computer had blurred the boundaries between mind and matter, between object and information, and the boundaries became permeable.

But dematerialization, the keyword of the knowledge economy, works both ways. Entire industries emerge whose products are pure knowledge – Google's search algorithm or Apple's software – and conversely knowledge becomes an industry.

Now Number 2, like the hunchbacked little man in the German folksong, could enter anyone's kitchen, storeroom or cellar, or even be included in prayers. He entered every person's brain and house, and his medium was electricity, which connected people and markets.

He grew out of all proportion. And finally, in May 2010, a surprised world realized for the first time what can happen when Number 2 has total control.

16

LIGHTNING

THE EGO MACHINES FUNCTION IN TEXTBOOK FASHION – AND START WARS

A chess grandmaster requires about 650 milliseconds to recognize that he has been checkmated. A normal person requires 1,000 milliseconds, one second, to react physically to a danger signal. In the best case, financial markets require as long as the chess grandmaster to react to a stock exchange crash.

Financial market transactions take place today at lightning speed. Traders install their servers right next to the computers in the New York Stock Exchange so as to shave off milliseconds. A transatlantic cable will reduce the transmission time for data between Wall Street and London traders to 740 nanoseconds (100,000 nanoseconds make 1 millisecond). To give an idea, it is the difference between taking one minute to make a decision and taking almost ten weeks. The trap closes a million times more quickly than the time taken for people even to realize that they have been caught in it.

'By the time the ordinary investor sees a quote, it's like looking at a star that burned out 50,000 years ago,' says one of the people who built these systems.[1] But no light comes on between the beats of this almost subatomic unit of time. The beats are filled with decisions, reflections, judgements and preferences that are transformed into money – 1 billion bytes on a single day.

The volume of data has exploded as time has collapsed. In four years, the average holding period for shares dropped from two months to 22 seconds. In the 1950s the average was four years.[2] In physical terms the economic universe is moving backwards towards the Big Bang.

The Lehman Brothers crisis already featured ultra-complex financial products whose physics was incomprehensible even to the initiated. The Flash Crash of 6 May 2010, the largest ever Dow Jones point loss in a single day, which still remains largely unexplained; the mysterious processes behind the failed IPO of the Bats trading platform; the stunning losses incurred by Knights Capital – these are all traps snapping shut, and only thanks to the fact that they opened again and the incidents could be more or less swept under the carpet have they left no traces in people's minds.

In August 2012, Knights Capital lost almost $1 billion in half a second (and mysteriously recovered 99 per cent of it later) and 75 per cent of its market value on account of puzzling trades ordered by its own computer. Science historian George Dyson likened it to someone being run over by a car and then suddenly getting up again and walking away.[3]

In February of that year, the physicist Neil Johnson had already warned of the collapse of the entire system that could be triggered by a 'global war between competing computer algorithms'. The market, he said, 'had evolved into a "lake full of different types of piranhas" devouring each other in a high-speed frenzy'.[4]

In all of the digital systems in which Number 2 has installed himself, from finance markets to Amazon, he is obsessed with predicting the moves of the other side, with reproducing them and responding with the aid of the Nash equilibrium. In financial algorithms, however, where tiny profit margins and gigantic amounts of money are at stake, as was the case with the Flash Crash, Number 2 was not acting *within* the market, he *was* the market.

If it had been a political system, the only comparison would have been the Cuban Missile Crisis. The smallest sanctions, the slightest pain in the negotiations, the tiniest deviation from absolute egotistical self-interest can unleash the monster. This 'algorithmic tragedy of the commons, in which all players, acting in their self-interest, had spawned a systematically dangerous market', had brought the world to the brink of a system failure.[5]

The real swarm in a world in which the market is the truth is not the collective intelligence. It is the millions of piranhas hunting our intentions, aims and desires. In a world known euphemistically as the knowledge economy, every question, every answer, every purchase or sale is a statement that tells more about people than they would wish.

As always, the finance markets also played a pioneering role here. Within a few years there was an explosion in the proportion of transactions taking place in 'dark pools' – in reality, uncontrolled stock markets – in which investors had once taken refuge from predators. An institutional fund whose algorithms decide to purchase or sell shares in large quantities immediately changes the price. Anyone who can predict this in fractions of a second can do good business.

There are algorithms that feed the sharks, offering themselves in small doses and in this way forcing the agents from the other side into a nanosecond spiral of rising prices. Others attack the sharks by sending out false signals. And others still disclose the buyer's intentions. Then there is the relentless barrage of systems with tell-tale names like 'Blast' that buy and sell simultaneously at inconceivable speed to tear the piranhas into pieces.

The investigative financial journalist Scott Patterson, who was possibly the first person to peer into the dark pools, describes how the creators of the predator algorithms were able to invent a new Darwinism, believed to have become extinct, even in the most fiercely contested market. It is not the Darwinist fight for survival of the Victorian age but a permanent war, the eat or be eaten of autonomous predators with lightning reactions, a 'frenzied dance of predator and prey'.[6]

The shockwaves rippling through the financial market social networks following the flash crashes of May 2010 and August 2012 were an indication of how unstable the systems were.

Perhaps even more worrying today, the unmistakable language in practically all sources shows that none of those involved had a solution that would not destroy the foundations of the system itself. They are the oldest fears of the Cold War transferred to a world whose paranoid knowledge technology produces not transparency but naked fear of monsters.

And as in the Cold War, there are skirmishes, threats of total destruction, proxy wars. Since the start of this century, crises have erupted twice in the automated systems, later to be known as algorithm wars.[7] Scott Patterson's reconstruction of the events in his book *Dark Pools* takes us right back to the Cold War. 'Deadly weapons' are developed that cause terrible damage in the algorithm wars, because the intentions and plans behind them are no longer recognizable; they are highly complex moves, in which everyone expects to be extinguished by the other side and tries desperately to establish a 'balance of terror'.

While politicians put up their own 'Star Wars' defence system in the form of rescue funds, an analysis of almost 19,000 high-speed and completely unexpected incidents on the stock market between 2006 and 2011 showed that the dome protecting the finance markets had 'ultra-fast "fractures"', as the authors put it metaphorically, that could lead to the 'slow "breaking" of the global financial system'.[8]

The main reason for this is that man–machine communication has been replaced by machine–machine communication. 'Darth Vader' Joseph M. Gregory was not alone in telling his staff that the only thing needed for profit was the 'machine'. Countless others did so as well.

Experts like George Dyson state openly today that no one knows anymore how any of these Number 2 mutants in uncontrolled orbit will develop. All they know is that a galvanic spark would be sufficient to set something in motion. 'And this could be happening all around us,' he says,

> not just in the world of finance. We would not necessarily even perceive it, that there's a whole world of communication that's not human communication. It's machines communicating with machines. And they may be communicating money, or information that has other meaning – but if it is money, we eventually notice it. It's just the small warm pond sitting there waiting for the spark.[9]

* * *

We fallible humans with all our deficiencies and false compromises were taken out of the loop and replaced by Number 2. Before leaving Wall Street, Dave Cliff – one of those who created whole generations of economic agents – warned that now Number 2 was in charge, one day the entire system would enter into an endless loop that no one would be able to interrupt anymore.[10] Systems that seek continuously to find out what their opposite number is planning and hiding, and then factor in that their opposite number knows that they want to find out what he is planning, and so forth ad infinitum, get bogged down. And because they get bogged down, they have to collect more and more information. This began on the stock markets; but it doesn't take much imagination to figure that wherever Number 2 evaluates and prices human transactions, the information collection mania will result in a system with self-perpetuating feedback.

Number 2 doesn't need the computer, because he is an automaton himself. All he needs is a game theory matrix, a table in which all conceivable moves and their risks are entered, and a few formulae. But technology makes his existence easier.

Within these systems, Number 2 lives a carefree life. He can read the reports on the latest press conference by a DAX company, the results of the last Champions League round or the news of protests by opponents of a new airport runway. News agencies like Reuters and Dow Jones offer him their texts in machine-readable language. But he also communicates with Twitter and Google, Facebook and YouTube to gauge the mood of entire populations.[11]

Most digital copies of Number 2 are still brutally simple (of zero intelligence), and we all work with them. They are designed to find out the cheapest flight and the best-priced restaurant, and many of them don't even work with different providers but just compare prices. Others evaluate intellectual work, as in the large Thomson Reuters databases that determine the importance of scientific work through parameters like frequency of citation in major journals – and even provide evaluations of entire universities, mostly on the basis of indexing by a single commercial supplier.

The more interesting agents, however, particularly those used in financial markets, are programmed to learn and change their behaviour. Altogether they are a variation of the great self-serving lifestyle of Mr Hyde.

Today it is impossible, even for IT business engineers, to predict how certain evolutionary economic agents operating in the markets will develop. The knowledge acquired by an intelligent first-generation Number 2 is optimized by the second generation without any human influence.

Thus the organisms that have been created have quasi-biological functions. Like real living beings, they are exposed to environmental influences (the market), and – again like real living beings – this pressure leads not only to the selection of superior egoists but also to mutations.

The systems contain not only increasingly well-trained agents as highly efficient ego-fighting machines but also, like calves with two heads or people with seven fingers, what Charles Darwin would have called 'monsters'. It is bizarre and revealing to see how the quarrel over the causes of unstable automated finance markets is being conducted within the industry exactly as Darwin argued in the nineteenth century in response to the criticism that the existence of such phenomena disproved the theory of evolution.

And so it is today as well. One side says that Number 2 has become a monster because he was always predisposed to become one and that something should therefore be done; the other side believes that Number 2 has mutated into something different, a random variation that is not 'systemic' or inheritable.

Darwin himself would no doubt have pointed out that there is a difference between creatures that are bred and those brought forth by nature. 'Domestic races of the same species ... often have a somewhat monstrous character,' he wrote, and his explanation why nature allows such a thing is extremely relevant to our subject. 'The unfortunate creation of freak animals is because "man selects only for his own good; Nature [by contrast] only for that of the being which she tends."'[12]

At the moment no one can answer the question as to what Number 2, in the shape of his algorithms, is really doing in financial markets. Some suspect that he is learning. But what? And what conclusions can be drawn?

The people I spoke with while researching this book were unable to say. And after three mysterious crashes, the confidence of thinkers is no longer that of the masters of the universe. On the contrary, some of the most important thinkers have left Wall Street and, like the 'über-quant' Emanuel Derman or Nassim Talib, have written books whose 'wake-up' character recalls the warnings by self-critical nuclear physicists in the 1950s.

It is true that some economists, unsettled by the force of the crisis, took a second look at Number 2, whom they had allowed to operate in place of humans in the models. Some, like the writers at the International Monetary Fund, concluded that a mad character from a novel would provide a better explanation for the crisis than Number 2.

The British economic scientist Geoffrey M. Hodgson has urgently called for a new economy *without homo oeconomicus*.[13] Behavioural economists have shown the contradiction between reality and models. And Gerd Gigerenzer, the great Berlin educational researcher, has demonstrated that people and nature are driven not by the mathematics of self-interest but by intuition and heuristics.[14]

It is all the more strange, therefore, that we allow into our social life the very thing that almost led to disaster in the first global automated markets.

There is good reason to believe that within the current financial and European crisis a much more fundamental conflict is brewing involving the application of neoclassical and neoliberal American ideology to societies, micro-markets and even the constitutional orders of Western Europe.

It is based on the conviction not only that governments know less than the market (which is just a large computer), but also that they can no longer express the will of the majority.

17

POLITICS

How to trap states in a cage

For almost two hundred years, since the publication of Mary Shelley's *Frankenstein*, our imagination was accustomed to the appearance of monsters. They looked like Boris Karloff, Godzilla or Ridley Scott's Alien. They took the form of current fears, and if the fears had no shape, they embodied a genetic mutation of them, like the beings under a nuclear cloud.

Information capitalism bred a creature whose genetic code reproduced itself relentlessly in 'toxic papers', which in reality were electronic signals. This creature was no longer in the habit of trampling buildings and entire cities. Instead it left behind a swathe of new buildings and entire city districts, whose human inhabitants had been evicted.

Like the clueless small investors who sat in front of their screens and watched as their old age pensions went up in smoke, people in the early years of the twenty-first century began to suspect for the first time that they were living not in Seattle or Solingen but in a single huge machine.

'We will socialize in digital neighborhoods,' Nicholas Negroponte, one of the pioneers of information capitalism, had said barely ten years earlier, 'in which physical space will be irrelevant and time will play a different role.'[1]

This is precisely what had happened, but in a completely different way than had been envisaged. Only the virtual space remained.

The new Big Brother, as the monster was called somewhat unimaginatively by some, did exactly what the sociologist Zygmunt Bauman had predicted: he practised exclusion,

> spotting the people who 'do not fit' into the place they are in, banishing them from that place and deporting them 'where they belong', or better still never allowing them to come anywhere near in the first place. The new Big Brother supplies the immigration officers with lists of people they should not let in and bankers with the list of people they should not let into the company of the creditworthy.[2]

Everywhere today it is a binary question of exclusion or inclusion: from Google search results, social networks and the nomadic Occupy tent cities in the heart of finance centres to the unsteady 'house of Europe', which threatens to evict some of its tenants and whose young people are deciding to move north.

To have an illusion means to write oneself a cheque for something one doesn't possess and in its place to buy something one can't afford. This is exactly what happened with the American real-estate bubble. These houses are distortions of reality, even if the owners are entered in the land register. They were products not only of financial mathematics – and in this sense they are harbingers of the new era – but also of the political economy. They were not only a financial experiment but also a social one.

One of the traders who caused the subprime bubble to burst described how the scales fell from his eyes, as he put it himself: 'How do you make poor people feel wealthy when wages are stagnant? You give them cheap loans.'[3]

The American homeowners who went shopping with money they had borrowed on houses they didn't own acted rationally until the crisis broke out. They were encouraged not only by banks but also by the media, scientists and Nobel Prize winners. It was in line with the theory of the new information capitalism.

The supposed knowledge society proposed the worldwide dismantling of physical barriers from companies, institutions and individuals.

The proportion of immaterial goods and virtual capital continues to rise. In her pioneering book *No Logo*, Naomi Klein describes the economy of markets that no longer produce but brand, lease, borrow and lend assets and people, so that some were even saying that future consumers would find the concept of 'property' old-fashioned.

This dismantling was not meant to be as it was with the new homeless. Suddenly people were standing naked and without a roof over their heads. And all that the over-indebted American mortgage clients had done was to put into practice sentences like 'use capital but don't own it', coined by influential businessmen (Jeremy Rifkin) and applauded at forward-looking congresses throughout the world. Logically, this also means 'use workers but don't hire them' (rather lend them out) and ultimately 'use your head but don't own it'.

What it meant was a most fateful operation in which the new economic thinking set up a world of labour for itself where identity and personality had long been jettisoned.

'Our identities,' a notorious manifesto of the Internet ideology summed it up, 'have no bodies, so, unlike you, we cannot obtain order by physical coercion.'[4]

To keep caged people happy, they have to be told that the world around them doesn't exist. Whether the foreclosure of American non-homeowners in August 2007 was a theoretical or real web mistake is moot. It is in any case impossible to determine because things moved so fast.

To describe what happened next as a self-fulfilling prophecy would be too fatalistic. At all events, it soon transpired that, for all the mental muscle provided by computers, ignoring the existence of the body and the physical world causes difficulties when real people are involved. The generation of people who had the smartest machines no longer knew what was going on. And then, all of a sudden, it was over, followed by this strange shoulder shrugging, this failure to understand what had happened, this confused argument by doctors at the patient's bedside, this political obfuscation, this sentence 'I hope it works.'

One of the most alarming signals is the fact that in the era of new rationality there are no rational answers anymore. On closer inspection, it looks as if the finance crisis, with its astronomical figures beyond human or political conception, has made us into occupants of the computer itself, in which we can only watch bewildered as strings of figures and codes flow by. This is what it must feel like inside the Matrix. After the Lehman Brothers crisis, neither banks nor their supervisory boards were able to distinguish assets and liabilities. 'Caught in a trap' is one of the most used phrases in connection with the finance and euro crisis – from the liquidity to the constitution trap.

The political actors were caught in the trap. They said so themselves, and so did the media, analysts – and anyone who switched on the news could see it as well.

How often do you have to say 'trap' before you realize that it really is one? The language – and the body language – of politicians since the financial crisis is that of people who are trapped. Trap language is one that prevaricates, pretends to find a way out when none exists, and simulates routine amid panic. Behind closed doors, politicians seek outlets, they go round in circles, use phrases that exclude other options ('there's no alternative'), utter the passive constructions of the suffering ('we are forced') and insist on a simple rationality ('if the euro fails, Europe will fail'), which then become the rationale of all the other occupants of the cage.

The Cold War has returned, but in the form of a cold war that society is waging with itself. Before EU summits, 'landing zones' are marked, 'rearmament' is offered or threatened, and real or imagined conflicts between political allies are orchestrated, followed by 'victory parades' in the form of press conferences by some EU states, interpreted by others shortly afterwards as 'capitulation', while at the same time the impact on the markets and on the countries' own population is being tested, either through reports in the media, sudden threats of plebiscites or bitter opposition to them – all political tactics that have been employed for years, all terms from current political discourse.

Interestingly, states, often without their politicians noticing it, have long been treated by the economy as mere participants in the market rather than overarching constitutional structures.

Heads of government are only partial rulers of their countries; Number 2, who knows how to play rational games, is also infiltrating here. Logically, investment banks advise their investors to regard the entire European crisis management not as politics but as a non-cooperative game that, once understood, can be exploited. In other words, don't believe anything, assume the worst and absolute self-interest and then see how far this strategy will stretch.

'Don't believe that the Soviet Union wouldn't attack us for some moral reasons,' people said in the Cold War. 'Only if we assume the worst can we find a rational strategy to outsmart the opponent.' As mentioned, it was the Nash equilibrium.

And today?

'You'll read plenty,' wrote the *Wall Street Journal*, as if it were not talking about the 2012 euro crisis but mutual deterrence, 'about how the euro won't break up because that would be bad for everyone – so in the end, leaders will get their act together and do the sensible thing. Don't believe it for a moment. A catastrophic outcome is quite possible. The only rational thing to do is to prepare for the worst.'

And because the newspaper is convinced of the higher wisdom of the markets and of the limitations of states, it recommends its readers to stick the film *A Beautiful Mind* in their DVD players to understand the euro crisis.[5]

One of the most important strategy games in the Cold War, which John Nash and his colleagues also investigated, was the 'chicken game'. Two cars head for each other at speed. Which one will give way first and when? How long is it possible to stay on course before the other swerves away? As always with these conceptual games, it was not about how a person reacted autonomously but how he gave the impression of fearless autonomy and left the other in the dark about his intentions. This needs to be known today to understand how states and their citizens are read by financial markets; the latter act as if the former didn't exist.

Citizens and states are no longer sovereign but just pretend to be. That is why parliaments become extras and the public become soundboards that are spoken to in order in reality to influence markets.

States are now as constrained in their scope for economic activity as the military was during the Cold War.

In January 2012 the chief strategist of the Chicago investment company William Blair described the European crisis policy as a 'sovereign game' in which politicians were interested not in money but in political self-determination. During the Cold War, strength had been demonstrated by an 'abundance of nuclear power'; now the new rivals – states and financial markets – were showing their strength through an abundance of supposed financial resources with which they could rescue or destroy failing states. 'The abundance, however, can be faked or bluffed, or it can actually exist,' warns Brian D. Singer, the author of the article.[6] Put plainly, do we have the money to back what we are guaranteeing?

Germany's game plan was to impose 'Teutonic fiscal prudence' on the entire eurozone. Southern countries needed money but had to give up some of their sovereignty. In the world of Number 2, the idea of allowing the world to choose for itself is a 'threat' because the market makes better computer choices than a plebiscite.

> Former Greek Prime Minister George Papandreou tried to threaten other countries with a referendum. Unfortunately, it was a bluff, and when it was called, he lost his job. [...] France has created a coalition with Germany to tap Germany's economic power. It is not trying to tear apart capital markets; it is playing a sovereign game – exactly as John Nash's model would predict. The leaders and their media partners are playing the game quite well. [...] Once the illiquidity problem has passed, many developed countries will be faced with chronic insolvency.[7]

Investment banks need not therefore fear regulation or 'retribution'. 'Like it or not, a good lawyer, a derivative, and a smart financial mind can get around just about any regulation that is put in place, unfortunately sometimes illegally.'[8]

Investment bankers aren't to blame for everything. They describe how investors can play the game, but since the euro crisis, states themselves have been playing the same game with each other. Even the proposition $1 + 1 = 2$ can be a bluff in this undercover game. It remains to be seen how long democracies can put up with these forms of public communication.

In the bunkers of their meeting rooms, the political class must plan five steps ahead and predict the next ten steps by the market, which in turn has forecast and factored in the next five steps by governments. Governments can only talk in tactical terms with their subjects; they bypass parliaments and laws; they have to lay false trails and maintain contradictory expectations, to pretend to have unlimited resources and stamina, to announce, implement and abandon regulations – just to confuse the opponent in the arms race with the markets, mislead it and force it to cooperate. Not to fall into a trap but to set one.

The opposite side uses precisely the same bluffs. As a master of game theory models, Number 2 has shown how to do it. The algorithms calculate future price developments from a plethora of information; reckon with the aid of other algorithms how its behaviour will be perceived by others and will change the future; and decide on that basis what kind of false information to put out and who will receive it. They attempt to predict the performance of companies before the companies themselves know it (dark pools) and send information themselves to the finance and political markets to provoke or prevent actions.

Most hedge fund managers, investment bankers and traders have no face and no name but effective weapons and a rationale on which the entire game is based: they don't want to lose.

Whereas social conflicts between the real economy, state and society were played cooperatively for decades, particularly in Germany, under the heading 'social market economy', the international financial markets are now increasingly playing an uncooperative zero-sum game with society: one side's profit is the other's loss.

This can be formulated in much more concrete terms. After a fifty-year Cold War between a social-economic and a centrally planned economic system, both with the atom bomb, we find ourselves now, following the end of Communism, in a new cold war between democratic nation states and globalized finance market bodies.

Both sides know that the other has powerful deterrents and weapons of mass destruction. They cannot talk directly with one another but have to reproduce the ideas of the other in their heads in order to react to them. They must both reason that the other side will not employ a destructive strike and that neither side wants the other to go bankrupt, although this doesn't prevent strategic first strikes, as Lehman Brothers, which believed in its relevance to the system, was to discover to its (short-lived) horror. The managers were convinced that the state would not allow them to go under.

We must abandon the idea that the crisis is an exceptional situation and that all political actions are special operations by a crisis intervention team. We are in a phase of containing a global financial expansion. The problem is that, in contrast to the 1950s, when it was a question of containing nuclear-backed Soviet imperialism, the most powerful ally of the time, the USA, is no longer playing today. Of all the bad news in Charles Ferguson's film *Inside Job*, without a doubt the news about the Obama administration is the worst. The American government has not only protected the financial elites but also made them members of its cabinet.

Within one decade, from 2000 to 2010, the balance of power between European politics and American financial markets shifted. It was not until the crisis that it became clear that politicians were acting in the same way as the game theoreticians in the Cold War. They communicate through moves not through arguments. And moves can be penalties, rewards, seeming self-sacrifice, withdrawal or attacks.

Like the players in RAND Corporation, they are playing not only with the 'opponent', or even the 'markets', but with their own subjects. Is there enough money for the bailout fund? Is there a red line? Should parliament be informed?

The fact, as the public is informed, that something has 'got out of control' and has to be 'contained', that money must be 'earmarked' and 'panic' prevented, that a 'protective umbrella' has to be opened based on decisions by legally immune 'governors' – this, along with the nuclear metaphors 'meltdown' and 'financial weapons of mass destruction', is the language not of the Federal Agency for Technical Relief or of Fukushima, but of an internal cold war.

18

MATRIX

'How do you create men like this?'

Is that the machine that is pressing Europe's politics and its citizens more and more against the bars of their cage? Is that the rationality to which entire states are increasingly having to adapt their own rational decisions? One would have expected a little scepticism, if only in the form of an inspection to establish whether the fabulous machine called 'the market' that was keeping everyone in suspense really worked as indicated in the old-fashioned operating instructions.

How, in the midst of a market crisis, could Angela Merkel's description of a 'market-conforming democracy' [*marktkonforme Demokratie*] sound like a vision, and why were there attempts at damage control in states but not in markets? The answer is that almost all political and social elites accepted as a natural law the theory that the market knows better than they did. Only because of this re-labelling did the meltdown of financial markets fail to raise doubts about omniscience but rather give birth to the political vision of a market-conforming democracy that would rise like a phoenix from the toxic ashes.

What we have been experiencing with the financial crisis since 2007 is evidently something other than a temporary irrational system error, more than the periodic evergreen of 'systems gone wild'. One cannot simply 'switch off' machines or, like after Fukushima, announce a change in energy policy. The reference to monsters reveals the degree to which the collective unconscious suspects that something living has been unleashed.

Field research by the Austrian sociologist Karin Knorr Cetina on the stock markets in New York and Zurich shows that traders see their digital trading systems no longer merely as a medium of communication but rather as a biological life form in its own right, something like a 'greater being'.[1] With the merging of man and machine, computer monitors are no longer just windows to the markets as they were in the 1990s, but the markets themselves, or, better, a 'building site on which a whole economic and epistemological world is erected',[2] a transformation that is also taking place in so-called 'private' social networks like Facebook.

Consequently, all definitions of the market are merging into a single definition. In a discussion with an experienced trader who has operated on practically all stock exchanges in the world, researchers asked the following question:

'What is the market for you?'

The trader's answer: 'Everything.'

'The information?'

'Everything. […] 'Who's selling, who's buying, where, which centre, what central banks are doing, what the large funds are doing, what the press is saying, what's happening to the CDU (a political party in Germany), what the Malaysian prime minister is saying, it's everything – everything all the time.'[3]

There is a strong suspicion in society that this merger is creating a new type of person. People sense the almost alchemic process by which individuals are being fashioned by the machinery of an unrestrained information market – particularly when these individuals are perpetrators, as was the case with the French stockbroker Jérôme Kerviel, who lost 2.8 billion euros for his employer, Société Générale, in 2008. At the height of the financial crisis, Kerviel was seen in the eyes of the French public practically as a Che Guevara, who blew up a system that demanded a certain type of behaviour by demonstrating precisely that behaviour. To judge by his supporters on Facebook or in the French media, it was almost like a chapter from the *Matrix* trilogy.

Kerviel was the epitome of the cyborg, the man-machine, who

perceived figures on his screen not just as fixed values but as pure liquidity, as a constantly changing electrical current. 'Tell me who you are. Who is Mr Kerviel?' asked the judge at the start of the trial.

After Kerviel had given evidence, his lawyer, Olivier Metzner, asked a different question, not without pathos but with a rhetoric that revealed the truth about the whole system. 'Who are you, Société Générale? Who are you? How do you create men like this?'[4]

It's not the first time this question has been heard. Exactly the same question was asked of Dr Victor Frankenstein.

19

MIND'S EYE

THE MARKET-CONFORMING DEMOCRACY BOOTS UP

What kind of politics does Number 2 espouse? Or, more precisely, what would his ideal state look like? What will we be living in when his work is finished and the social institutions have everyone under control? And for those who know that controversial political utterances are nothing but game moves, what does 'market-conforming democracy' mean?

It goes without saying that Number 2 and his millions of clones are no longer simply satisfied with what their customers want. The flash crashes showed that the mercenaries had got out of human control. This is no accident but was exactly what the creators of these mercenaries wanted; they would not have gone through the Chicago machine if they had wanted to command an army of automatons.

What they wanted was quite decent: a society in which people were free to live according to their desires and passions – including the agents and dummies. Many of those who built evolutionary agents in financial systems no longer know what their creations are doing except that they are most probably still acting according to the simple rules of self-maximization that were programmed into them.

As long as they remain grounded in the 'constitution' – self-interest means profit maximization, a constitution for the world of automatons described most fundamentally by Ken Binmore – the agents can do what they want. And because everyone basically mistrusts everyone else, the squirreling of information about what people are thinking or planning replaces communication.

Deceit in this world is a non-ethical matter, and planned untruthfulness is the least of the problems. In an era of big data – the complete interconnection of all data about people and things – self-deceit, illusions and strategies with which people mislead themselves also fall into this category.

Companies who fool themselves and others are seen through by the stock markets and punished, unless they manage, as was the case with Lehman Brothers and AIG, to remain at the poker table. Where classic 'lies' are told, it is easy to make legalistic and moral judgements. The situation is quite different, however, when the participants themselves don't yet know what they know.

People have been living for generations with the paradox of unintentional consequences, and an important aspect of the legal establishment of the truth is finding out what was planned deliberately and what was committed unconsciously. This line moves when technologies arise that can name this implicit knowledge but are used by people who are convinced that bluffing is normal social behaviour.

The programmer Alex Pentland develops and proposes appliances that can read human signals. 'Signal' sounds harmless and sterile. What is meant, however, is information that people don't even know they have.

Scientists like Pentland are not Frankensteins. They present technologies that can be used for both the dark and the light side of power. 'Pentland suggests that this kind of monitoring might be useful for identifying people who are potentially headed for burnout and who therefore require more detailed monitoring.'[1]

But information in markets is always collected and evaluated in the context of 'undercover games': the players fail to reveal something or keep something to themselves so as to gain an advantage. No company or organization would say it wanted to find out what its employees were keeping secret. Game theory in a normal working environment then sounds more like this:

Because people tend to hide stress, it can be difficult, if not impossible, to detect. [...] In a trial study, Pentland and student Michael Sung fixed physiological sensors on students playing poker for real monetary stakes and monitored bodily movements, skin conductance and heart rate. They found that they could identify moments of especially high stress [...] with 80 percent accuracy. They could also tell about 70 percent of the time when players were bluffing.[2]

The experiment is important here only because it is nothing other than the transfer of the lie detector to the Game of Life as it affects us directly. Data mining, the extraction of all kinds of digital information, has long merged with what Alex Pentland calls 'reality mining'.[3]

Everybody knows from politico-military scenarios how lie detectors are used today. The new war against terror, which replaced the Cold War, is full of examples. However strange it might be for hundred-year-old women in wheelchairs to have to undress at airport security controls because they could be concealing a weapon in their vehicles, we are basically willing to accept the principle of fundamental mistrust at such key communication or transport sites, to allow ourselves to be searched by complete strangers, to take off our shoes, to open and close our briefcases, and to have our fingerprints taken when entering the country.

Don't get me wrong: we are not talking here about the undoubtedly legitimate fight against terrorism. At the same time, this treatment by intelligence agencies is very much an integral part of the information economy: control through the body scanners at airports, or, in the case of Los Angeles airport, through monitoring grids based on game theory; and through economic agents when purchasing online.

The 'market-conforming democracy' project is being worked on in practically all Western industrialized countries. As with the automated financial markets, the social networks and the search engines in the commercialized Internet, the new information state is developing robot-controlled methods based on the pre-crime analysis model for predicting and monitoring. The broadcasting centres of twenty-first-century information capitalism are in Silicon Valley and Wall Street. A third, the most powerful of all, which is constantly occupied with human thought, is in Virginia at the headquarters of the US National

Security Agency. Today the best brains work for the NSA – the Carnegie Mellon project, for example, was financed by DARPA, the Defense Advanced Research Projects Agency – and Google poaches its managers there.[4] The former bunkers and monitoring apparatus of the Cold War are now housed in the much more solvent structures of the NSA. Whereas the Cold War game theoreticians played economic games with the Soviet Union, the NSA goes one step further. It has become an essential component of the information economy and, like the people at RAND, is in the process of rewriting social contracts. One of its most important masterminds, although not himself a member of the NSA, even sees new constitutional rules being created, which will shake the foundations of democratic nation states.

Philip Bobbitt calls these new states 'information market states'. As an attorney, he is an influential political thinker, a former member of the Security Council, a Democrat and anything but a 'Big Brother'. He worked for Bill Clinton, and George Bush included Bobbitt's ideas in his 2004 State of the Union message.

Two years after the Lehman Brothers débâcle, Bobbitt demanded something that was applauded by Henry Kissinger, Niall Ferguson and the American political establishment and which a financially softened-up Europe is just now reacting to. He designed and foresaw a new constitutional order that would replace nation states, the transformation of our world into 'information market states'.

For Bobbitt, the lesson to be learned from the current crises is not that the intelligence quotient of the markets should be questioned but rather the contrary: markets have delegitimized states because the latter no longer understand modern financial and information processes. Information states have a quite simple message: give us information about what you are thinking, planning or consuming and we will offer you new opportunities for your development and career. At the same time, the modern information market state guarantees only minimal welfare entitlements.

Bobbitt doesn't say that he endorses this development. He describes it as a natural law; more precisely, he sees all social change today as the result of technological determinism.

The fathers of Number 2 viewed the market as a single giant computer, an information-processing machine that fixed fair prices. Bobbitt goes one step further: he sees the state as a computer which – now available in the form of a kind of Apple super-iMac with a high-speed chip, better graphic card, faster data transmission and cool design – imposes certain behaviour on us, just like the mobile phone, computer, Facebook, Vaucanson's duck, Frederick the Great's automatons and Watt's steam engine.

When Bobbitt wrote about a 'new constitutional order', he was not talking about Mr Hyde and he was mindful of a certain diplomacy, but the echo of the fathers of Number 2 can be clearly heard in sentences like these: '[The information market state] will outsource many functions. [...] In part this is a matter of shifting the basis for the state's legitimacy away from assuring mass welfare and maximizing individual opportunity, and by adopting methods of warfare and defence unavailable to nation states.'[5]

This is a perfect description of the reduction of human behaviour by Number 2 and the state his people should live in. Best of all, as Bobbitt repeatedly demonstrates and, as is apparent to everyone who feels America's all-seeing drones, its 'eye in the sky', watching over them, the technology of war is an information technology – a theory that should not surprise opponents of the algorithm wars. In the moment that this WORD is written, high-frequency algorithms worldwide are concluding hundreds of thousands of transactions, and high-frequency algorithms of the information market state are screening the movements of its citizens. The information recorded by the tens of thousands of drones in the skies above America and countless CCTV cameras is interpreted in the same way as Russian troop movements and vehicle convoys during the Cold War or share movements in automated markets. Number 2 is no longer a being with incomplete information.

Mind's Eye, a Pentagon project, plans to fit all monitoring systems in daily life with visual intelligence. It is the social equivalent of what the radar crews did in the 1950s, and it will finally transfer the system of symbolic actions and transactions to human life.

Only recently, researchers at Carnegie Mellon University presented a system that not only decodes surveillance videos in seconds but also attempts to predict what could happen next.[6] Video recordings are cut up into individual segments and then given semantic tags like 'pick up', 'bury' or 'carry'. If someone 'picks up', 'buries' or 'carries' a body, the system warns the operators, who will then carry out further machine-like actions as a function of the situation.

Game theory models play only a marginal role here at present. They are probably involved in behaviour predictions and social strategies but are just one of many ingredients. Image recognition processes, statistical analysis and perhaps even neural networks are much more important for the 'eyes' in the sky. But this is only a question of the degree of organization. As we have seen, Hal Varian is not the only person to believe that behaviour can be predicted using the Nash equilibrium.

In the security architecture of Los Angeles airport, this need not appear as a threat to us.[7] There, the task of averting attacks by an 'intelligent opponent' (terrorism) with limited resources has been solved with game theory models that deploy security forces using a highly complex randomization principle – always with the objective of increasing the 'costs' incurred by attackers (for example, they would need to take account in their strategies of a continuously changing routine) and forcing them to resign in this way. But such applications, which ultimately aim merely to spread out scarce resources (police), could also under other circumstances be used for monitoring. What if our entire life in the era of big data were to be screened and recorded by drones and digital signals? Statistics are one thing – and at present are one of the main factors alongside game theory – but the analysis of the material from the point of view of needing to know no more about people's motives other than that they seek to maximize their profit is on a different ethical level. In every Charles Babbage there is a Sherlock Holmes, and in every Sherlock Holmes there is a general suspicion of a world that has something to hide.

No, it is not Orwellian, or at least not as long as the West lives in democracies. And yet it could be more dramatic: systems that predict human behaviour can only resort to game theory models.

In other words, all these cold eyes in the sky and on earth must by definition think the worst of the people they watch. It is now time to look at what this means.

20

COORDINATION

In the 'twilight of sovereignty', markets give power to the people

In the latest update of information capitalism in the machine age, the brain, the market and the state have become computers with the same software. This is all extremely plausible for society, because almost everyone already lives inside the machine. Like Frederick the Great with his wind-up automatons, we think we know the clockwork that drives the world.

But it is no longer the machine of the revolutionary 1990s with its digital utopias of limitless communication, transparency and friendly, increasingly intelligent swarms. No doubt, hope still lives on of a knowledge economy in which people, at no cost, benefit from one another through cooperation and altruism. For reasons of 'technical' impossibility, this type of person is not programmed. And there is a difference between assuming that people are driven by pure self-interest and programming an entire population in that way.

The automated market analyses preferences, and whether it is about the choice of books or of governments, for this market it is just a question of price. The argumentation is always the same: information capitalism inserts the genotype of the synthetic *homo oeconomicus* into all conceivable systems – from the individual to global economies

– and runs an increasing risk of producing endemically self-fulfilling prophecies.

Walter Wriston, head of Citibank and the most powerful banker of his time, announced gleefully in 1992 the 'twilight of sovereignty', a world in which the state would capitulate in the face of market knowledge and the rationality of *homo oeconomicus*. He predicted what William Blair's investment bankers established as fact in 2012. States now only play 'sovereignty games'. 'Markets,' wrote Wriston, 'are voting machines; they function by taking referenda.'[1]

This was written, it should be pointed out, before the dawn of the commercialized Internet. At a time when the expression 'worldwide web' didn't even exist, Wriston extolled the market with the same words with which Internet Inc. is extolled today. The 'information' produced by the market is a 'running tally on what the world thinks of a government's diplomatic, fiscal, and monetary policies'. In other words, it is the markets that give 'power to the people'.[2]

The market as a symbol of democratic participation was the original idea of the fathers of Number 2, economists like Kenneth Arrow or Milton Friedman. In consequence, the state will become a market, otherwise it will no longer be able to exist.

Bobbitt clearly points out that a market-conforming policy in the information state is not the same as the laissez-faire of Ronald Reagan or Margaret Thatcher. Comparisons like this have always played down the real situation. Supporters of pure neoliberal theory would shudder with fear if they knew what Number 2 really wants. 'The market state is classless and indifferent to race, ethnicity and gender, but it is also heedless of the values of reverence, self-sacrifice, loyalty, and family.'[3]

Elections are thus to a certain extent popular assemblies for an abstract general idea. Consumer preferences are expressed through collective communication on the Internet, in the media and through the 'markets' themselves. As both – communication on the Internet and media reports in the popular press unfortunately aimed increasingly at click counts and information cascades – are quantified and selected by algorithms, the sinister self-fulfilling prophecy loop closes.

Those in any doubt need only look at the first examples in practice. The way in which the energy revolution took place (particularly where nuclear energy was criticized), the fact that in the 'choice' that was offered, the political solution was the precise opposite of what had been promised (from the restructuring of the Bundeswehr to the minimum wage, for example), the way in which the Greek plebiscite was dealt with and also advice given to the Greeks to postpone their elections out of consideration for the 'markets' – these are all the birth pangs of a new information market state.

These are not isolated phenomena but the result of the spread of Number 2 to the social and political world. Only when the state (or what is left of it) generates its reality from the market computer through a consumer plebiscite will it have arrived at where it should be, claims another early RAND strategist who is deeply involved in our story.[4]

The 'impossibility theorem' by the would-be left-wing Nobel Prize-winning economist Kenneth Arrow proved mathematically that the wishes of all market participants cannot be summarized in a realistic *volonté générale*. This means as well that, unlike markets, elections do not express the sum of individual wishes.

As noted in Chapter 9, Philip Bobbitt foresaw a state that would 'respond to ever-changing and constantly monitored consumer demand rather than to voter preferences expressed in relatively rare elections'.[5] For this reason alone it has continuously to produce 'transparency' to provide its members with the necessary information and to protect them from damage. To do this, of course, it has to get into the heads of the market participants – formerly citizens – since the information market state has constantly to make predictions on all possible future scenarios 'so as to predict and exclude risks'. It is a risk assessment machine and hence precisely what a modern stock market is.

Sentences like the following one about the need for behaviour predictions could just as easily come from a financial market analyst or social network operator: 'Rarely before have governments had to rely so heavily on speculation about the future because a failure to act in time would have such irrevocable consequences.'[6]

Social networks have the power of the masses, automated financial markets the power of money, and now the global information market state, the third in the alliance, has the power of military and legislative force. With all the authority of an ex-member of the National Security Council, Bobbitt's main distinction is between 'intelligence producers and consumers'. Everyone has to be assessed as an intelligence producer and an intelligence consumer, and in this way the circle is closed: citizens, job applicants or tourists have exactly the same experience as people who consult the Internet and are monitored so that their behaviour can be predicted.

The information market state likes to speak in tongues, preferably in those of its idealistic enemies. Bobbitt and others therefore demand a digital parallel universe for the secret services and security forces in the new state. And because the game also involves saying something that means something else, he uses terms sacred to the pioneers of the Internet: 'open source' or insight into the algorithms, a global search engine and 'creative commons', the licence-free use of information.

In this way, the information from all secret services in the 'free' world is bundled on a single platform and made accessible only to those who meet the security requirements. Among the demands of the American National Security Agency are a 'Google for intelligence services' and an open-source directory that collects information on the Internet and makes it available for just a short time, and above all uniform jurisdiction. This platform will not only control the monitoring of 'intelligence consumers' and 'intelligence producers' but also evaluate this intelligence like a stock exchange. With the aid of mathematical recommendations, information about risks, such as a cyberattack or possible terrorist plan, is 'hedged' – for example through the manipulation of news made public – in the same way as funds. To some extent, stock exchange, Facebook and secret service algorithms use the same weighting; the only difference is the pricing, the 'truth'.

The best way of understanding what this means is to identify the subject worthy of investment, to use a financial term. This is done with the aid of data mining and predictive algorithms – used today on all passengers entering the USA, for example. If in the world of information market states an independent jury – like Friedrich Hayek's proposed 'council of wise men' for modern democracies – is persuaded that an interned terrorist has lied, then, according to Bobbitt, coercive methods can be used, such as 'sleep deprivation, isolation and the administration of drugs. Where there is no severe pain, there is no torture.'[7]

To be fair, it should be pointed out that in these specific cases Bobbitt provides for a series of legal constraints ('no torture for political purposes') and bases his comments on a 'ticking bomb' scenario, a situation in which a suspect knows where a ticking bomb is hidden. At the same time, this concession is cancelled out again by the fact that, as Niall Ferguson admiringly points out, he doesn't discard the use of truth serums and 'mild torture' but merely criticizes the absence of a legal basis for them. They need to be regulated like a financial market. He describes the American practice of kidnapping suspected terrorists and having them interrogated by the secret service in third states in which torture is allowed as 'outsourcing to the unregulated market'.[8]

He makes it clear that he rejects such methods because they are outside the law. The law must adapt, and in practice this means that this jury of responsible anonymous people 'chosen randomly from the largest number' should decide on the way in which information is obtained from terrorists. They would represent 'not the government, but the society in whose name the government is acting'.[9]

It is clear that this entire system depends on *who* is a terrorist. If we ignore the obvious cases, it is evident that everything depends on the categorization. Bobbitt himself points out that someone like the French Resistance hero Jean Moulin was treated by the Nazis as a terrorist and that it was the Nazis who coined the term 'terrorism' in reference to the French Resistance. But he does not say how, within the new conception of the enemy in an international war, to prevent innocent people from being classed as terrorists. And the current practice in Guantánamo does nothing to allay this fear. What happens if the jury decides that the suspect is a terrorist and that he knows where the ticking bomb is hidden? In a world full of possibilities for digital simulation, identity theft, entire wars legitimized through lies about weapons of mass destruction and, finally, as has been seen on financial markets, the possibility of systematic deception, this is not exactly comforting.

Bobbitt's organizational form of the future is not the surveillance state but surveillance markets in democratic states. They screen not only the potential danger from without but also the popular consensus, which is nothing other than the consumer decision of a permanent voter.

One is not possible without the other, and a lot of money and technology has to be invested in both. It is precisely here that the next hype is beginning to take shape.

21

BIG DATA

NUMBER 2 IS FLYING IN A HELICOPTER ABOVE OUR HEADS

In 2013, business consultants McKinsey announced a new phase of 'capitalism' and forecast a similar Big Bang in information and speed for social markets to the one that took place in financial markets after 2004. The latest trend is called 'big data', a huge universe of interconnected information that can be bought and sold in data supermarkets and has the potential for relating and linking all kinds of things, from morning coffee to vibrations, noises, blood pressure and even flaming on the Internet, and for devising analytical models for just about everything that has been recorded anywhere. McKinsey reckons that by 2018 in the USA alone there will be a need for at least 200,000 data analysts to study systems in depth. Added to this are a good 1.5 million data traders who will use, format and trade in data.[1]

The computer offers the opportunity for reading all of human society like a machine – or, to put it another way for drawing all of human society into the innards of the machine. Researchers at *The New York Times* state that 'The most optimistic researchers believe that these storehouses of "big data" will for the first time reveal sociological laws of human behavior – enabling them to predict political crises, revolutions and other forms of social and economic instability, just as physicists and chemists can predict natural phenomena.'[2]

The significance of this is explained with remarkable openness and enthusiasm by Harvard sociologist Nicholas Christakis:

If you had asked social scientists even 20 years ago what powers they dreamed of having, they would have said, 'It would be unbelievable if we could have this little tiny Black Hawk helicopter that could be microscopic, fly on top of you, and monitor where you are and who you're talking to, what you're buying, what you're thinking, and if it could do this in real time, all the time, for millions of people, all at the same time.' [...] Of course, that's exactly what we have now.[3]

This all sounds exciting for technocrats but scary for humanists, who see the shadow of Big Brother growing so quickly and so darkly that one of the people involved in the design of the new industry has pointed out cautiously that George Orwell didn't go anything like far enough when he wrote *Nineteen Eighty-Four*.

But the fear of a science-fiction future fails to take sufficient account of the present day. Obviously, it's not wrong to prepare for the worst – the stormtroopers, anonymous masses and icy machines with which Apple advertised its first Macintosh in a celebrated publicity film by *Alien* director Ridley Scott in 1984 as a way of saying that 1984 wasn't *Nineteen Eighty-Four*. It's not about the Great Dictator turning society into a prison. It's about society getting itself into a trap that it can no longer escape from.

To complain that the big data computer inadmissibly reduces human behaviour to mathematical models as if people were shares and their actions transactions, and to say that efforts should be made to limit this computational approach to humanity, is but a belated demand for more time to react. It does an injustice to the computer and is too forgiving of the society that created it. Big data will work with multi-agent systems that cannot do otherwise than to analyse the social world with the ego of Number 2 and game theory formulae.

Our new technical world reproduces in detail the economic world view developed by neoclassical and neoliberal economists since the 1950s. What is happening today is not a technical or physical revolution.

Every iPhone, every Google Glass, every ingenious financial, advertising or search algorithm is primarily the result of social physics and serves to place people in a new economic system. A person who has been simulated in machine-readable form is then open to simulation by a machine.

Anyone who reads this book as an e-book will see this immediately. The data from e-book readers – underlining, pages or chapters skipped, reading time – are reported back to a head office, which draws conclusions – so specifically that books are already being rewritten on the basis of this feedback. The minute e-book readers start to read, they becomes agents on the market.

Since the Reagan era, the neoliberal pioneers of the new information capitalism have been talking about the computer in this way. They proclaimed the age of social (quantum) physics, the 'conquest of matter' and the 'modernization' of the marketplace, a holy trinity designed solely to optimize profit.

It is an unsettling triumph, and one made no better by the ideological claim that it benefits mankind. Dirk Helbing, who is seeking to establish FuturiCT at the ETH in Zurich, one of the largest data collectors on the planet, and has applied for a billion euros from the EU, describes unashamedly what is happening: 'It is [...] very important actually that we learn how to measure social capital, such as trust and solidarity and punctuality. [...] This is actually very important for economic value generation. [...] If we would learn how to stabilize trust, or build trust, that would be worth a lot of money.'[4]

The mistake in this vision is most apparent in the blind spot that enables the social engineers of big data to ignore the problem of their self-fulfilling prophecies. They have learned nothing from the experiences of the financial markets except a hunger for even more data, even more interconnection, even more real time. And yet, particularly in the area of epidemic forecasts, about which they are so proud and which is repeatedly cited as a political justification for even more data, they have produced hugely incorrect results. The statistician Alexander Ozonoff from the Harvard School of Public Health has discovered a significant correlation between diseases and their discussion in the media: the more one reads about them in the newspapers, the more frequently they occur.

'The more a particular condition is on people's minds and the more it's a current topic of conversation, the closer the reporting gets to 100 percent.'[5]

There is a lot of evidence that this was responsible for the rapid spread of swine flu. The more the media are controlled by clicks and algorithms and comment in real time, the stronger this tendency will become. In the era of big data, Black Fridays with their self-reinforcing panic will become more rather than less frequent.

Apart from mass suggestion, however, the friends of big data are often surprisingly bad at what they claim to do best, namely forecasting – not just on the stock market but in practically all areas where we can verify the quality of the forecasting (and it is horrifying to consider all those areas where we have no idea whether forecasts are evaluated at all).

ECRI, an influential forecasting institute that appears frequently in stock market programmes, commends itself with the comforting sentence: 'Just as you do not need to know exactly how a car engine works in order to drive safely, you do not need to understand all the intricacies of the economy to accurately read those gauges.' It recently made the headlines for a dramatically incorrect forecast that Nate Silver, one of the most serious American statisticians commented on laconically: 'Who needs a theory when you have so much information? But this is categorically the wrong attitude. [...] [ECRI] had a random soup of variables that mistook correlation for causation.'[6]

Here again the financial markets were merely the pioneers. We know next to nothing about the predictive software used in tax or immigration offices, banks or HR departments. But from what we know of other areas such as medicine, we have a right to be suspicious.

Silver mentions a study published in 2005 examining medical forecasts on drugs being tested. To the annoyance of experts, it showed that most of these forecasts were wrong. And the study would soon have been forgotten if Bayer had not confirmed the results even more emphatically a short time afterwards: two-thirds of the positive results claimed in medical trials (published in leading journals) could not be replicated experimentally.[7]

The same applies to the real estate bubble in the USA. The rating agencies had predictive software and had installed a complex market-surveillance system. They later explained the fact that they nevertheless rated toxic papers so positively by referring to 'unforeseen circumstances', the so-called 'black swan'. Nothing could be further from the truth. As Nate Silver shows, the real estate bubble was anything but a black swan. It was an elephant in the room. Even more importantly, everyone realized that something had gone wrong.

The real estate bubble burst in 2007. 'Google searches on the term "housing bubble",' writes Silver,

> increased roughly tenfold from January 2004 through summer 2005. Interest in the term was heaviest in those states, like California, that had seen the largest run-up in housing prices. [...] Instances of the two-word phrase 'housing bubble' had appeared in just eight news accounts in 2001 but jumped to 3,447 references by 2005. The housing bubble was discussed about ten times per day in reputable newspapers and periodicals.

Three years before the 'surprising' event, it should be noted.[8]

The answer to the puzzle is that there was no shortage of knowledge or information. They were used incorrectly, as a weapon for the agenda of the omnipresent Number 2.

Moody's profits increased between 1997 and 2007 by 800 per cent thanks to derivative products.

According to Frank H. Knight's formula devised in 1921, risk was something that you could stick a price label on. Risk, said the poker players at RAND Corporation, was something that could be reduced if one nailed down the opponent to his egotistical survival interest. Risk, said the people at Moody's, is something whose price must be made so costly that no one can afford to set off a bomb.

22

SUBJUGATION

WE ARE THE SUM OF OUR DESIRES, AND WE KNOW WHAT WE DESIRE

We have seen so far how Number 2 became big and strong and how he has done everything to manage our identity, our preferences, passions and wishes for us. A strategic masterpiece of mental imperialism, the only thing that still counts in an information economy that celebrates the 'subjugation of matter'.

But there was a problem that Number 2 couldn't solve alone in his ethereal airiness. There was already someone sitting in people's heads, where he was implanted. Some called it the ego, others the self.

Although the so-called 'postmodern' philosophers in particular had weakened the fortress with their assaults, the ego was quite resistant. It wanted things that had to do with identity: long-term employment contracts, for example, or to go home in the evening, like generations of people, and to say that it had sold its labour but not its soul.

Like Ellen Ullman, a programmer who began to work enthusiastically in Silicon Valley in the 1990s and experienced all this: the utopia of cooperation, the new thinking, the idea of being part of the creation of a new world. She is one of the few early examples of the digital *homo nuovo* who has reported on her hours and years with and inside the great machine that is Silicon Valley.

Her book is 'an exquisitely melancholy cry', as one critic wrote, 'from a body disappearing into the machine'. It is a fascinating testimony by a woman who, like many of her generation, believed in the short summer of a free Internet that 'we could smash the machine and replace it with a better one', only to find herself in the 'great engine of commerce'.[1]

> I'd like to think that computers are neutral, a tool like any other, a hammer that can build a house or smash a skull. But there is something in the system itself, in the formal logic of programs and data, that recreates the world in its own image. [...] It is as if we took the game of chess and declared it the highest order of human existence.[2]

That is precisely what has happened. Not through the computer itself, but through access by the information economy. Ullman's feeling, as has perhaps become clear by now, is not some side-effect of a technology that we simply still don't know how to use properly. Who could have been more prepared than a programmer like her? It is, rather, the logical consequence of an economic imperialism that found the perfect instrument in the calculating machine. Reduced to a soundbite: We thought Silicon Valley would conquer the world. No, a certain type of economics (at heart neoliberal but much further developed than that) has conquered the world – and is now conquering Silicon Valley. One of the reviewers of John Davis's fundamental study of the extinction of the individual in the 'political economy' sums it up in a nutshell: 'For neoclassical economists [...] this is all irrelevant. [...] Davis might as well be writing about [...] chess pieces, because the abstract, atomistic individual isn't as complex or related to the real world [...] as checker pieces.'[3] This is what Ullman felt intuitively, and if literary Dadaism existed today, it would portray people as chess pieces playing poker.

This is why rational choice and game theory were so well received in Silicon Valley. Since the primeval days of RAND Corporation, the digital elite had made a series of assumptions about rationality, from pure computer science and information theory to design: Bauhaus architecture influenced Silicon Valley more than any theory – in a way it swam like a fish in the ocean of 'rationality'. How could they resist a theory that reduced people to their preferences plus their egotistical desires to achieve them and that regarded everything other than maximization of personal benefit as non-rational?[4]

We want what we want – neoclassicism is not interested in why we want something. Our interests come from outside, and this is where, in the digital era, information economy sits at the helm. Hence the recommendations 'like it', 'your preferences', personalized search. Google – and also many finance algorithms, Facebook and the filter functions of surveillance software – claims somewhat arrogantly that it discovers our preferences: its predictions, recommendations and controls are like a mirror that reflects our wishes.

Let us take, for example, what Google CEO Eric Schmidt says about 'autonomous searching'. Our smartphones, he says, search constantly on our behalf, and can predict what we should or want to do. 'It knows who I am. It knows what I care about. It knows roughly where I am. So this is the notion of autonomous search – this ability to tell me things I didn't know but am probably very interested in is the next stage of search.'[5] Or look at the new functions promised by Google Maps. An app functioning as a navigation device tells us not only what we can see but also what we will like. 'Around the corner behind you is where a scene from your favorite movie was filmed' is an example cited by *Atlantic Wire*.[6] It is impossible for such systems to function without assumptions being made about the user. They can only be assumptions that are also made in rational choice and game theory.

It should not be forgotten that for Number 2 there is no need for anything more: not for consumption but also not for environments remote from the market, such as elections or social contacts.

A lot of this is fine, not just for Internet searches. One day Google will find out that we want to go to the cinema and will simply pick us up in a self-driven car and take us there. And so there is no misunderstanding: the recommendations from Google and above all from Amazon function very well at the moment. Assumptions about rationality, intentions and the human (or user's) ego are in any case unavoidable. People used to rely on their bookseller; now Amazon suggests a few other books. Designers of databases for libraries know that it is impossible to code huge amounts of detailed information about every single reader. It might be possible sometime, particularly in the era of the e-book, but until then simplifications are inevitable. This also applies to political information, social discussion, arguments and theses. The key question is not how to avoid simplifications but what kind of simplifications are acceptable for us and what interests they serve.

But what if what we saw with the flash crashes happens? What if the system doesn't reflect our preferences but actively shapes them? Then technological determinism will have become social determinism. Then we are what others consider to be our preferences, not only Amazon but also friends on Facebook, family, the personnel department, the bank, authorities, or – as we shall see – career portals like LinkedIn. And then we can say as much as we like that there are lots of things that don't serve profit optimization and self-interest – a world that reveals and sells our preferences for us gives us no chance, if we want to be seen as rational beings, as being anything other than ego machines. Everything will then be subject to market laws, including political and social preferences in a permanently screened society. But questions of relevance can never be answered exclusively through markets. They are political decisions.

Ellen Ullman was only the prototype created by the new information economy. Jérôme Kerviel in front of the judge is the criminal counterpart (see Chapter 18). People cannot be exposed to an environment of automated self-interest for long before paying the price, which is what it is all about. Our civilization constantly projects its wishes into its tools, but technology is always dependent on institutional targets and aims.

What did people like Ullman think, and what do many people still think today? It's the old story of technology as Trojan Horse. But it doesn't work like that. It has never worked like that. It only functions when institutions and powers use technology, like Frederick the Great used automatons, to infiltrate them as Trojan androids into the minds of his subjects.

The tools flourish, they become increasingly powerful, but the individual actually becomes more and more dependent and possibly weaker. The Californian psychologist Raymond Barglow describes how the information economy strips the individual of identity, leaving just the dream of a high-tech Silicon Valley worker: 'Image of a head

... and behind it is suspended a computer keyboard attached to it ... I'm this programmed head!' As the sober Manuel Castells noted in one of his less emotional moments, it is the picture of 'absolute solitude'.[7]

Ullman describes a social experience in *Close to the Machine* – and it doesn't matter whether the machine is a computer or a person instructed by computers (which anyone will discover if they try to oppose it). There is nothing that can be called to account less than a computer, and there is nothing that can be called to account less than the market it represents.

Computers and markets are always right, as was shown on a large scale during the financial crisis, even when they can't be right. In terms of game theory, those who cancel the download in frustration pay the price for their involuntary cooperation that allows everyone else to continue to play the game.

In terms of morality, in a world where no appeal is possible, we must seek 'responsibility' in ourselves. This is the core of the new ideology and the essence of the winner-takes-all society: everyone can do anything – become a YouTube star, *Fifty Shades of Grey* bestseller, an overnight sensation by means of a good joke or video, make money by lending empty promises and buying houses with it, etc. Only when everyone believes this and is willing to leave the game as the loser without blaming anyone except themselves or chance, is the great round of poker really under way.

If anyone were to say that in so many words, no one would voluntarily play along. Number 2 discovered that in spite of all the theoretical preparation, the resistance of this ego was enormous. It therefore had to be overcome in another way. Not, to quote Susan Sontag, by killing it, but by extinguishing it.

PART II

OPTIMIZATION OF THE INDIVIDUAL

23

THE SECRET

INSTRUCTIONS FOR THE GAME OF LIFE

To understand a machine, we read the instructions. The new information capitalism offers them in an unexpected place.

There is an entire sector that makes recommendations in the form of slogans. Among the most successful in the last decade: 'The ultimate secret for obtaining absolutely everything', 'no limits', 'orders from the universe' and 'the Secret'. They guarantee that, as *Newsweek* unenthusiastically noted, 'you can manipulate objective physical reality – the numbers in a lottery drawing, the actions of other people who may not even know you exist – through your thoughts and feelings'.[1] Everything is possible; there are no limits. Temptation is the emotional counterpart to globalization.

The rapidly growing number of these recommendations – sales of 50 million lifestyle guidebooks for business alone – leads one to suspect that the opposite is true: more and more people evidently have the feeling that they have fewer opportunities and they therefore resort to products from the cosmic supermarket. What they promise is in such marked contrast to every experience of life that the labels have to be back-translated: the 'ultimate secret for obtaining absolutely everything' actually means that it is no secret that there is absolutely nothing to be obtained.

Surprisingly, there are few complaints to the universe or to the authors, because they manage to persuade buyers that it's their own fault if the product doesn't work.

The journalist Barbara Ehrenreich, who has visited some of these self-discovery factories, says that one of the most lonely moments in her research was when she told a coach 'It doesn't work', to which the coach replied with a smile: 'You mean it doesn't work for you?'[2]

You enter the glittering lobby of the 'Secrets of the Millionaire's Mind' and then, when you find yourself going out again straightaway through the revolving door, comes the mocking rejoinder: 'Everything is possible, just not for you.'

The ability to make matter from ideas was an ancient dream from the era of magic. One is inclined to dismiss a promise stating that anything imaginable can be supplied if only the demand is well enough articulated as the social humbug of American business philosophers. Given the scarcity of resources and scepticism about future growth, who, apart from a few unworldly daydreamers, can believe that there are endless raw materials in an immaterial world that can at any time be made real? The answer is that it is not the daydreamers who believe this but the dominant economic and political elites in the Western world.

This is precisely what happened on Wall Street when virtual money multiplied its nonexistent value by being loaned.

At the individual level, what the critics of Number 2 and of game theory predicted is now a reality: we all have to become the manager of our own ego. We have to reinvent our identity, as if in an endless game of poker, through tactics, strategies, bluffs and moves. The cosmic supermarkets are only the most obvious and hence the most treacherous addresses in a new and fateful superstructure that is completely changing our relationship to society – and to ourselves.

The world has been dealing with the disastrous consequences of this thinking for more than a decade. Many people point to the moral failure of individuals as being responsible for the fact that we appear to be losing the ground under our feet and that all certainties are becoming volatile. The financial crisis is associated with the greed or avarice, in other words the weaknesses, of a few individuals – which is once again like saying that it works, but not for everyone.

This is clearly wrong, however. The apparent human weaknesses are strengths, because they are rewarded with the only thing that counts, namely with more money and with power that is great enough to destroy entire states.

Terms like 'weapons of mass destruction' and 'nuclear meltdown' have been used to describe the financial crisis, replacing the word 'crash' from 1929. As a metaphor, 'crash' comes from the world of traditional physics, where metal collides with concrete. The new words show that information capitalism is not about money clattering to earth but the transmutation of matter.

Without really understanding what they were doing, it was the Germans who started this revolution. They celebrated the fall of the Wall as the belated victory over a political system (except, of course, for those who saw it as a capitulation to the other side). And because they were involved for a decade after 1989 with themselves and with reunification, they believed that the old bipolar political world would merely be replaced by a new one. In reality, it was a victory over a physical world view.

While we are talking about geography, a revolution of a completely different kind took place during the administrations of Reagan and then of Bush Sr. As long as Communism existed as a political force, there was also the positivism of the nineteenth century with its work ethos, its muscles and its tangible things. This was now replaced by a completely new political physics based no longer on the coal mines of the Dickensian era but on the sand of Silicon Valley.

The chemical compound silicon dioxide was to introduce a change in the landscape, against which the mines and underground galleries of the nineteenth century now looked like sandcastles.

As long as it existed, the Wall was the impassable border in which the previous century was cast. It confirmed the Newtonian theory that all matter consisted of solid particles, 'so very hard as never to wear or break in pieces, no ordinary power being able to divide what God himself made one in the first creation'.[3]

In 1989, people and markets still believed that only tangible things existed, just as they believed that the sun rose and set, but already the threat of the American SDI space programme had made them realize that an immaterial physics could shake the solid world of bricks and mortar. Even if SDI was only an idea, the hypothesis alone had made defensive walls and offensive systems seem old-fashioned.

This became clear to the whole world when Ronald Reagan pronounced his most famous sentence: 'Mr Gorbachev, tear down this wall.' In reality, it was not aimed in the first instance at Gorbachev himself but at Russia's young elite, whom Reagan had addressed a year before, on 31 May 1988, in what he described as the most important speech of his life.

In front of a huge bust of Lenin at Moscow University, which was too heavy for his advanced guard to remove from the sight of the cameras, Reagan announced a weightless revolution that would 'fundamentally alter our world, shatter old assumptions and reshape our lives'.

It was to be a 'market revolution', however, that used the very technologies that had enabled SDI to make the Soviet military-technological complex obsolete.

In a deliberate recasting of the computer terminal within the atomic bomb silo dramatized in so many Hollywood films, Reagan said: 'One individual with a desktop computer and a telephone commands resources unavailable to the largest governments just a few years ago.'

It was not about resources, minerals or products, however, but about just one thing: the alchemic transformation of the soul into any desired material.

Reagan used the image of the pupation of the butterfly, the ancient symbol of the metamorphosis of the soul, to show that it was no longer a question of the manipulation of things by science but of the manipulation of the soul by a kind of digital alchemy:

> It's been called the technological or information revolution, and as its emblem, one might take the tiny silicon chip, no bigger than a fingerprint. [...] Like a chrysalis, we're emerging from the economy of the Industrial Revolution – an economy confined to and limited by the Earth's physical resources – into, as one economist titled his book, 'The Economy in Mind,' in which there are no bounds on human imagination, and the freedom to create is the most precious natural resource. Think of that little computer chip. Its value isn't in the sand from which it is made but in the microscopic architecture designed

into it by ingenious human minds. Or take the example of the satellite relaying this broadcast around the world, which replaces thousands of tons of copper mined from the Earth and molded into wire. In the new economy, human invention increasingly makes physical resources obsolete. We're breaking through the material conditions of existence to a world where man creates his own destiny. Even as we explore the most advanced reaches of science, we're returning to the age-old wisdom of our culture, a wisdom contained in the book of Genesis in the Bible: In the beginning was the spirit, and it was from this spirit that the material abundance of creation issued forth.[4]

In the context of the information society, 'man creates his own destiny' is not mysticism but a new definition of work. If one no longer needs anything but oneself to obtain everything, this also means that those who get nothing make their mind superfluous, like a redundant worker in the days of Henry Ford.

Arrogant European intellectuals joked at the time that in his speech Reagan offered the Russian people American television and radio shows 'in seconds' by satellite. He was not talking about the private mythology of a Hollywood actor, however, but about the screenplay for a new world order, which in a fine-sounding but completely unsentimental manner revoked the distinction between mind and matter and declared the ego to be the decisive marketplace of the future.

The fragments of the Berlin Wall, signed by statesmen and finding their way like splinters from the Cross to all corners of the world, were not only souvenirs of a failed socialist human experiment but the start of a new one. Every fragment at the macro-geopolitical level illustrated what had long become common scientific knowledge at the micro-level.

And even the largest concrete wall in the world built by human hand and guarded by huge military forces couldn't do anything about it: information breaks down walls.

Without the information theory of computer science, founded in 1948 by the inspired mathematician Claude Shannon, the SDI missile defence system would not have been imaginable even as a hypothesis. It was a small step to adopt at the political level the term that Shannon and later other areas of physics considered that matter was made of: the bit. As an immaterial particle it had the advantage of being able to win over with physics even those who suffered from materialism.

Naturally, politicians were not particle physicists or information technologists. All they did was to compute the military potential of the technology that had emerged from California and Seattle into the now limitless world markets.

'Information' is not in the least what viewers hear and see on the news. Information that can be duplicated at will can be anything, particularly money, which is transformed with such speed into bits, so much so that at the end of the twentieth century Jeremy Rifkin was able to write 'Less than 10 per cent of the American money supply is still in the form of currency.'[5]

Websters defines 'frontier' as 'a region that forms the margin of settled or developed territory'. This is almost a perfect definition of where the computer industry stands today: 'The broad expanse of this region is almost limitless.'[6]

Ronald Reagan said this on 2 May 1961. For almost ten years, from 1953 to 1962, he presented *General Electric Theater*, a television show sponsored by the American electronics giant General Electric. At the invitation of the company he gave a publicity speech for ERMA, the first super-computer, which could read and process cheques. A few weeks earlier, the Russians had launched the first man into space, and a few months later the Berlin Wall was erected.

On that much later day in Moscow, the triumph of the information age must have seemed for the American president like a providential occurrence.

People and political analysts celebrated the end of the bipolar world, but while they celebrated, a new world was reorganizing itself in the form of the smallest measurable quantifiable unit of yes and no, 1 and 0, all or nothing. The chip, which wired communication as a complex system of yes and no states, soon became more than the fingerprint of a working world restricted to hands and arms. It was, as a pioneer of the new era was soon to write, nothing less than the image of entrepreneurs themselves.

24

SUCCESS

GOD WANTS YOU TO BE RICH. WHY AREN'T YOU?

Since 1968, the student demonstrations and protests of a Western counterculture, the critical predictions of the 'end of growth' and an environmental movement with increasing political success, post-war capitalism has found itself confronted by mounting contradictions.

From the mid-1970s, conservatives, of all people, began to condemn materialism, with diverse references to quantum physics and information theory and in the name of immaterialism, albeit with completely different intentions than the Left.

The establishment was horrified to observe how quickly the protest movement of the 1960s had managed to hack its way into the power system. Twenty years later, many of them had changed sides and found a platform in the form of *Wired*, and the new information technology ideologies were infecting the codes of the anti-establishment mood like a computer virus. These new ideologies evolved within a few years into the 'new economy' and 'neoliberalism'.

Just ten years after Reagan's speech in the heart of Communism, the arch-conservative American businessman George Gilder, an adviser to the President, who had also informed him of the 'economy in mind' (and wrote the foreword to the book of the same name), gave a speech in the Vatican.

The digital revolution had been proceeding at breathtaking pace; moreover, the Internet had turned walls into networks. Gilder entitled his speech 'The Soul of Silicon', and it was a sermon about the new economy in mind. 'There is no longer anything solid or physically determined in the prevailing theory of the atom,' he said. 'At the root of all the cascading changes of modern economic life [...] is this original overthrow of material solidity in the science of matter itself.'[1]

Gilder derisively attacked the 'morbid anxieties' of the new social movements about 'nonrenewable energies, finite reserves and the limits of growth'. Those who spoke like that, he said, glorified matter and flesh and failed to recognize the new message of science and the old one of religion: 'The world is not entrapped; man is not finite; the human mind is not bound in material brain.'[2]

What applied to globalization now applied to every individual.

Apparently it didn't occur to the audience he was speaking to that the immaterial, the soul, was now itself becoming the market. Gilder, at the time one of the most influential pioneers of the new economy and a welcome contributor to *Wired*, left no doubt that 'destiny' in this new world without limits was what people made of their lives. Neither material limitations nor – even more decisive – unforeseeable circumstances could stop or save them if things went wrong.

What followed was a spectacular real-time experiment, comparable with the former socialist laboratory: the return in the twenty-first century of the notion of magic with the aid of science.

Reagan didn't yet talk about the mail order service from the universe delivering refrigerators that stood in the kitchen by dint of the imagination (as entire imaginary houses were built during the real estate crisis), but it was clear who was responsible if the kitchen was empty: individuals themselves.

On the fifth anniversary of the American magazine *Wired*, which like no other publication combined the aura of the counterculture with the new economy, Gilder announced the end of the 'tyranny of matter'. He was supported in an editorial entitled 'The State of the Planet', a direct reference to the pessimistic reports by the Club of Rome.

'In this economic system our ability to create wealth is no longer limited by physical boundaries but only by our ability to develop new ideas – in other words it is unlimited.'[3]

At the same time, the journalist and ex-hippie Kevin Kelly, a former member of the Whole Earth movement before he became editor-in-chief of *Wired*, prophesied that the 'made world' would be saturated with the pure force of the 'global spirit'.

The dominance of mind over matter is not new. It is the dogma of the advertising industry, which over the course of a century had perfected the manipulation of the mind. Now it has become a business model not only for cyber-prophets but also for local used car dealers.

In *New Rules for the New Economy*, the most influential book of the era, Kelly wrote that the principles that dominated the world of software, media and services 'will soon command the world of the hard – the world of reality, of atoms, of objects, of steel and oil, and the hard work done by the sweat of brows'.[4]

An ethic that makes individuals responsible for their success or failure has always existed. The successful succeed because, as *The Secret* postulates, they have attracted success – exactly like a friend in a social network.

'One individual with a desktop computer and a telephone,' said Reagan, 'commands resources unavailable to the largest governments just a few years ago.' *The Secret* and other tracts took this literally. 'You can have anything' means: your bicycle, your refrigerator, your television, your job and your soul are broken, and you are still waiting to be invited onto television, because you are broken yourself and need to be repaired.

In 2006, two years before the Lehman Brothers bankruptcy, *Time* magazine summarized the mood of great expectation in a title story 'Does God Want You to be Rich?' The answer was yes.

In the same year, a man named Mike Gelband discovered what it meant to doubt divine will. He was responsible for the real estate department at Lehman Brothers. In his annual interview he said unexpectedly and in a state of high alarm: 'We have to rethink our business model.' He was promptly fired.

25

ALCHEMISTS

TRANSFORM YOUR SOUL INTO GOLD, BECAUSE WORK IS WORK ON ONESELF

These hopes of a new economy of endless wealth through inexhaustible resources and entropy-free energy were not new. And once again, as with Galvani, Salvá and all the others, with this technology, which was meant to fulfil all dreams, there were the initial much more direct and realistic attempts – like twitching frogs' legs and, in the case of the spiritual economy, shining like gold.

What we are experiencing is a replica, the second attempt by modern society to reawaken magic with the aid of modern science.

The first attempt had disastrous consequences.

Back then, in the early twentieth century, the door appeared to open overnight to a world of fantastic surfeit in which physical boundaries no longer existed. Honorary members of the Royal Society and Nobel Prize winners suddenly bent over alchemist tracts, seeking ways of turning lead into gold and making matter out of nothing.

All this was prompted by the nascent discipline of nuclear physics. In a laboratory at McGill University in Montreal in 1901, the chemist Frederick Soddy and the physicist Ernest Rutherford had discovered that a radioactive element could turn into another element. Soddy's biographer describes how the later Nobel Prize winner for chemistry experienced the moment of discovery: "'I was overwhelmed with something greater than joy – I cannot very well express it – a kind of exultation." He blurted out, "Rutherford, this is transmutation!" "For Mike's sake, Soddy," his companion shot back, "don't call it *transmutation*. They'll have our heads off as alchemists."[1]

What happened instead is described in Mark Morrisson's fascinating study *Modern Alchemy*: scientists and society became crazy about alchemy, metaphysics made by physics. 'After Rutherford and Soddy's 1902 publication, such attitudes changed dramatically. Even religious skeptics began to wonder if the alchemists might have understood something about the nature of matter that nineteenth-century scientists had missed. Could radium have been the fabled Philosopher's Stone?'[2]

This was the start of what Morrisson calls an academic Gold Rush. If just a few words are replaced, the hype sounds like a parody of the pioneers of financial markets who in the twenty-first century wanted to make gold from nothing with the aid of computers and algorithms.

Suddenly, modern chemistry and physics were being mixed with esoteric subjects, sometimes by the same people. For our purposes, what matters is that people believed that in 'transmutation' they had discovered an 'energy', which, as a report on meetings of the Chemical Society states, would lead directly to the primordial matter and hence to having available all energy to create the world.

There is a certain bizarre attraction in experiencing this circuit full of doppelgängers and encountering a revenant at every door. In his book *The Interpretation of Radium*, Soddy claimed to have discovered, together with the new technology, the 'end of work', which in the screenplay is in fact not foreseen until the start of the third millennium.

'A race which could transmute matter would have little need to earn its bread by the sweat of its brow. [...] Such a race could transform a desert continent, thaw the frozen poles and make the whole world one smiling Garden of Eden.'[3]

For almost thirty years, the public was captivated by the idea of alchemic transmutation. Morrisson shows how scientists, the media and science fiction writers dreamed the dream of surfeit. It could be a vision of inexhaustible energy reserves – crossing an entire ocean with the energy of a test tube of radioactive matter – or the actual transformation of base materials into gold.

Next, alchemy infected economics. What would happen if gold, whose value was due to its scarcity, were to be available in surplus? In 1922, *The New York Times* felt obliged to publish the report by an American federal authority on its front page:

> The recent revival of interest in alchemy and published suggestions that artificial gold might become so abundant that the natural metal would lose its value as a basis for currency brought from the United States Geological Survey today a statement that no occasion exists for chemists to hope for nor economists to fear the prospect of the precious metal being produced in the laboratory.

When in the 1930s the (subsequently repudiated) news was disseminated that the German Adolf Miethe had managed to make gold, *The New York Times* ran a headline 'Synthetic Gold Might Disrupt the World/Commercial Use Would Mean Chaos in Finance'.[4]

Although it might appear merely a historical footnote, it is worth mentioning here because it heightens awareness of unintentional consequences of the main script. The history of unforeseen results in technologies that are meant to save the world is as important in a world of calculation as, for example, the adverse effects on a drug information sheet.

One of these is described by the author H.G. Wells, who was fascinated by Soddy's discovery and even more by his alchemic theses. He was interested not only in the transmutation into gold but also in the prospects of limitless energy.

He published the novel *The World Set Free* in 1914 and dedicated it to Soddy. The book, very poorly written but also highly prescient, tells the story of the first nuclear war taking place in the 1950s. Cities on both sides are wiped out; the gold created spontaneously as a result of the explosions destroys economies, and in the face of a weapon that produces no winners but only losers, the nations decide – no, not to employ game theory, but to institute a world government.

Soddy himself was hugely impressed by the book. In the 1920s he coined the term 'virtual wealth' and formulated a theory of unreal capital, which anticipated the 'economy in mind' in a remarkable fashion.[5]

In 1932, the young physicist Leó Szilárd read Wells's book and was also suitably impressed. A year later he discovered the atomic chain reaction and handed the patent to the British government, because, as he said, he had understood what Wells was saying. Seven years later, it was Szilárd, once again explicitly referring to Wells's book, who was responsible for the creation of the Manhattan Project and the building of the atomic bomb.

So much for intentional and unintentional consequences of technological utopias, which almost all dream the same dreams.

It may nevertheless be said that over time they became more realistic and profitable for the dreamer. Soddy's transmutation failed to produce gold but instead produced the atomic bomb, and with the atomic bomb came the new rationality in the guise of game theory.

At the second attempt after the Cold War it was no longer a question of trying to produce real gold in the real world. Now the computer and its game theory agents hinted at the Midas touch: everything you touch through me will turn to gold ...

'The rich,' wrote George Gilder, 'have the anti-Midas touch, transforming timorous liquidity through the alchemy of the creative spirit into capital and real wealth.'[6] This was similar to the 'virtual wealth' that had already spirited itself into the thinking of the 1920s.

In his book *Bad Money*, describing the 2007 debt crisis, Kevin Phillips showed the extent to which the actors on Wall Street were operating increasingly in a mentally deranged world and yet initially were just becoming more and more successful.[7]

Of all the resources claimed by the new capitalism to be inexhaustible, money was the one resource that appeared to corroborate the theory that everyone could have everything. The increase in virtual money meant that debt grew and savings shrank, while at the same time apparently making it possible for every wish, from a car to a home, to be fulfilled.

The extent of the transmutation contradicted all laws in force hitherto. The computer historian George Dyson highlighted this anomaly by musing on the possibility of buying a house without money and spending the non-existent money into the bargain. Entire industries that no longer owned their own plants but outsourced production confirmed this supposition.

It is no coincidence that at the absolute high point of the hype, Rhonda Byrne's popular book *The Secret* climbed a few rungs higher on the chutzpah bestseller ladder. The rich deserved their success, she wrote, because they attracted it.

It was already clear shortly before the crisis in 2007 that the promises of the new economy were not being fulfilled. Information capitalism had produced winners, albeit winners in a winner-take-all society. Although everyone could see that in America and Europe for the first time middle-class income appeared to be shrinking and most salaries were no longer linked to the growth in productivity or profits, this did nothing to alter the boundless optimism of the elites.

Germany, a country without the religious revivalist tradition of the USA, borrowed from the toolbox of the 'economy in mind' above all those elements that appeared to fit best with its own intellectual history. With trivial but misleading social programming, every expert group talked of the 'knowledge society' and made 'lifelong learning' a duty.

It was trivial because the school of life was a cliché – and more than ever in a culture that had produced the *Bildungsroman*. It was also misleading because society in the third modern industrial age no longer knew what people were meant to know and how they should learn.

Looking more closely, however, it can be seen that the slogans had the same architecture as the world code created on Wall Street and in Silicon Valley, which taught that the world can be controlled by the mind.

Work is basically work on oneself, a mental process, but one organized according to the laws of the marketplace. Those who became unemployed were to a certain extent liberated from their own soul. To sell one's labour but not one's soul was the spark that gave the twentieth-century world its identity. 'Become who you are' was its philosophical counterpart.

What something is cannot be separated from what it does – this realization of the new physics destroyed identity in an unparalleled fashion and laid the foundations for modern humanity's nomadism.

The body as tomb of the soul – *soma/sela* – is one of the basic Platonic formulae of the Western world. Venture capitalists and Internet theoreticians were convinced that the dissolution of the bodily shell would crush to pulp not only concrete structures but also the architecture of organizations, bureaucracies and businesses of all types and put the individual on an equal footing with those in power.

It is surprising how few people recognized that the game could have a different outcome. Just as the idea of deregulated communication was immediately scuppered and became the driving force behind deregulated financial markets, so the equating of the individual with businesses did not make business more human; it made humans more like businesses.

What is happening can no longer be explained on the 'scientific' basis of a new world view; nor is it possible in this way to explain the disturbing fact that the immaterial economy allows or even inevitably causes losses that eat up states while rewarding the perpetrators.

It can only be explained by once again harking back to the laboratory discussion over a century ago. The return of alchemy, which had long disappeared from daily life and was then revived in financial markets of all places, is no coincidence.

Making gold from nothing: that is what everyone is being asked to do today, and the miracle of transmutation judges the value of your soul. While Number 2 is imposing on everyone a world of irrefutable logic, everyone knows that you can't catch Number 1 with logic. Logic tells us that it doesn't work. It can be placed in people's mind only by magic, the magic word that accompanies the computer and the iPhones like a celestial body.

We need now to take a look inside the laboratory.

TRANSMUTATION OF THE SOUL

LIFE AS A FAILED EXPERIMENT

'No one can escape the transforming fire of machines.' This is the first sentence of Kevin Kelly's book *New Rules for the New Economy* published in 1998, a highly influential essay containing both linguistic and conceptual cues as to what Silicon Valley and Wall Street were planning with the new world.

This basic essay on the new economic rationality uses the idiom of magic. Kelly begins with a sentence that could have been taken from the works of alchemists. They believed that the soul transmuted in a 'transforming fire'. Kelly and his like-minded contemporaries on Wall Street argued using mystical terminology, but in reality they were demanding quite simply the alchemic transformation of humankind through the technology of the digital markets.

The new magic of the codes had hardwired the digital workplace from the outset with the four elements: earth (the sand from which microchips are made), fire (electricity including firewalls, burning of data storage media, 'software smithies'), air (wireless transmission) and water (the information flow itself, which drowns those who don't know how to navigate).

Magic was also urgently required because the contradictions of the new economy were so unmissable and their relationship with disdaining neoliberal governments so close that without phoney magic people would never have been persuaded to organize their own lives on a market basis.

I hey had to be promised the great transformation, which in the alchemist's laboratory also meant the transformation of human flesh into a substance of unimaginable perfection, an act of 'spiritual rebirth and physical immortality'.

The cyber-prophets promised nothing less than the realization of the oldest dream of humanity – with the small proviso that it could be achieved only with digital doppelgängers, at least as long as people breathed, ate and died in reality.

It was a perfect division of labour between the 'economists in mind' (or service society), who wanted to turn deindustrialization into a new market, and the digital evangelists, who wanted to do the same with the disembodied and exanimate ego, in which Number 2 had taken over control.

Economists preached the transformation of the marketplace, politicians and journalists the transformation of workplaces – economic transmutation on the one hand, social transmutation on the other. Most of the battle cries were shared: 'outsourcing', 're-engineering', 'downsizing'.

The motivation was evident: if everything was immaterial and just a question of information economy and communication, the real world could actually be transformed into the symbolic space in which Number 2, the computer and game theory could operate as in the Cold War.

Kevin Kelly can be seen as one of those progressive pioneers who are not only responsible for the entire mishmash of technological and biological metaphors but have also attempted to reach out over the abyss in the long-standing cultural war that separates the counterculture and Wall Street. That the technical systems have become new life forms, that the Web always knows more than the individual, and that only the totality of the unfathomable knowledge can reveal the truth – all this was indeed a 'neo-biological' metaphor, 'the analogue for the network being was the market as theorized by Hayek'.[1]

Kelly did a lot to make Number 2 less scary (an example of a functioning system that he loves is Sim City). He describes a world led not by humans but by agents of the Darwinian fight for survival – as he illustrates, for example, in an immortal passage in which the price of an egg is fixed – while *homo sapiens* leans back and dwells on thoughts of 'co-evolution and cooperation'.[2]

No one escaped Kelly's alchemic arts; no one suspected the price to be paid for the new ideology; and no one laughed when Kelly called Benetton a new 'economic superorganism' with reference to the personalization of pullovers and shirts.[3]

The return into people's minds at the start of the twenty-first century of demons, elves, dwarves, magicians and vampires after their long period of exile must be seen as the precursor of a fundamental ecological change. The climate of reason, which they were unable to withstand, has changed in their favour.

On millions of screens, on which thoughts can be transferred by touch, and money by light, creatures are appearing that were last hatched from the alchemists' glass retorts.

The scruffiest of seventeenth-century magicians, out of work for a couple of centuries, would feel completely at home in today's world. They would be masters not only in computer games.

No one would have to explain to them a world in which all of the information about every single soul, including how long they spend reading particular words on their e-reader, can be transformed into money.

The fact that they had arrived in a world in which, as the Nobel Prize winner for economics Joseph Stiglitz put it, 'financial wizards' produced 'monsters' in their 'Frankenstein laboratories' with mathematically impenetrable 'toxic' formulae on their screens, merely meant to them that they had finally returned home.[4]

This is hardly surprising. After all, when financial marketing literature spells CPDO, it is using the same incomprehensible mystical alphabet that the alchemists once employed, in this case for offering clients the 'hottest alchemical method for transforming plumbous yield premiums into the gold of market-beating returns'.[5]

The alchemists never distinguished between mind and matter. According to the magic books, those who wanted to turn lead into gold required not only certain essences and formulae but also screens, 'projections', that calculated the magic code on the basis of strictly defined symbols. A screen that made the transformation visible: the inner power of imagination, the legendary *imaginatio* with which the power of the soul could be exploited.

If Gabriel Clauder, the personal physician of the seventeenth-century Elector of Saxony, were to step into the twenty-first century, he would be pleased to note that alchemy had made astounding progress. He would see that money and power are produced where the human soul is broken down according to strict rules into individual formulations and then reassembled. He would see the algorithms that determine our existence today merely as improved versions of his alchemic recipes.

Clauder's essay *Die universelle Tinktur oder der Stein des Weisen* [The universal tincture or the Philosopher's Stone] is just the incremental code for making something from nothing. The Philosopher's Stone was not a stone but a fluid, pure liquidity. To obtain it the magician needed the 'universal spirit', which was unfortunately volatile, invisible and ethereal.[6]

To condense it, a piece of earth had to be dug up from a field at midnight in April or May, when it had not rained for weeks, and then exposed to the sun for three hours with the aid of a burning lens, the evaporating water being absorbed by a linen cloth, which was then wrung out over a glass vessel. Just a few drops of this tincture, provided they were used by a trustworthy person, would transform a few ounces of mercury into pure gold.

These days, anyone who wrote an email after midnight containing the words earth, shovel, dig, burning lens, mercury, linen and gold, would no doubt be directed by Google to garden implements – or arrested by Homeland Security on entry into the USA – but the transmutation from nothing into money or power will nevertheless have taken place.

Scipione Chiaramonti, a seventeenth-century mathematician who believed in witches and would like to have seen Galileo burnt at the stake, was convinced, long before Google, Facebook and Apple, that one could determine and predict people's thought, character and intentions through their voice and movements, the weather, place and syntax.

The discovery by American researchers that one could tell just from automated data on movements and places recorded by a mobile phone that a person was likely to catch the flu, or from seemingly unconnected emails that he would be fired from his job sometime in the future, would have seemed to Chiaramonti like a logical conclusion of his theses.

In 1670, a man called J.L. Hannemann attempted to revive the forgotten idea of a 'collective world soul'. This collective psyche was for him a simulation of the natural world. Our discovery of a 'networked society' would probably have evoked no more than a tired yawn from him. In the great universal organism everything was linked and everything communicated, even across continents. If the arm of a man whose tissue had been used to correct someone else's nose became putrid, the other person's nose would also putrefy, even if he were far away.

There are any number of essays on numerology, cryptography and gematria, and the widest variety of codes with which the esoteric patterns of human behaviour control have been calculated and predicted, substances manipulated and programmed, many of them thought up and disseminated by some of the best mathematicians of their time. The distinction was not between magic and science but between areas of one and the same brain.

The estate of Isaac Newton, one of the greatest mathematical geniuses of his time, contained a million words on magic and alchemy, none of them, as one of his biographers stated succinctly, with any substantive value. They were all written, he said, in the same twenty-five years in which Newton conducted his mathematical studies and would have been as rational as them if their entire content and sole intent had not been magic.

Medical and cultural pandemics both tend to have precisely localizable origins. The magical science that replaced the natural magic of Merlin's worlds and mutated in its turn into the scientific age was triggered by one of the first great open-source movements in history.

In the thirteenth century, the writings by Islamic scholars translated into Latin on astrology, fortune-telling and above all alchemy arrived in Europe from Catalonia and Mallorca. (In Britain alone, 3,500 such writings have survived.)

The intellectual infection of the twenty-first century also has two precisely localizable origins: San Francisco Bay and the southern tip of a small island in New York, in other words Silicon Valley and Wall Street.

Many people labour their entire lives and still never manage to understand why *it* doesn't work. Why can't they have what everyone has been promised? They feel like an experiment that keeps on going wrong. The transformation of lead into gold doesn't work, and those who claim the contrary turn out to be charlatans. And yet people follow the regulations and instructions precisely, they study, they learn, they struggle at work, they communicate with friends, they go to the right places, but sooner or later most of them realize that the entire undertaking is a failure – at the latest when, in their 'retirement', the entitlements they have acquired during their lives disintegrate.

The problem is that most people read the codes of the information society, like those of the alchemists, as metaphors. They don't understand how serious it is when information can no longer be distinguished from things and can be measured and calculated. In the words of Theodore Roszak, information has become a fetish.[7]

As long as external forces – gods, kings or governments – could be held responsible for misfortune, the disappointment gave rise to revolts and revolutions. The new capitalism, however, has managed to turn the responsibility back onto the human ego.

Thus, more and more people feel that they have not exploited their full potential in life, while the structure for realizing their demands insists that 'we have lived above our means'.

As we know, this is not intended as an economic argument, because the question of 'who' has lived above their means would then need to be answered. It is a purely ethical argument and, as can be seen from the most popular idea of sin, also a religious one: it doesn't work because you have sinned.

The bemoaned lack of flexibility, discipline and responsibility are not systemic failures but character faults, and they can be eliminated. Only in this way is it possible to explain how the dismantling of the welfare state was supported even by those who would soon be in need of it. The American example in the 1990s, as Thomas Frank shows, illustrated the role reversal of entire classes.

'The rich, the former leisure class,' wrote *Wired*, 'are becoming the new overworked. And those who used to be considered the working class are becoming the new leisure class.'[8]

In the alchemy laboratory only the worthy could hope to master the transmutation of matter into gold or spirit. To have a chance, a person had to be healthy, patient, intelligent, devout and disciplined.[9] He had to be capable of taking in all information without drowning in it. Those 'passing from one opinion to another, and from one wish to another wish ... are so mobile that they can hardly finish the slightest thing that they intend'. The alchemist had to be creative and 'of constant will in work, so that he does not at one time presume to try one thing, and another time another'.[10]

Even if that was taken fully to heart, all efforts were in vain without God's blessing. The problem was that He was quite an unpredictable boss, who 'filled with all justice and goodness extends [His divine power] to and withdraws it from whomever He wills'.

It should not therefore be surprising if no gold was produced: the decisive doctrine was that it was more important to transform the soul than to transmute metal.

These tricks, centuries before advertising and branding, were possibly the first time that mental work was combined with industrial tasks.

Many alchemists were entrepreneurs associated with the flourishing mining industry. Work on the self, the regeneration of the soul, called for a form of spiritual devotion to fashion. There had to be a permanent willingness – hence the comparison – to shed the old existence like one would discard old clothes. This took place in the fire of the alchemic smithy: a metamorphosis of the self, which became the product in future work processes.

The alchemic transformation was communication, and even the practical results in the laboratory, as research has shown, were read as a language, as this was the only way of explaining the interaction between man and matter. Hence the secret writings and codes, algebra, and finally also prayers. In the merging of the spiritual and the material what remained was exchange – or communication – as the essence of everything. Doing is thinking, thinking is doing.

In this way a magic system arose. What used to be called 'initiation' is now 'communication' via digital channels. Yesterday's 'adept' is today's 'talent', and yesterday's 'completeness' today's 'perfection'.

'Talent', the favourite word worldwide in recruitment, is an eternal promise, pure potential. Obfuscating terms like 'knowledge' or 'creativity' by misguided journalists, who believe that knowledge is education, often cited as indicators of an advantage in the Darwinian survival scenario, just randomly serve the needs of unpredictable bosses, who give or withdraw their loyalty as the mood takes them.

They are no longer terms describing freedom but rather social control, which decides whether the process achieves the desired outcome or not. Self-transmutation is just as little in the hands of the individual today as it was in the times of black magic.

The ego, which must seek the reasons for its failure in itself, is an interface not only for accessing the world but also for being accessed by it. Action depends on thousands of details, on physical and mental health, how honest one is with oneself, the time of day at which entries are written in Facebook or emails are sent, the location and all the locations where one has ever been and which make it possible to predict where one will head in future.

One need only look at the puzzled faces of students scaling the summits of knowledge, at skilled workers, engineers and journalists who suddenly realize that 'knowledge' is merely part of a process whose material results decide whether the knowledge is useful or not. Money is also information with both a religious and a profane value, as in the world view of the alchemists.

As Hans Christoph Binswanger explains in an elegant interpretation of Goethe, money is (just) an invention, possibly the only thing that has a direct influence on reality.[11] European societies have discovered that an information explosion can be followed by a financial explosion.

It is thus hardly surprising that Ken Binmore's vision of the future, what he calls 'non-cognitive learning', is learning that no longer needs to be 'understood'; it is reason, which swaps knowledge for information and in which it is no longer a question of understanding the incoming information signals but just of receiving them and passing them on.[12]

Information is in some way similar to the substances and chemicals stirred by the alchemist. He doesn't know what they consist of and cannot explain how they work, but with unshakable conviction he knows what will come out if he mixes them; from love potions to poultices.

In this way, the individual has become a workpiece in the information era, which gains value only through processing and exchange.

27

DEATH DATING

CREATIVE DESTRUCTION AND THE ENGINEERS' ART

The theoretical abolition of mind and matter in the economy of the twentieth century has a very real history. In 1932, the greatest industrial nation in the world found itself in a depression that was much more than a cyclic economic crisis. The fact itself and the extent of the disaster gainsaid all of the promises that for almost half a century had accompanied the great epoch of technological miracles.

For many people, 1932 was a template, as if the monstrous crisis of self-confidence in the world of that time in some way anticipated the world of today. A massive collapse in housing prices and the reluctance by the American public to consume had brought the economy to the brink of ruin. Even the boom years prior to the world economic crisis were driven by fear of overproduction.

People still bought things because they needed them and not because they wanted them, but it was already evident that something would have to be done to increase the rate of turnover.

The record years of industrial production before the world economic crisis saw the mass production of cars, refrigerators and vending machines, but beneath the level of tangible things that could be bought, for the first time tools were being made that could penetrate into the mind and shape it like a piece of wood or metal.

The discovery of mass psychology for the advertising market – by Sigmund Freud's nephew Edward Bernays, who invented the term 'public relations' – brought about the colonization and exploitation of an emotional continent that had been thought for centuries to be unpredictable.

At the time it was just a question of mental raw material and not the mathematical models that IT experts in the computer era would use eighty years later with the aid of psychologists and anthropologists. Of decisive importance, however, was the fact that the success of the new methods could be calculated in dollars and cents and determined on the basis of sales.

Long before Google and algorithms existed, the recognition that individuals as part of the masses were predictable and that their behaviour was to a certain extent determinable, was something like the nuclear fusion reactor of social change, with enormous political consequences. The two atomic nuclei involved in the fusion were the psyche and the product.

The inventors of these instruments, called 'advertising' and 'PR', saw themselves, as Edward Bernays put it, as an elite, a 'relatively small number of persons' who were the only ones to understand the 'mental processes and social patterns of the masses'.[1] After the experience of the emotional mass mobilization in the First World War, this was a claim of enormous significance.

The social engineers, as they liked to call themselves, consistently described their services as 'technologies'. They were effective and mercilessly neutral.

Naturally these 'hidden persuaders' overestimated themselves, and in fact their claims about the controlling power they had over people might have been one of their best publicity stunts. An entire library of studies has put the picture of the manipulators into proportion. They couldn't do what they claimed, was one widespread thesis, because people are richer, more profound and contradictory than the simplified concepts would have it. But that is not the issue. The issue is whether the world can be shaped so that it fits these simple concepts.

Mass psychology had shown that the mind could be manipulated so that neutral things appeared in a different light. Now came the second stage: things could also be manipulated so that they changed the psyche and the entire behaviour code. Nothing bothered the mind engineers of the 1930s more than the morality of their customers, who believed that things should not be wasted and that they should last for ever.

A decisive proposal was made by a real estate broker called Bernard London, who in 1932 published an essay entitled 'Ending the Depression through Planned Obsolescence'. By this he meant a product becoming broken or no longer up to date. London suggested that every product should have only a limited and government-ordained service life. Then it would be 'legally dead' and would be disposed of or destroyed.[2]

In processes that are still only known fragmentarily today, engineers began to build 'death dates' into their products. Death dating determined the service life of an object – be it a toy car, a light bulb or a radio. Even the journalist Giles Slade, who narrated the story of obsolescence in America, did not manage to identify the highly efficient processes behind these built-in technologies. A few internal memos from General Electric in the 1930s show, however, that everyone seems to have been aware of what was going on.

Breaking down: light bulbs after a certain time (because the luminescence was too weak), tubes in radios, electronic components that were timed to give up the ghost when the battery needed changing. The main thing was that now a second control authority was established.

The advertising psychologists claimed to control people's minds, but the manufacturers controlled the service life of the hardware, just as psychology does with people – as soon as they are transformed from luxury to consumer items.

In 1880 the light bulb was a luxury. It cost half a day's wages. Edison's first customers were J.P. Morgan and the Vanderbilts. Then, as houses were gradually connected to the electricity grid and production methods improved, industrial production was possible.

In 1924, the members of the Phoebus cartel, including Osram, Philips and General Electric, met in Geneva and decided together to artificially shorten the life of light bulbs. Vance Packard quotes a memo stating: 'The design life of the 2330 lamp has been changed from 300 back to 200 hours. [...] It is understood that no publicity or other announcement will be made of the change.'[3]

For the first time, engineers had built 'creative destruction' into the objects themselves, thus designing not only something functional but also something non-functional. The boundaries to which the premature death of the light bulb were stretched is now legendary. In 1901 a light bulb was switched on in a small fire station in Livermore, California. It is still burning, 111 years later. The fire department website shows how many generations of fire chiefs the small, now weakly glowing bulb, has survived.

The desire of industrial giants to decide themselves how long something functioned was both a technical and a psychological operation. They resorted to formulae, some of which are still used today. With simple appliances they might be in the form of algorithms relating just to the material or to the functionality. Sometimes it was sufficient for the product to quickly become dirty and unappealing.

With complex products the trick was to manipulate the weakest link to sabotage the functionality of the device. But psychologically the death date was only a means of producing surplus through redundancy, albeit so effectively that a member of the US Congress expressed sympathy for the millions of people whose household appliances fell apart.[4]

In the wake of the public discussion after the Second World War, provoked in particular by Vance Packard, planned obsolescence was dealt with more carefully. Failure as a principle of superfluity was now a three-stage process, perfected by engineers, advertisers and designers. The entire sector spoke with unparalleled openness about the three options: planned failure through quality; ageing through function because new devices were better and faster; and 'psychological failure' because a product had become undesirable, out of date and therefore redundant. This applied to all changes in design and fashion, which were sold through advertising and example as necessary. Harley Earl, one of the first industrial designers, described 'planned or dynamic obsolescence', as he called it, as follows: 'Our big job is to hasten obsolescence. In 1934 the average car ownership span was 5 years, now [1955] it is 2 years. When it is 1 year we will have a perfect score.'[5]

Decades before the arrival of a world calculated by computers, a cultural machine was built that functioned in a deterministic fashion and produced surplus through its own redundancy. It produced, at least in the eyes of the manufacturers, calculated self-destruction, the result of profit maximization that knew no chance, no right or wrong utilization or way of life, and no fate – it came with the power of predetermination. It changed the categories of reliability, loyalty and longevity for material items, well before the modern media society, politics and the new economy did it with immaterial ones as well.

Many newspaper articles and readers' letters at the time show that large sections of the public were aware that the world into which they had entered as consumers would be one of broken loyalties.

Department stores and companies suddenly stopped promising lifelong warranties – an advertising message that before the world economic crisis had been of existential importance for mass products. Fewer than ten years before the theoretical collapse of the entire system had been mapped out by the Stock Exchange crash, Henry Ford, the originator of mass production, had said:

> We cannot conceive how to serve the customer unless we make for him something that, so far as we can provide, will last forever.... It does not please us to have a buyer's car wear out or become obsolete. We want the man who buys one of our cars never to have to buy another. We never make an improvement that renders any previous model obsolete.[6]

As Giles Slade describes minutely, the old promise of a lifelong warranty was cancelled and replaced by a new one, instant gratification. It was the final transfer of the thing in itself to the brain, where hormones are released and dependencies created.

Above all it created a new, simple and simplified law of history that, in spite of the widespread scepticism about technology, has taken over even those areas of human society – from stock markets to social groups – that would normally firmly reject the law of predetermination: technological progress is self-justifying. Those who don't keep up lose touch.

In his book *The Filter Bubble*, the journalist Eli Pariser points out that this apparent fatalism is even reflected grammatically in the preferred use of the passive mood: 'Technologists [...] rarely say something "could" or "should" happen – they say it "will" happen. "The search engines of the future will be personalized," says Google Vice

President Marissa Mayer, using the passive tense.'[7] Pariser, who reproaches Google, Facebook and Amazon a little harshly for not telling us about new things, gives a hint of the much more fundamental problem, unfortunately without digging deeper. He writes that in the depth of their codes they have a 'bad theory of you'.[8]

In a world in which information capitalism markets the inside of our heads, it is no longer the product but people themselves who are exposed to planned obsolescence. Therefore their experience, their work references and loyalties no longer count; instant gratification replaces lifelong loyalty; 'liquidity', the liquefaction of figures, identities, careers and jobs, is the order of the day.

To the extent that people have to function like machines, death dating has become the central, grossly underestimated basis of our social world. One 36-year-old writer understood intuitively that it is no longer about the manipulation of things but of people, and this recognition is behind one of the key texts of our modern society. In 1932, the same year that London's essay on planned obsolescence appeared, Aldous Huxley's novel *Brave New World* was published, a far more realistic view of our modern world, as Neil Postman pointed out years ago, than George Orwell's *Nineteen Eighty-Four*.[9] Indoctrination machines whisper in the ear of people as they lie in a trance that 'ending is better than mending'. In a society in which not only clothes and machines but above all people have production defects, human skills, talents, emotions and loyalties can evidently be programmed with limited life cycles. In Huxley's novel, this occurs through changes in genetic information. Fortunately, it hasn't yet come to that in reality, but we are not far off. As we shall consider in detail, digital information about us is acquired and evaluated and is capable of predicting how long a worker will remain loyal, whether in ten years' time he will still be capable of carrying out the task he has been hired for or whether he will be redundant. The mechanics of life cycles has long included a switch that can turn people on and off without them even knowing why.

Transmutation is the constant switching on and off of capabilities and characteristics in the great gene pool of social life. Reid Hoffman, founder of LinkedIn and one of the most important international marketers of career résumés, gave an unsentimental summing up of what is at stake today: 'There is not a "true self" deep within that you can uncover via introspection and that will point you in the right direction.'[10]

One should resist the temptation to regard such assertions merely as the private philosophy of successful businessmen who also want to write a book one day. On the contrary, they lead directly to the heart of the new ideology, where multinational structures produce the essence of the new individual.

Doing means doing and not thinking about it, as one commentator puts it. This is not a psychological view of the world but a physical one. It is what computers would say if they could talk about minds.

To the applause of the cyber-protagonists, R.G. Collingwood described the new physics as the impossibility of separating what a thing is from what it does. The abolition of this distinction, he said, was also the abolition of mind and matter. In this way, what people are automatically becomes a moral value judgement that can be inferred only from what they do.

Because identity is no longer based on what one is, it cannot get broken like a toy that has been dropped on the floor. In the modern cyber-era, people are switched on and off when they are disconnected from the nodes of the information network.

Historically, the first signs that people were instinctively sensing these changes were to be found in precisely the same place in which Silicon Valley planned its new ideology.

On 2 December 1964, a young man stood up to the microphone in front of protesting students and cried a couple of sentences that were to become legendary: 'We're a bunch of raw materials [...] that don't mean to be made into any product, [...] to end up being bought by some clients of the university. [...] We're human beings!'[11]

His name was Mario Savio and he spoke these sentences on the campus of the University of Berkeley in California. The Free Speech Movement (which was to develop into a worldwide student revolt) was aimed initially at the marketing of mind, soul and knowledge for the military-scientific complex. This is precisely what the elites, with a candour inconceivable today, had predicted for the young generation at the time.

The pronouncements in a lecture series in 1963 by Clerk Kerr, chancellor of the University of Berkeley, the main target of the protests, give an idea of the amount of prior planning that had gone into the concept of the information society, from the idea to its implementation.

In 1963, Kerr described a world that barely differs from today's reality. He predicted the emergence of a digitized 'knowledge industry' in which the 'intellect has also become an instrument of national purpose [. . .] a component part of the military-industrial complex'.[12] Spoken at a time when the Vietnam war was being waged in Southeast Asia, it was clear that thinking was now synonymous with warfare. The new knowledge no longer meant what it had for generations. It did not even presuppose theoretical thought.

The philosopher Gilbert Ryle, whom the university chancellor cited, blamed what he believed was a fatal distinction between mind and body for this misconception. An action carried out without further reflection is also a form of knowledge. Intelligent action consists of the application of rules: doing is a mental operation.

This is no different from the ideas hatched in the candlelight of the alchemy laboratory, except for the fact that the laboratory has now changed completely. It is the 'machines', the 'appliances' and above all the mainframe computer that transformed symbolic action immediately into reality.

The students of that time understood this instinctively. Round their necks, many of them wore punched cards with which universities managed students and staff. One of them bore a modified version of the warning written on the cards: 'I am a student. Do not fold, spindle or mutilate.'

Decades later, Reid Hoffman said that every person should be a 'startup company'. His words echoed those of the cyber-protagonist Marc Andreesson: 'Markets that don't exist don't care how smart you are. Similarly, it doesn't matter how hard you've worked or how passionate you are about an aspiration. If someone won't pay you for your services in the career market, it's going to be a very hard slog. You aren't entitled to anything.'[13]

The mantra of the new identity said that you only are what you do, you only do what there is a market for, and there is only a market for what you are paid for.

In the alchemy laboratory, every experiment started with the idea of chaotic primary matter out of which something was to be created.

Information capitalism locates the chaos in the individual: 'You're not in a calm lake. You're in a chaotic ocean. [...] Lofty questions about identity and moral purpose [...] take time to work out, and the answers frequently change.'[14]

It is logical that anyone who thinks like this is proclaiming an 'era of the unthinkable'. Unthinkable in the most fundamental meaning of the word: a world in which thought becomes action because it immediately leaves digital traces that can only be evaluated mathematically – for example by LinkedIn. But in this way life itself becomes a stock market.

The stock market crashes of today, the 'black swans', the cracks appearing in the dome of the system, show in the eyes of Reid Hoffman, the administrator of millions of career résumés, that volatility, sinking and falling life market prices, are becoming the new norm of existence: 'Fragility is the price we pay for a hyperlinked world where all the slack is optimized. The economy, politics and the job market of the future will host many unexpected shocks. In this sense, the world of tomorrow will be more like the Silicon Valley of today: constant change and chaos.'[15]

According to Hoffman, people are permanently in radar mode. They know that their life form is fragile and that if they are not constantly willing like a stock exchange trader to take opportunities, they risk 'a major dislocation at some point in the future'. We will now become a complete embodiment of Number 2. We will screen our co-players, driven by the same ambition and the exclusive wish for profit maximization, and we will write our own risk insurance policies: 'By introducing regular volatility into your career, you make surprise survivable. You gain the "ability to absorb shocks gracefully".'[16] In short, we become the traders of our own lives.

Volatility that is measurable mathematically in milliseconds is no longer just a feature of stock markets but also of human identity.

In a truly perverse carry-over of the causes of economic crisis, we are expected to act like the stock markets of the world: we must invest in ourselves and take enormous risks and if necessary artificially incorporate crashes and shocks in our careers.

How can one live a life like this?

The new elite suggests saying 'yes' as the default setting: 'What would happen if you defaulted to "yes" for a full day? A full week? [...] Remember, if you don't find risk, risk will find you.'[17]

28

RE-ENGINEERING

THE DISASSEMBLED INDIVIDUAL IS A GOLDMINE

Yes, you are not an online mail-order shoe seller. But you sell your brain, your talent and your energy. And you do it under the fiercest competition. This is the mantra of Reid Hoffman, and there can be no doubt that this is the doctrine of the new information capitalism.

In future, people will live with a new division of labour: they will become the workers and managers of their own mind factory. They are surrounded by people who want precisely the same thing, who use Twitter and Facebook, who write blogs and send photos, just like you do.

In view of this constant exchange-like flow of information, which can all be exploited in a volatile labour market, the only survival strategy is the one recommended by Number 2: reduce everyone else to their self-interest, to a bluff, a hidden plan with which they hope to win the Game of Life.

Looking at current communication on the Web, the jubilant accusations and hate messages, it is evident that this game is already being played.

In information capitalism the ego now assumes the role not only of despotic factory owners but also of their workers and even the means of production. The material used for production consists of information, the modern-day gold. But – as if to make the nightmare of Soddy's contemporaries come true – gold that is available in excess. Curiously, this doesn't reduce its worth but increases it.

For thousands of years, humanity unthinkingly overlooked huge amounts of murky unpleasant, evil smelling or useless matter. At first it tried unsuccessfully to turn the unattractive materials into gold. Later it learned what the raw materials coal and oil could be used for.

The American physics Nobel Prize winner Arno Penzias explained this with a nice joke: 'If I see some brown, sweet, gelatinous stuff on your tie, it's dirt. But if I put that same stuff in a dish, it's chocolate pudding. Data is like dirt, but once you put it in its proper place, in order, it becomes information.'[1]

Not only is every event in the life of a person information; the same is also true of the exchange of these events with countless others recorded digitally. Not only the stain on a tie, but also the hand movement to try to remove it, how soon it's brought to the dry cleaner, how often it gets dirty, the type of dirt, the occasions when the tie is worn – all these are potentially usable and marketable pieces of information. And we are only talking about a single tie. What about the countless tie wearers, waiters in restaurants, cabin crews in aeroplanes, the manufacturers of chocolate puddings and the makers of the ties themselves?

More and more people today are finding themselves involved in social networks they would never have entered but have been drawn into because others have published photos in which they and comments about them can be seen. What applies to photos also applies to any form of information. 'If I give away [my genetic] data,' said a senior researcher at Microsoft involved with big data, 'I'm giving away some of my brother's data, my mother's data, my future kid's data.' In fact, she muses 'Who owns the email chain between you and me?'[2]

It has long been evident that this also applies to the working world. Every manipulation, every movement, every nod of the head produces knowledge whose interpretation we are ignorant of; every thought; every sentence, every email produces a narrative that we understand only when it is presented to us as a story of our own actions, as an investigating judge might do. Then sick leave is correlated with codes for feelings, movement and soon even glances, body language and gestures. Google's recent invention Google Glass could well give birth to apps that decode the authenticity of a smile and the messages of body language.

The data flow now also includes information from brain scans, with which companies like Lucid Systems claim to be able to determine the 'unspoken truth'. This also destroys another boundary of matter: the past.

Everyone would say that what happened in the past was inevitable, because otherwise there would be no houses, temples, works of art, books, cities or countries. Now, however, people are interested in why things happened as they did and how they might have been.

'From a scientific point of view, therefore, if we want to understand what might happen in the future, it is critical to consider not only what did happen but also what *could have* happened.'[3]

Everyone can understand why a share analyst might look at the price development in the past so as to extrapolate it for the future. Today, however, such analyses are being applied on a small scale to human experience – in the investigation of financial fraud in Wall Street firms, for example – and possibly in the human resources departments of large companies.

When it comes to the accumulation of big data, we are still in the pre-industrial age, as Google engineer Martin Wattenberg claims.[4] Such 'transaction data', the results of communication both between humans and things and between humans and humans, are stored in huge supermarkets, and if you look closely you will see that it is hands, arms and legs, movements and thoughts that are waiting there to be converted into money. They are the automatons in Merlin's museum demonstrating the movements of their arms, hands and eyelids.

Companies like the American firm ClearStory offer information like this tailored to any desired form by combining publicly available data with data made available to them by businesses. 'Where should McDonald's locate? Who will go there? And what will the customers eat?' is one of the more harmless inquiries.

'We're about making data consumable,' said Sharmila Shahani-Mulligan, ClearStory's founder and chief executive in an interview with *The New York Times*. We shouldn't be placid about the boring word 'data'. It signifies the transmutation of human thoughts and micro-actions into consumable matter. Mulligan also makes it clear what the transmuted mental material is in reality: 'The gold locked up in thirty years of relational databases.'[5]

It is true, as Earl Shorris once wrote, that this is the age of information. However, information is not the precursor to knowledge but the tool of salesmen.[6] If, in the new world view, the entire universe is a computer that just processes information, the macrocosm and microcosm will merge in a way they haven't done since the age of magic.

It is not true that money is the only thing that matters: everything is money – from the individual sequences in the genetic code to conceptual associations and all forms of movement in space and time. There is no longer a structural need for classic workers, or for most intellectual work. There are job opportunities for the analysts who evaluate the information about information, be it on Wall Street or in companies.

People are no longer cogs in this machine but its product. 'The naïve prejudice,' writes a mathematician from MIT, 'that physical objects are somehow more "real" than ideal objects remains one of the most deeply rooted in Western culture. [...] A consequence of this belief [...] is that our logic is patterned exclusively on the structure of physical objects.'[7]

A distinction is being denied here that is part of our everyday experience and common sense. If it is the mind that manipulates and controls the elements, then the mind can also be manipulated and controlled like the steel that is shaped into car panels. Even the IT specialist Danah Boyd, who carries out research at Microsoft into big data, speaks of an 'odd moment of creepiness'.[8]

In a world in which information is the only solid fact, the human senses no longer function as survival tools or even reliable pieces of evidence.

Look, over there are some people talking. They are exchanging information, they are laughing, they are doing business, perhaps they are talking about nothing special The important thing is that through conversation they form a shared social space. An American company has specialized in the analysis of such spaces, and its digital label nTAG records who converses with whom and for how long.

The exchange between mind and matter, between software and hardware, takes place through routines. This is the reason why all religions attach such importance to spiritual exercises and rituals. Everything is defined in them, every hand movement and every word, an eternal algorithm, which in most cases aims at transforming matter into mind or mind into matter. It is an exchange extending from the Last Supper to the alchemist's laboratory and Zen Buddhism.

In everyday life, however, most people are agreed that routines are better carried out by slaves. Ever since Henry Ford built the first conveyor belts, routine has been said to destroy people. Everybody thinks of the mindlessness of assembly-line work, better suited to machines than thinking beings. Now, in an era when this slave is a computer searching our entire lives for routines that it can perform for us, the advocates of the new working world go one step further.

They now suggest that our entire conventional life, which is based on a stable identity and regular work, is nothing other than a routine. 'Twenty years of experience,' says Andy Hargadon, business management expert at the University of California, 'is really one year of experience repeated twenty times.'[9]

In this vision, the ego is in fact only a disruptive habit, an automatism that makes people dull and sluggish. Because people are only what they do and because they have constantly to do something new, they become permanently volatile. In the language of applied information theory, the individual ego is just 'noise': 'We don't want the name,' said a Google manager to The New York Times. 'The name is noise.'[10]

This suggests, in the logic of the 'Californian ideology', that people are avatars and, free of the constraints of repetition, become disembodied, a pure idea with time and leisure for contemplation and creativity, and – incidentally – deprived of the excuse of grinding hard work when they no longer have the strength to be creative.

It is worth looking at this on another screen, on one where people have to eat, are born and die. All the data offered for sale in the data supermarkets come from conveyor belts on which devices have separated them from people, like incandescent wires.

Whereas in the real economy robots assemble, weld, paint or pack cars or coffee machines from countless parts and stamp them with a brand at the end, on the conveyor belts of digital capitalism devices dismantle people into their constituent parts. If people are what they do, the converse must also be true. One can discover what they are by observing what they do. And with sufficient information it is possible to know what they are going to do before they know themselves.

As Sigfried Giedion points out in his fundamental history of the machine age, the conveyor belt has always been thought of as an automated unit in which the individual is just an observer.[11] The presence of human workers was seen as a stopgap until machines could master complex processes.

In the midst of the world economic crisis in 1929, the American industrialist L.R. Smith took the next logical step and published an essay entitled 'We Build a Plant to Run without Men'. It is not so much Smith's vision, which now appears banal, that is interesting as the way it occurred to him:

'Its answers rested in the subconscious mind of engineers. [...] It is highly probable that watching our workers do the same thing over and over again, day in and day out, sent us on our quest for the 100% mechanization of frame manufacture.'[12]

Perhaps education systems today are required to train more and more specialists simply so that machines can learn from and ultimately replace them.

'A human specialization,' wrote Hugh Kenner, 'sufficiently well observed, is mechanically reproducible, and when a man has *become* his specialization, that man [...] is himself mechanically reproducible.'[13]

This will apply particularly if the cognitive capabilities of computers increase to the extent that specialist cyber-evangelists are predicting today. In the information market state, the fact that we are 'observed' today by machines is almost always due to three overlapping reasons: as far as surveillance is concerned, the aim is to obtain knowledge of future social behaviour in order to control us; in the consumer sector, it is to obtain knowledge of shopping behaviour in order to advise (or manipulate) us; and in production, it is to obtain knowledge about our knowledge in order to replace us.

In the era of big data, it is no longer human observers at the conveyor belts but devices that we carry around with us, which track us and observe our actions and thoughts, analyse them, store them in digital warehouses and reassemble them as required for customers.

In contrast to the factories described by Sigfried Giedion, modern technologies executed via a computer interface not only carry out

actions for humans but also translate each of these actions into information. They write an unending novel about what people do with and
through them. Now it is no longer just a button being pressed but a
whole text being written.

The modern language of work asks: when, where, how long, in what
mood, with whom, how often, how quickly? It is not only the worker at
the machine who is described and read by this subtext – as is now being
commented on even in the most uncritical social media communities
– but every person participating through the digital machine in the
market of thought and speech.

The first person to point out this phenomenon was Shoshana Zuboff,
who in the late 1980s invented the term 'electronic text' to describe
these working environments.[14] Since then, not only the working world
but all of human life has been shadowed by electronic text.

Only a very few people are aware of this text. We are practically all
illiterate with regard to the novel of our own lives, written in a language we don't understand, encrypted like the Holy Scriptures and
interpreted by exegetes whose standards we cannot question.

Employers, Homeland Security, but also Google, Apple or Amazon,
are unlikely to show their cards when things get serious in this suppos-
edly transparent world. They are like priests who jealously guard the
real meaning behind the Word of God. At the same time, power in the
modern world – as Shoshana Zuboff presciently noted decades ago –
depends on who interprets these texts and by what rules.

The rules are equivalent to what one could call human controlling:
it is all about efficiency and optimization, be it in purchasing, or risk
prognosis with shares or diseases. The electronic text is used to determine the conscious or unconscious logic of human behaviour. Above
all it is used to discover the *contradictions* in our behaviour.

29

YOU

How the essence of a person is read and marketed

Whenever you, dear reader, have problems in future – be it at passport control, in your job or when applying for a loan – it will always be a matter of contradictions. The entire career of Number 2 and his instruments based increasingly on game theory are a conceptual operation designed to eliminate contradictions.

Neoclassical economists have always insisted on the inherent consistency of Number 2, the *homo oeconomicus*: he could not behave in conflict with his own egotistical actions; even his altruism was self-interested.

There is a logic to everything, even to contradiction, failure or the attempt to be someone different. Even if generations of economists and psychologists (who had a completely different picture of the human ego) disagree with this finding, in an era of predictability it is more relevant than ever. Wherever the thinking or conscious or unconscious actions of people appear contradictory, it is possible to identify their 'true' intentions, which are their self-interested goals.

Only occasionally – for example, when technology is used to provide legal evidence in court cases in the USA – do we gain a small insight into the depths of the analysis.

'The work can be likened to reading different pieces of the cross-referenced diaries of insanely prolific diarists,' wrote Elizabeth

Charnock, CEO of Cataphora.[1] For years her company had been analysing data for court cases, particularly those involving Wall Street.

Now that she has sold this department, she is one of the few people
who can talk openly about her systems. It really is a special kind of
diary: 'However, the overall effect is vastly more potent, in part because
so many real-life actions seem to be taken almost on autopilot. As such,
a portrait constructed from these actions captures the essence of a person's true nature with far greater clarity than anything he's consciously
composed ever could.'[2]

It was 'diarists', writers in fact, who since 1900 have been predicting
the collapse of life narratives. Oscar Wilde's *Picture of Dorian Gray*, in
which the hero looks strikingly youthful while his portrait grows older
and unattractive, is in the eyes of the analysts a pact with the Devil that
many people enter into today without thinking.

'A similar divergence,' writes Charnock, 'often happens between the
meticulously groomed digital personas people construct for themselves
on social networking sites and the portrait of their digital YOU constructed from pulling together all available bits of data from all available
sources that relate to them.'[3]

From Oscar Wilde and Kafka to Aldous Huxley, George Orwell and
even Max Frisch, the story of the loss of identity was still able to rescue
the identity. For all their pessimism, sociologists like Richard Sennett,
who in the late 1990s was demonstrating the disempowerment of the
individual in the globalized working world, continued to believe in a
game played by human actors.

Now there is a new author. Charnock and her team discovered to
their own surprise that they were 'clinically capturing the character of
both individuals and organizations'.[4]

This is the operations report in which the story of our personal lives
will be written. You might have revised, studied, bought a new suit or
dress for the job interview, but the digital you doesn't wear a suit or a
dress, and your references and certificates consist of digital data rather
than academic qualifications.

What, asks Charnock, who since 2002 has looked at 'hundreds of
thousands of interesting e-mails and other types of electronic data' –
'Possibly even some of yours, dear reader!', as she openly admits – is
our response 'to Google determining that you're obscure?'[5]

The new life stories are no longer I-stories but you-narratives. A vast and to some extent highly mathematical literature brings this digital you to life and transforms it in a breathtaking and imperceptible process into a participant in Number 2's great Game of Life.

Number 2, the analytical algorithm, and the digital you (ourselves), Number 1, oppose one another, just as the USA and the Soviet Union once did during the Cold War – with the difference that it is almost impossible for us to analyse Number 2's moves, even if we suspect sometimes that we are being played with, which makes us more careful in our communication. But Number 2 knows about the power of habit and that we cannot control our behaviour all the time.

These algorithms don't understand what people mean when they use words like 'sad', 'bad' or 'annoying'; they don't know the feeling people have when they are 'happy' in their emails, laugh scornfully or answer certain emails first in the morning and leave others to gather dust. Nor do they know what it 'means' when a stockbroker whose emails are being investigated by the SEC recommends stocks to customers and a minute later complains of 'depressed markets'.

They don't need to understand all this and are thus in complete agreement with neoclassical economists.

What Number 2 actually does will come as no surprise to anyone who has followed his progress so far: he translates communication into an economic model. Below the surface of the words, an economy of give and take is at work mechanically, 'please' and 'thank you', 'yes' and 'no', but in an infinite number of contexts, an economy of profit and loss, bluff, punishment and reward.

> After we had been doing this work [with algorithms] for a while, we began to understand that we knew more – *really* knew more – about our targets than their spouses or closest friends did. Perhaps more than they knew about themselves. We not only knew whether they were happy or unhappy, but what made them that way and how they behaved in either state. We could observe the consistency of their viewpoints over time and whether they expressed the same opinions regardless of who was listening. We saw who was overgenerous about sharing credit and who endeavored to grab credit for anything short of inventing the Internet.[6]

We are now in the heart of the machine and we can vaguely hear Ken Binmore's complaint that people want to be seen in a good light and are horrified when they are compared with the egotistical Mr Hyde.

The good news for Binmore and the rest is that how people would like to be seen is completely irrelevant. It makes no difference if we write books about altruism and the welfare state; let us not forget that those who offer their services to others do not contradict the theory but hold on determinedly to their own interests. Number 2's market calculating machine is trained to spot a bluff – all the more so, since Dr Nash's equilibrium formula, in cases when he doesn't know his opponent and cannot speak with him.

Charnock describes how difficult it would be really to understand the nature of people's goals if we were only to speak with them. But as we have seen, Number 2's world is not about psychology, it's about strategically analysing people's behaviour so as to be able to understand the means and the moves behind their perpetual self-interest.

This might still seem abstract to some, but in the practical work of an analytical data miner it is quite concrete:

> After all, most people want to be seen as nice and sensible – even those who, in reality, are mean-spirited and short-tempered. [...] But we have a unique advantage. Rarely do we actually meet our 'targets'. Instead, we study a comprehensive set of their electronic artifacts, sometimes dating back years. [...] For most people this amounts to hundreds of thousands of data items.[7]

People in work situations want recognition, success, money, power; it is a social economy that is transformed and evaluated with the aid of social physics.

But Number 2 can transform all this into commodities. He can use utilities and determine how and to what extent the Nash equilibrium is achieved in digital communications. He is playing the Cold War, eternally and with the same effect: 'The digital you,' says Charnock from experience, 'is much more likely to be caught lying, cheating and stealing in the workplace than the real you.'[8]

It is useful at this point to note that with this instrument Charnock's Cataphora uncovered real cheating and real lies, including incidences in major finance scandals. Her openness is to a certain extent counter-revolutionary and deserves great respect, because she shows basically how systems work on everyone to whom they are applied.

When Cataphora is investigating, the employee receives a 'freeze' letter from the state attorney prohibiting any further digital communication or the deletion or modification of existing data. It has long been clear, however, that the same operations are being carried out on living beings in real time and without pause.

'What does he know that I don't know?' This is the question traders ask their computers. In the game theory environment of the Pentagon and on the stock exchange, after analysis of the information about one's counterpart, who is as unknown as Charnock's 'goals', the 'hidden game' begins – the manoeuvring in which things no longer mean what they mean but are there to send signals that provoke moves desired by the person sending them. As is the case here:

> The fact that this portrait [of a person] is painted with sophisticated computer programs gives it the imprimatur of objectivity. The attorneys and investigators with whom we work use our various computer-generated archaeological exercises and personal portraits in their witness interviews, depositions, and even in trials. Key witnesses and actors in a big case expect to be asked certain obvious questions relevant to that case. Their attorneys will coach them accordingly. What they don't expect is some off-kilter question about why they changed some subtle habit at a particular point in time. In other words, 'When did you first suspect that there might be a defect in the product?' is obviously going to be a key question in a product liability case. But a question such as 'Why did you stop having lunch with James on Fridays?' or 'Why did you start deleting e-mails at the end of every month?' often flummoxes opposing witnesses into a perplexed stupor that benefits our clients as they cross-examine them.[9]

In the economy of mind, no one has time to wait for someone to make a mistake. Mistakes are already interference with reality. Their counterpart in the digital self is 'contradictions'. And nothing enthrals the code more than to discover and make them visible.

In the twentieth-century world, many of our contradictions disappeared, unnoticed by us and our environment. In the information ecology of the twenty-first century, contradictions are not only signalled but are simply unavoidable. In a system of pure mind, in which thoughts are transferred by contact, they will inevitably become actions and breaches of the rules.

It is an underestimation of the analysis to believe that contradictions are merely conceptual incompatibilities. The software examines not only vocabulary and syntax but also emotions that are in conflict with actions, and even on a time axis that indicates the extent of a good or bad mood.

What people have done, what they are doing, what they will do: the deconstruction of people turns them into a vast bundle of data, which in the economy of mind no longer have a body or identity, are just a file, an option, a future, calculated by Number 2 on the basis of a value composed of different actions. Just as engineers in the 1930s translated repeated movements into robot movements, the codes translate repeated patterns into discrete information packages. They permit not only analysis of the past but also predictions about the future.

In models used to describe work, consumer behaviour and major geopolitical changes, people already live in a defined future which, like a share, determines its value in the present, which in turn models the future in a self-fulfilling prophecy.

It begins with the genetic prediction of diseases and ends at work, in schools and with mortgages. And there is already a toy that does this.

Jeremy Bailenson from Stanford University calls these systems 'Veja Du': we see in simulations what happens to bodies, products, people, extrapolated into the future.

This is the great transmutation machine, which is not yet promoted in Germany only because, unlike in the UK or USA, the real economy can play the role of common sense.

But in the English-speaking world, the automation of human life no longer differs greatly from L.R. Smith's 'factories without people', except that it has become a factory made of human thoughts, dreams, hopes, lies and strategies.

30

MASS DELUSIONS

SURPLUS, WEALTH FOR ALL AND THE KNOWLEDGE SOCIETY

Robinson Crusoe's self-sustaining economic system served economists for a long time as a model showing how people can work and function.

It took hundreds of years before a reader discovered the now famous mistake in *Robinson Crusoe*: the eponymous hero swims naked to the ship to fetch the tools he needs to survive, which he puts in his pockets – which he doesn't have because he is naked.

No one knows how Daniel Defoe made this mistake. Perhaps he was distracted. Or maybe he was a sadist. There is nothing worse than the sentence 'Take as much as you can carry', when you don't have anything to carry it in.

Perhaps Defoe also wanted to gently indicate that the entire story, related not by him but by a certain Robinson Crusoe, was just a figment of the imagination.

The same mistake has slipped into the stories of human life. Today they are told not in words but through formulae and numbers. Everyone is a kind of statistically average Crusoe, a slow-witted and lethargic shipwreck stranded on the shores of the information society and globalization.

'No man is an island', 'The world won't wait for us', 'The era of palm trees and hammocks is gone' – these are the messages of the *über*-author, the composite voice of newspaper articles, talk shows and politico-economic admonitions.

Robinson Crusoe also followed the information economy of his time. Through the Bible, which he fetched from his ship, the former unbeliever found God, and what we call knowledge today was for him 'destiny'. It goes beyond the scope of this book, but the Bible, which Crusoe opens at random to seek answers, might be seen in the book as the all-knowing search algorithm.

With head, hands and information as the main tools of civilization, it is said, anyone can prevail in the capitalist jungle. We have everything we need in abundance if we just use our heads, jump into the water and fetch tools and information from the Noah's Ark of the knowledge society. Crusoe managed on a desert island, and today, as a modern Defoe would have it, even 'a Masai warrior with a cell phone has better mobile phone capabilities than the president of the United States did twenty-five years ago'.[1]

Why then, one might ask, is he not a president of some kind?

The problem is that on the way from the rocky shore to the Noah's Ark of the knowledge society, the authors of the new biographies mislaid something.

For the people who win and lose in information capitalism, this moment between shore and ship is crucial. You are told that if you want to you can achieve anything. It's about the missing link in the transformation of the naked man, the raw material, into one who, like Crusoe, pedantically lists information ('Bible, four compasses, charts, books of navigation'), reboots and creates a paradise for himself.

Today, this transformation is called 'knowledge', 'creativity' and 'talent'. It used to be called education or history, but now it means much more than it has ever done. 'Knowledge society' means: swim out naked and take what you can.

Crusoe brought ashore exactly what he needed. Everything is merely a question of navigation instruments and the Bible, two technologies, one providing a link to everything and the other all the answers.

The knowledge society loves immaterial goods and virtual capital, dismantles the individual and entire companies, and its Darwinist mantra is lifelong learning. In reality, lifelong learning is a wonderful but trivial concept.

This terminological deceit is possibly the saddest collateral damage from the crisis, because it misled so much idealism and exploited the best pages on the Internet for its own purposes. Behind the obligation to lifelong learning, which in reality was just a commitment to continuous adaptation, was a realization of the ponderousness of institutions.

The eight-hour day in the traditional working world shaped not only the day but also the year and the entire life. Today it is no longer possible to live in an era of simultaneity and still believe that the economy of a person's own life is not affected by it.

The continuing erosion of time sequences in a world of high-frequency action and real-time communication eats its way out of the micro-level and into the macro-level, where the distinction between work and leisure is blurred.

Lifelong learning establishes in the head the idea of continuous simultaneity. It sounds non-stressful and placid, but it is often the opposite of what it appears to connote, representing in reality the ability to unlearn what we believed in yesterday, including our own identity. What we were supposed to learn, apart from the equally mis-used term 'creativity', was puzzling even for the education authorities, which within a few years completely and confusingly rewrote school syllabuses.

In California, for example, state subsidies for universities fell by 30 per cent within three decades, leading to the bizarre situation that in the El Dorado of the new thinking, the state contributed one third more to prisons than it did to universities.

Ironically, the era of the knowledge society has also seen the downgrading of German universities and their students through the suppression of sought-after creativity.

Not only was the economic utility of education recalculated; a fundamental change in perspective also took place. The idea of learning and education was to create stable identities that would last a whole lifetime. After all, general education that does not aim immediately at industrial utilization costs society less and has the longest-term impact on life.

This, however, is the individual perspective. In the fluid communication and work situation today, identity is disruptive because it demands loyalties that can no longer be guaranteed. Only a relatively narrow sector of society benefits from highly specialized fast-track education, as the anthropologist Joseph Tainter has shown in his pioneering studies of the 'collapse of complex societies',[2] while the costs are spread through the system.

One cannot talk about immaterial goods and believe that the contents of one's own head have nothing to do with the future development of markets. For centuries, lifelong learning was insignificant, before it was reinterpreted by Wall Street and now means adapting second by second to new market situations.

'Knowledge economy', 'information' or 'service society', 'one-person company', 'excellence initiatives', are the kind of inflationary and undefined terms that are being fed deliberately into our brains. It is true that in the twentieth century the Left managed, often with great concessions, to appropriate concepts like freedom, emancipation and progress for themselves – even in cases where the opposite was apparent, as in socialism as it actually existed, for example.

But the appropriation of terms that no one can contradict is continuing in the twenty-first century by the other side. Who can have anything against education, learning, knowledge? And what else is it but a 'permanent revolution' when identity becomes as fluid as the figures on a trader's screen?

It is always a question of *who* is talking about a life: ourselves or those whom we are meant to recruit, pay and promote. In the first case it is psychology, in the second sheer economics.

On Wall Street, people like the globalization prophet Thomas Friedman walked on the shore and identified the losers who were incapable of learning. 'The turtles represent the real threat to the stability of this whole movement toward high-tech, free-market, global capitalism. [...] There are a lot of turtles out there trying to avoid becoming roadkill on the information superhighway.'[3]

His turtles were pensioners in Russia or villagers in developing countries, who 'eat' rainforests and our scarce material resources in general.

Earlier we would have asked what else they could have done. But not in the new era: in the age of the information economy an inexhaustible raw material has been created that enables a turtle to become a gazelle merely by the power of its mind. The miracle drug that makes this happen is information itself, digested by networks and transformed into any desired product.

It was only when Wall Street brokers discovered that in the globalized world money is also just information – which, as someone once said, makes every computer into a machine for printing money – that the explosive mixture of money, mind and investment arose, long before schools, universities and ministries of education jumped onto the 'human capital' bandwagon. It was investment bankers, economists and software tycoons who now became specialists of the mind, not as analysts but as shamans.

Sigmund Freud, they mocked, had explained the soul using metaphors from the age of the steam engine, with 'forces', 'drives' or 'pressure'. Now they performed their magic with bits, with 1 and 0, yes and no, in and out, on and off, and disputed that identity can be anything other than constant movement.

This really marked the birth of TINA – There Is No Alternative. 'I don't think,' radioed Friedman from his small island to those throughout the world unwilling to learn, 'there will be an alternative ideology this time around. There are none.'[4]

In the telescopic vision of globalization ideologies, individual ideas of fairness shrink to the size of a turtle. The fact that in a crisis profit is privatized and loss socialized is not only something that offends the economic reason of every individual. At its core it is an attack on the idea of democracy itself.

In this way, according to the super-quant Emanuel Derman, who created some of the models that have now become out of control, the link between capitalism and democracy has been broken. 'We have seen corporations treated with the kindness owed to individuals and individuals treated [...] as things.'[5]

Hence the new world view, the privatization of public life, the economization of the most private sphere.

American and German media celebrated the revolution in which the 'power that for generations lay with a few thousand white males [...] is now being seized by Everyman and Everywoman. [...] It's not only changing the way we invest, it's changing the way we work and live too.'[6]

However scientific the programme might sound, it is in fact magical.

Just as quantum physics replaced Newton's matter, quantum economics is replacing Newton's matter in the creation of wealth. Whoever said that, you might think, can't be right in the head, even if his name was George Gilder, one of Ronald Reagan's closest advisers.[7] And yet, as everyone knows, this is precisely what happened: it was the quants on Wall Street who began to make something out of nothing.

Ray Kurzweil (futurist), Richard Branson (founder of Virgin), Jeff Skoll (co-founder of eBay) and Arianna Huffington (founder of *The Huffington Post*) are all fulsome in their praise of *Abundance*, one of the latest bibles from Silicon Valley. 'Abundance,' it says, 'is about creating a world of possibility: a world where everyone's days are spent dreaming and doing, not scrapping and scraping.'[8]

Within the theory that everyone can have everything, there is also plenty of room for the good works performed for the world by Jeff Skoll, Ray Kurzweil and Arianna Huffington.

The idea that dreaming is doing might have been expected of ordinary people, but not of the think tanks of Palo Alto and Wall Street. 'Like primitive tribes, they worship things they can see and feel,' it says in a book that is designed to win over investors, not for Greenpeace but for Greenspan.[9]

In retrospect, it was an ingenious chess move after the end of Communism to counter the critics of the ultra-materialistic American system at the subatomic level with the light waves of quantum physics. Where matter no longer exists and everything becomes information, people are endowed with enormous power to create wealth.

This is all the matrix of an ideology which began by being 'Californian' and in spite of all discernible setbacks and sacrifices has inexorably become consolidated and globalized in people's minds.

And how does this ideology work in California itself, where the new alchemy comes from? Not very well, it would appear.

'You start to ask: What is a city? Why do we bother to live together?'[10] This question was asked by the despairing mayor of one of the wealthiest communities in Silicon Valley, predicting without irony that soon a single employee would service an entire city, presumably with a focus on all-consuming pension payments.

In a community whose elite members write books like *Abundance: The Future Is Better Than You Think*, the idea of an administration serving the public interest gradually becomes literally inconceivable.

The eulogies to the benefactors, the 'techno-philanthropists', who have made it consume gigabytes. But at the south end of the Valley, an alpha journalist and economics expert meets the mayor of San José to find out whether what has happened in Europe could also soon affect the USA. The under-financing of public budgets, exploding pension obligations, the political impossibility of increasing taxes, have resulted in the city considering proclaiming a public state of emergency – in a community, it should be added, with the highest per capita income in the USA after New York.

And here, where the economy in mind was born and where we, in the triumphant words of Reid Hoffman, are experiencing 'the world of tomorrow', we can see how the *oikos* is suddenly changing into a haunted house. In contrast to the theory, there are bricks and mortar but no people. The mayor calls it 'service-level insolvency'. The new city hall has been completed but it will never open because there is no money for the employees. Libraries, not a bad place for a knowledge society, will be closed three days a week. 'I think we've suffered from a series of mass delusions,' the mayor says. 'We're all going to be rich. [...] We're all going to live forever. All the forces in the state are lined up to preserve the status quo. And here – this place – is where the reality hits.'[11]

We will read in future history books about the competition in the first decade of the new millennium between those who used the new technologies socially (the users) and those who used them economically and capitalized the social aspects.

It now appears that those who possess the new communication platforms have won. They have achieved what no arch-capitalist has yet managed: they have sold an idea, applauded by an avant-garde that ought in fact to be its enemy, an idea they don't stand for themselves, as a business model.

It is true that the Internet is a never-ending source of knowledge and that there are impressive examples of collective intelligence. But as always in the information society, this picture changes immediately when cyberspace is annexed by the markets. The weaker the social institutions that decide on the value of indifferent education become and the more they delegate to the web marketplace, the less chance there is of escaping. The confidence in one's own knowledge of how the world works disappears.

The search for an identity, which in Germany, for example, produced the tradition of the *Bildungsroman*, is, as the sociologist Manuel Castells has noted, a force that is as powerful as technological change itself. But while Castells, possibly the most influential network theoretician of our time, still talks of 'structural schizophrenia' between the individual and the network,[12] for some software tycoons the split has already taken place. To insist on one's own identity, they say, as if they had transformed Number 2's neoclassical theories into a philosophy of life, is for losers.

In the end, the question remains: how do we explain this trance in which Number 2 is given such free rein? Why is he everywhere? In the afterword to his *Black Swan*, Nassim Taleb asked with regard to financial markets how a technological civilization could have produced the idea of wanting to find out precisely why people come up with ideas. He found the answer in Asperger's syndrome, a mild form of autism.

It might be disputed whether autists really have problems identifying with others and instead prefer to quantify all aspects of people and things. But Taleb points out pertinently that the alleged knowledge society keeps on developing new grammars to fit the universe to its models.

And if any proof were needed of how the spiral is tightening, the influential economic scientist Tyler Cowen announced that the symptoms of crisis in the new economy are caused not by too much but by too little autism. He sees in the history of economics, starting with Adam Smith's sewing needle factory, in which for the first time repetitive work operations were carried out, the longing for the 'cognitive strengths of autism'. Computers, from stock exchange terminals to PCs, are merely tools that imitate the capabilities of the autist. They train us for a world in which survival depends on following a single goal, as in a life-and-death game. 'Today a new kind of person creates his or her very own economy in his or her head.'[13]

31

EGO

KILLING THE PUPPETS

The light of the Twilight Zone is slowly dimming, and the links have led us safely to where our search began. The indoctrination machine of the American radar crews, which was conceived merely as a training device, now transforms individuals, in Tyler Cowen's words, into people who are taught by the machine in the same way as the machine was taught. As computer pioneer Alan Turing wrote of the first computer, the machine should be treated like a child.

'Our hope is that there is so little mechanism in the child-brain that something like it can be easily programmed. The amount of work in the education [of the machine] we can assume, as a first approximation, to be much the same as for the human child.'[1]

And as bizarre as it might still appear to some people today, one of the basic questions for our future will be why we are educating machines so that they grow up, not only in automated finance markets but also in all other areas as well, to such an extent that they will educate us.

We cannot wait, as in Heinrich von Kleist's essay 'On the Marionette Theatre', until we arrive on the other side in a Garden of Eden after having 'passed through infinity'. In view of what has been said here, the question of what we have become is a little worrying.

Who likes to lose a game? By claiming that in decisive moments we all play games, the masterminds of the Cold War managed to reduce the motivation for human rationale exclusively to self-interest. Only when everything is seen as a game played according to the rules of self-interest can people and their world be calculated on the basis of precise mathematical formulae. All the signs indicate that today, now that the logic of the Cold War has taken over civil society, we are merely at the beginning of this transformation. The next step is gamification, the idea of transforming our entire life into a game of badges, rewards and promotion. In Chore Wars, people living together organize their entire day, from taking out the rubbish to washing the dishes, on the basis of a competition for virtual badges and points. Health insurance companies are considering rewarding healthy behaviour, providing people are willing to have their life evaluated in real time. The quests and missions in computer games are then transferred to real life: run 10 kilometres on the home trainer and advance to the next level.

Because in information capitalism every citizen is merely a consumer, gamification, the little and more domesticated brother of behaviourism, is now transforming politics, the largest market of all. Talk shows that offer a prize to the guest with the best arguments are just the beginning. Gabe Zichermann, the most important pioneer of the gamification industry, already has precise plans as to how elections in the USA should be organized in the future. Prizes and badges will be awarded for attending party events, visiting politicians' websites or taking part in question-and-answer sessions with politicians. But the most radical idea is the organization of voter lotteries. Voters would receive a lottery ticket with their voter registration. After the election results have been announced, a public draw would take place on television with a first prize of $10 million, 'a drop in the bucket in the cost of a US federal election' but a huge incentive to counter voter apathy. Additionally, there would be all kinds of symbolic consolation prizes, an invitation to the Capitol or White House, for example, or dinner with the President.[2] Philip K. Dick's *Solar Lottery* was not science fiction after all.

Once again, the question arises as to whether it matters at all if one has forgotten what one has lost. The question is not trivial. And in spite of the conservative attitude to culture, unlearning is an elementary component of self-enlightenment.

If that were not the case, we would be haunted by other ghosts than those who are walking abroad on these pages.

It's a different matter if we delegate cognitive capabilities in the computer era to a system called the information market and cannot then teach the machines working for it what we consider to be right.

We must protect ourselves from those who not only invoke mistrust and the cult of self-interest but also want to install a bizarre price-tagging machine for our thoughts.

The belief that the market is a huge computer that knows more than all of the participants in it had a function in the days before the total planning experiment failed.

The new era has made of it a statistical monster in which the 'truth' is not determined via individual content, careers and experience, but via statistical patterns interpreted purely in economic terms.

Cataphora's algorithms also just make statements about the mental economics of character. And George Dyson believes that the market, the most powerful driving force in the real world, is now becoming the most powerful driving force for our thoughts:

> If you had to say what's the most powerful algorithm set loose on planet earth right now? Originally, yes, it was the Monte Carlo code for doing neutron calculations. Now it's probably the AdWords algorithm. It's a sort of statistical sampling of the entire search space, and a monetizing of it, which, as we know, is a brilliant piece of work.[3]

*   *   *

And in this way the last metaphor appears on the horizon, over which the new big data star is rising in the luminescent colours of inevitability. With this metaphor, Number 2 is in the process of redefining the automaton and his own role: as a system of social insects.

The new multi-agent systems have learned. They don't give up a single one of their selfish genes, but they merge the systems themselves with biology. J. Doyne Farmer, whose legendary Prediction Company, the first prognostic software smithy, was bought by UBS, believes that the crisis is forcing consequences on us in the economic models as well.

He and others, writes *The New York Times*, have started to develop so-called 'agent-based' models of the economy, which ask how the seemingly random behaviour of individual ants can create structures with an objective, form and intelligence.[4]

In an article entitled 'Twitter in the Ant Nest', ant researcher Deborah M. Gordon stated that in contrast to what many people believe, ants do not communicate information with their antennae, as Francisco Salvá attempted to prove with his frogs' legs. All they do is to draw statistical algorithmic conclusions from the interaction and odour of other ants – evaluating news, so to speak, whose content is less important than its statistical distribution. It is similar to what happens in media societies through the pay-per-click system from AdWords.

Time to think of a way out. As things stand, the only option is to dissociate ourselves from the economization of our lives through the image of the self-interested and devious individual which has become hardwired into the system. The 'learning mind' is something other than the learning machine produced by market processes. 'A child learning to speak,' wrote Hugh Kenner referring to Turing's education metaphor, '[...] would resemble a mysterious device that accepts as input "very scattered and inadequate data", and generates as output an amazingly uniform product, exceeding the input in quantity and very often in quality (were Shakespeare's teachers more eloquent than he?)'[5]

Perhaps it's quite simple: don't join in the game, at least not according to the rules imposed on us by Number 2. It is a decision to be made by each individual – and by politicians. The chances in Germany are good, because it is still the real economy that drives our welfare. It would almost seem as if the country that was the birthplace of idealism could now shape a new realism as a counterweight to the economy in mind.

The answers in the first stage are highly pragmatic: they range from the construction of European search engines and the redefinition and renaming of 'data protection' to questions of interference with the human genome.

For this to happen, politicians and non-economists would have to recognize that markets, above all financial markets, in the words of Karin Knorr Cetina, have become something completely different to what they were in the past and as information machines can no longer make a claim to the 'truth' – because information itself will possibly never again be what we have always taken it to be.

It is becoming the result of a negotiation process, an auction, a bidding and bargaining procedure that takes place at high speed in more and more areas of human life, until it is ultimately codified through the authority of a rating agency.

How will we recognize it when the information economy goes bust? Everyone knows that states, businesses and people are bankrupt when they have no more money – but what about the economy in mind? The answer is not easy. It is possible that John W. Campbell hit the nail on the head when he warned against a culture of hidden games because they would lead to terrible psychological problems (see Chapter 15).

We might smile at the thought that big data protagonists not only dream of machines that produce social capital and trust but also, as we have seen, add that it is 'worth a lot of money'. Without putting too fine a point on it, the idea is that we build robots that are loyal to us, even when no one else is. But people like Dirk Helbing touch on a sensitive point. Evidently, normative values like trust, equality or fairness are being demanded on markets because they are no longer sufficiently available in the classic places in society. What trust, for example, can young people have in the personality-shaping effect of an education that is subjected by the society educating them, even while it is doing so, to a kind of death dating? Will trust and fairness be produced like cars, with price labels and in different qualities?

As Philip Bobbitt's reflections indicate, the question is by no means academic. In a world in which we are rational and can be reduced to our interests and in which all of the data we produce can be interpreted in this way, everyone is potentially under suspicion. In this world, trust could become a luxury that is attributed, for example, on social networks and fed to the machines: values would then only have a monetary significance.

Fortunately, a new debate has begun among economists that 'such things as fairness and equality have normative value irrespective of whether they increase preference satisfaction'.[6] Ken Binmore's idea – that altruistic or just fair behaviour is worthwhile because it is in a person's own interests – can be modelled mathematically, but because it can be applied in digital real time to everyone and everything, it undermines the belief in any form of non-market-driven, non-economic, normative power within a society. It erodes not only parliaments,

constitutional courts or constitutions themselves but also the sovereignty of the individual simply to be the person he or she wants to be.

'For Marx and the political economy that followed him,' says Evgeny
Morozov, who was the first to consider the bankruptcy of the information economy,

> it was important to know who had the means of production. Today,
> because of the information economy and virtualization, what is impor-
> tant is who controls the sensors and algorithms. It must be understood
> that we have reached a point where the models of our rationality reduce
> us to such an extent that we believe that we are no longer capable of
> finding out for ourselves what we want.[7]

* * *

Paul Valéry (1871–1945), whose works are deeply rooted in the
European idea, invented a Monsieur Teste. His stock exchange speculations and his endeavours to become pure mind cannot serve as a
model, except in one respect: 'He had *killed his puppet*.'[8]

'Who knows,' he says at one point,

> whether most of those prodigious thoughts over which so many great
> men and an infinity of lesser ones have grown pale for centuries are
> not, after all, psychological monsters – *Monster Ideas* – born of the
> naive exercise of our questioning faculties, which we apply to anything
> at all, never realizing that we may reasonably question only what can
> actually give us an answer?[9]

With the simplest of sentences, the merciless logic of an automated
society and economy can be incapacitated and new freedoms created,
be it with regard to sure-fire speculations about the future or markets
or predictions about people and their passions.

The sentence that will kill the puppets is: The answer was wrong.

ACKNOWLEDGEMENTS

Many people have helped me with ideas, suggestions, explanations and corrections. I should like to thank Emanuel Derman, Michael Hudson, Stefan Klein, Frank Lübberding, Torsten Eymann, Edo Reents, Frank Rieger, Thomas Schmidt, Tilo Eckardt and Ulrich Genzler from Blessing Verlag and Matthias Landwehr and Thomas Schmidt.

Evgeny Morozov, Philip Mirowski and Shoshana Zuboff not only made important suggestions but also allowed me to read their current projects. I should like to thank a few people who wish to remain anonymous because they allowed me a look at the digital shark tank in finance platforms. I am grateful to my colleague Rainer Hank for his valuable advice and criticism. And I have Evgeny Morozov once more to thank for some of the most fruitful inspiration that a writer working on his own can possibly imagine. Finally I should like to thank Rebecca Casati. So much for the acknowledgements. The responsibility is naturally all mine.

Appendix

SHORT HISTORY OF THE DEVELOPMENT OF ARTIFICIAL AGENTS IN STOCK EXCHANGES

The pathway to the machine was lined from the outset with the only bait that really attracts people: with bargains. It started in 1991, three years before the term 'worldwide web' was invented.

The economist Brian Arthur and the game theoretician Ken Binmore published a paper about 'designing economic agents that act like human agents'.[1] The aim, said Arthur, was to construct an artificial agent whom the observer could no longer distinguish from a person – at first glance not a difficult task in view of the fact that already all that remained in the prevailing models of people and their unpredictability were self-interest, profit orientation and fear.

The artificial agent was designed to perform best at auctions in the same way that humans do: through the game theory calculations of the Nash equilibrium. Two years later, in what is now regarded as a classic experiment, the economists Dhananjay Gode and Shyam Sunder created an artificial market under laboratory conditions, in which Number 2 acted in two ways.[2] In one version he also spent money that he didn't have, but in the second version there were restrictions preventing him from going over his budget. In both cases his IQ was zero. He bought, sold, abided by the rules of the market and of Professor Nash.

The results showed that the second version did not differ from human digital traders – a triumph not only for the software but also for neoclassical economics. Even with zero intelligence it is possible to act rationally by observing the rules of the market. 'Markets as a partial substitute for individual rationality', the two economists called it.

But as the finance markets went digital and the network became a trading platform, it was realized that zero intelligence and reliance on the market were not sufficient on their own to turn digital agents into terminators.

In 1998, the physicists Dave Cliff and Janet Bruten declared that the time had finally come for game theory. According to them, the agent, for all his self-interest, should not be a cretin. He must know that others wanted to pull a fast one on him and be able to react immediately.

> In a competitive market, the environment is clearly dynamic and unforgiving. Relevant information (such as other traders' profit margins, or the information held by other traders) is rarely known or predictable, and it is unlikely that any trader will experience acts of kindness or selfless altruism. In real markets, traders that consistently fail to make profits will not last long. [...] If you're a trading agent, you can't be sure of anything except that the world is out to get you and that if you snooze you lose.[3]

Everything else was now just a matter of the formula. Like Darwin's species, Number 2 had to learn in an evolutionary manner, and he did so by obtaining ever greater rewards, in other words profit, as he learned. He had to be fit in the Darwinian sense, that is, capable of survival. In the language of his optimizers: 'When economic agents act in a market environment, the formulae for reward and fitness can be compared directly with "profit" and "utility".'[4]

Needless to say, this practice could only be maintained in closed systems. But there were also mixed forms, mostly controlled by human intervention, for example when it was a question of accessing overloaded networks and the like, including negotiations in the microeconomy of the data cosmos about the distribution of information and about who should have access to this information and at what price – not in terms of money but, for example, also in terms of the qualifying period.

The situation changed dramatically at the end of the 1990s. There were already trading algorithms in existence, but they were one-dimensional, small 'single-cell organisms acting according to a basic set of rules'.[5]

But then, in 1999, Goldman Sachs bought Hull Trading, a company that, apart from its expertise in artificial intelligence and algo-trading, was known to have a number of first-class physicists working for it at Fermilab near Chicago: people who had been involved in the discovery of quarks and who had migrated after 1989 to Wall Street in the wake of government cost cuts. The purchase by Goldman Sachs of Hull Trading was like the Vatican acquiring a share in a clone factory. Or as Scott Patterson later described it: 'It marked a massive shift inside Goldman – the quintessential old-guard white-shoe Wall Street firm – towards electronic trading. The shift would pave the way for Goldman's rise to power in the 2000s, when it emerged as one of the most aggressive and sophisticated trading goliaths in the world.'[6]

In what was later to be known as the dotcom bubble, finance markets and computer networks began for the first time to pursue the same interests, and the network itself (Google made the first tentative steps) began to assume a critical mass as a market. Economic computer experts, who with the quants designed the electronic markets of the future, said clearly and concisely that in open systems only self-interested agents had a chance.

NOTES

Preface

1 S.M. Amadae, *Rationalizing Capitalist Democracy: The Cold War Origins of Rational Choice Liberalism*, p. 295.

2 Amadae, *Rationalizing Capitalist Democracy*, p. 296.

3 Otto Mayr, *Authority, Liberty, and Automatic Machinery in Early Modern Europe*, p. 124.

4 Ken Binmore, *Game Theory: A Very Short Introduction*, p. 31.

5 Dimitris Milonakis and Ben Fine, *From Economics Imperialism to Freakonomics: The Shifting Boundaries between Economics and Other Social Sciences*, p. 1.

6 Milonakis and Fine, *From Economics Imperialism to Freakonomics*, p. 107.

7 Nathan Berg and Gerd Gigerenzer, 'As-If-Behavioural Economics: Neoclassical Economics in Disguise?'

8 I am aware that I am simplifying the historical complexity. The new rationality was not inspired solely by game and rational choice theory. It was the product of countless and sometimes loosely connected disciplines: computer theory, statistics and cybernetics have gone their independent ways and are only marginally linked with game theory. It is true that Neumann's work would have been

inconceivable without Alan Turing's computing machine and the resultant question of what is computable and what not. In 'The Ontology of the Enemy: Norbert Wiener and the Cybernetic Vision', for example, Peter Galison describes how in the Second World War the 'rational' enemy became a conceptual figure with all the characteristics that game theory later attributed to it.

Chapter 1 Trance

1 Sharon Ghamari-Tabrizi, 'Cognitive and Perceptual Training in the Cold War Man-Machine System', pp. 289–90.
2 See George Dyson, *Darwin among the Machines*, p. 21.
3 Ghamari-Tabrizi, 'Cognitive and Perceptual Training in the Cold War Man-Machine System', p. 289.
4 Don Murray in a 1955 report on the first radar systems in which he described the 'bluff' of a non-identified aeroplane on its way to Los Angeles. See Ghamari-Tabrizi, 'Cognitive and Perceptual Training in the Cold War Man-Machine System', p. 270.
5 Caitlin Zaloom, *Out of the Pits: Traders and Technology from Chicago to London*, pp. 136f.
6 Fred Kaplan describes the division of labour between economists and mathematicians as follows: economists would 'study the "utility functions" of consumers and the actual behaviour and values of various nations. The mathematicians, who certainly knew nothing of such things, could then incorporate their findings into the matrixes of game theory.' *The Wizards of Armageddon*, p. 67.
7 David Riesman, *The Lonely Crowd: A Study of the Changing American Character*, p. 25. Cf. Ghamari-Tabrizi, 'Cognitive and Perceptual Training in the Cold War Man-Machine System', p. 271.
8 For example, Amadae, *Rationalizing Capitalist Democracy*, p. 157.
9 Ghamari-Tabrizi, 'Cognitive and Perceptual Training in the Cold War Man-Machine System', pp. 284f.

Chapter 2 Game

1 See the standard work by Gebhard Kirchgässner, *Homo Oeconomicus: The Economic Model of Behaviour and Its Applications in Economics and Other Social Sciences*. Fascinating insights into literary fantasy are provided by Laurenz Volkmann, *Homo Oeconomicus: Studien zur*

Modellierung eines neuen Menschenbildes in der englischen Literatur vom Mittelalter bis zum 18. Jahrhundert. The literature is vast; of central significance for the post-war revolution are Michel Foucault's lectures of 21 and 28 March 1979, contained in *The Birth of Biopolitics: Lectures at the Collège de France, 1978–79.* S.M. Amadae deals in detail with the transformation through rational choice and game theory in *Rationalizing Capitalist Democracy.* Philip Mirowski's *Machine Dreams: Economics Becomes a Cyborg Science* describes the transformation of *homo oeconomicus* into an information-processing agent no longer distinguishable from a computer. John B. Davis's masterly two volumes *The Theory of the Individual in Economics: Identity and Value* and *Individuals and Identity in Economics* open up a new perspective and are highly recommended. The last four studies consider the underlying question in this book, namely the extent to which the 'model' makes assumptions about the identity and individuality of *homo sapiens* that in the digital age jeopardize their survival.

2 See Axel Honneth, *Freedom's Right: The Social Foundations of Democratic Life*, pp. 181–91.

3 Lynn A. Stout, 'Taking Conscience Seriously', pp. 158–9. See also Stout's book embellished with many personal anecdotes, *Cultivating Conscience: How Good Laws Make Good People.*

4 Apart from John B. Davis, more recently, for example, Ben Fine, *Social Capital versus Social Theory: Political Economy and Social Science at the Turn of the Millennium*, and Michael J. Sandel, *What Money Can't Buy: The Moral Limits of Markets.*

5 See Milonakis and Fine, *From Economics Imperialism to Freakonomics*, pp. 20–2.

6 Foucault, *The Birth of Biopolitics*, pp. 267ff.

7 John B. Davis, *The Theory of the Individual in Economics*, pp. 81–103.

8 Jean-Pierre Dupuy, 'Cybernetics Is an Antihumanism: Advanced Technologies and the Rebellion against the Human Condition'.

9 Davis, *The Theory of the Individual in Economics*, p. 89.

10 Davis, *The Theory of the Individual in Economics*, p. 89.

11 Milonakis and Fine, *From Economics Imperialism to Freakonomics*, pp. 20f.

12 I thank Evgeny Morozov for his helpful suggestions.
13 Hendrik Hertzberg, 'Comment: Tuesday, and After'.

Chapter 3 Prophecy
1 Mirowski, *Machine Dreams*, p. 505.
2 This tradition remains today in hacker groups and, to some extent, in systems like Wikipedia.
3 Michel Callon, 'What Does It Mean to Say That Economics Is Performative?', p. 322.
4 Vance Packard, *The Hidden Persuaders*, p. 240.
5 Packard, *The Hidden Persuaders*, p. 231.

Chapter 4 Monsters
1 Joseph Stiglitz, *Freefall – America, Free Markets, and the Sinking of the World Economy*, p. 6.
2 George Dyson, 'Conversation: Technology: A Universe of Self-Replicating Code'.
3 Manuel Castells, 'Information Technology and Global Capitalism', p. 56.
4 The most extensive and comprehensive source material can be found online in the documentation of the American Senate hearings: *http://www.hsgac.senate.gov*.
5 I thank Philip Mirowski for allowing me a preview of his book *Never Let a Serious Crisis Go to Waste: How Neoliberalism Survived the Financial Meltdown*.
6 Scott Patterson, *The Quants: How a Small Band of Maths Wizards Took Over Wall Street and Nearly Destroyed It*, pp. 263–4.
7 Patterson, *The Quants*, pp. 264–5.

Chapter 5 Screenplay
1 Patterson, *The Quants*, p. 263.
2 Patterson, *The Quants*, p. 263.
3 Zaloom, *Out of the Pits*, p. 99.
4 Patterson, *The Quants*, pp. 53–4.
5 Patterson, *The Quants*, p. 162.
6 Satyajit Das, *Extreme Money: The Masters of the Universe and the Cult of Risk*, pp. 258–60.

7 Zaloom, *Out of the Pits*, p. 109.
8 Zaloom, *Out of the Pits*, p. 132.
9 Michael Lewis, *The Big Short: Inside the Doomsday Machine*, p. 251.
10 James Gleick, *The Information: A History, a Theory, a Flood*, p. 249.
11 Susan Sontag, 'The Imagination of Disaster', p. 221.
12 Steven Belletto, *No Accident, Comrade: Chance and Design in Cold War American Narratives*, p. 104.

Chapter 6 Reason
1 Kaplan, *The Wizards of Armageddon*, p. 66.
2 The fascinating story is told in Mirowski's *Machine Dreams*.
3 Anthony Downs quoted in Amadae, *Rationalizing Capitalist Democracy*, p. 5.
4 Sylvia Nasar, *A Beautiful Mind*, p. 108.
5 Nasar, *A Beautiful Mind*, p. 109.
6 Kaplan, *The Wizards of Armageddon*, pp. 66–7.
7 Philip Mirowski, 'A Revisionist's View of the History of Economic Thought: Interview with Philip Mirowski', pp. 92–3.
8 Mirowski, *Machine Dreams*, pp. 338–9.
9 Douglas Rushkoff, *Life Inc.: How the World Became a Corporation and How to Take It Back*, p. 151.
10 Hal R. Varian, 'Economic Scene: You've Seen the Movie. Now Just Exactly What Was It That John Nash Had on His Beautiful Mind?'
11 Ariel Rubinstein, *Economic Fables*, p. 129.
12 Philip K. Dick, *Solar Lottery*, p. 1.
13 Fred Kaplan, *1959: The Year Everything Changed*, p. 108.
14 John von Neumann turned first to the military with his *Theory of Games and Economic Behavior* because the overchallenged economists showed too little enthusiasm for it.
15 Mirowski, *Machine Dreams*, p. 330.
16 Mirowski, *Machine Dreams*, p. 425.
17 See p. 111.
18 Dick, *Solar Lottery*, p. 18.
19 Rubinstein, *Economic Fables*, p. 137.
20 Rubinstein, *Economic Fables*, p. 32.
21 David Mendell, 'Obama Would Consider Missile Strikes on Iran'.

Like countless other American politicians and commentators, Obama saw the attacks of 11 September as the end of the strategic rationality of game theory, in which neither side would risk suicide.

22 Belletto, *No Accident, Comrade*, p. 102.

Chapter 7 Social physics

1 Joseph Pimbley, 'Physicists in Finance', p. 44.
2 Pimbley, 'Physicists in Finance', p. 46.
3 David Kaiser, 'The Postwar Suburbanization of American Physics'.
4 In 1953, for example, 'each physicist received an average [federal support] of $11,000, while the corresponding figure for a chemist was $1,900; the average biologist received $4,900, and in geology and mathematics the amounts were $1,800 and $1,700 respectively.' Philip Mirowski, *Science-Mart: Privatizing American Science*, p. 113.
5 Paul N. Edwards, *The Closed World: Computers and the Politics of Discourse in Cold War America*.
6 Kaplan, *1959*, p. 65.
7 Jennifer S. Light, *From Warfare to Welfare: Defense Intellectuals and Urban Problems in Cold War America*, pp. 3f.
8 Kaplan, *The Wizards of Armageddon*, p. 223.
9 *http://www.sciencenews.org/sn_arc99/11_27_99/bob1.htm*.
10 Patterson, *The Quants*, p. 38.
11 Patterson, *The Quants*, p. 38.
12 Das, *Extreme Money*, pp. 140–1.
13 David Colander et al., 'The Financial Crisis and the Systemic Failure of the Economics Profession', p. 253.
14 Mirowski, *Machine Dreams*, pp. 14–15.
15 Philips, 'The Monster That Ate Wall Street'.

Chapter 8 Massacre

1 Zaloom, *Out of the Pits*, p. 132.
2 Zaloom, *Out of the Pits*, p. 155.
3 Katrin Knorr Cetina, 'How Are Global Markets Global? The Architecture of a Flow World', pp. 42–3.
4 Jean-Pierre Hassoun, 'Emotions on the Trading Floor: Social and Symbolic Expressions', p. 108.

5 Variants of game theory make different assumptions about the individual. Non-cooperative games played once – the origin of the theory – reduce the complexity of human agents. More recent approaches – games that are endlessly repeated and allow cooperation ‒ do human agents more justice. It is important to note that these are not the versions used in financial models, which exclusively employ non-cooperative and one-time games. See also Davis, *Individuals and Identity in Economics*, ch. 5.2.
6 Rubinstein, *Economic Fables*, p. 125.
7 Philip Mirowski and Edward Nok-Khah, 'Markets Made Flesh: Performativity, and a Problem in Science Studies, Augmented with Consideration of the FCC Auctions', p. 196.
8 Sylvia Nasar, *A Beautiful Mind*, p. 357. For the story of the Nobel Prize and Nash, see Mirowski, *Machine Dreams*, p. 333.
9 Ken Binmore, *Game Theory and the Social Contract: Volume 1: Playing Fair*, p. 24.

Chapter 9 Blood circulation

1 Gail Turley Houston, *From Dickens to Dracula: Gothic, Economics, and Victorian Fiction*.
2 Houston, *From Dickens to Dracula*, pp. 74, 118.
3 Houston, *From Dickens to Dracula*, p. 119.
4 Houston, *From Dickens to Dracula*, pp. 112–13.
5 Mirowski, *Machine Dreams*, p. 9.
6 Callon, 'What Does It Mean to Say That Economics Is Performative?'
7 Hugh Kenner, *The Counterfeiters: An Historical Comedy*, p. 41.
8 Introduction: Machel Callon, 'The Embeddedness of Economic Markets in Economics', p. 51.
9 Philip Bobbitrt, *Terror and Consent: The Wars for the Twenty-First Century*, p. 87.
10 Dyson, 'Conversation: Technology: A Universe of Self-Replicating Code'.
11 Steven Levy, 'Secret of Googlenomics: Data-Fueled Recipe Brews Profitability'.
12 Marcel Mauss, *The Gift: The Form and Reason for Exchange in Archaic Societies*, p. 98.

13 Paul De Grauwe, 'Economics Is in Crisis: It Is Time for a Profound Revamp'.
14 Luc E. Leruth and Pierre J. Nicolas, *The Crisis and Miss Emily's Perceptions*, p. 2.
15 Leruth and Nicolas, *The Crisis and Miss Emily's Perceptions*, p. 2.

Chapter 10 Nervous system
1 Mary W. Shelley, *Frankenstein*, p. 11.
2 Dyson, *Darwin among the Machines*, p. 140.
3 Laura Otis, *Networking: Communicating with Bodies and Machines in the Nineteenth Century*, p. 121.
4 Otis, *Networking*, p. 10.
5 Otis, *Networking*, p. 228.
6 Bram Stoker, *Dracula*, p. 70.

Chapter 11 Android
1 Simon Schaffer, 'Enlightened Automata', p. 136.
2 Schaffer, 'Enlightened Automata', p. 138.
3 Michel Foucault, *Discipline and Punish*, p. 136. Quoted in Schaffer, 'Enlightened Automota', p. 140.
4 Schaffer, 'Enlightened Automota', pp. 143–4.
5 Minsoo Kang, *Sublime Dreams of Living Machines: The Automaton in the European Imagination*, p. 111.
6 Kang, *Sublime Dreams of Living Machines*, p. 111.
7 Thomas Hobbes, *Leviathan*, p. 7.
8 Foucault, *Discipline and Punish*, p. 136. Quoted in Schaffer, 'Enlightened Automota', p. 140.
9 Schaffer, 'Enlightened Automata', pp. 139–48.
10 Margaret Schabas, *The Natural Origins of Economics*, p. 47.
11 Nancy Cartwright, *The Dappled World: A Study of the Boundaries of Science*, p. 1.
12 Schaffer, 'Enlightened Automata', p. 142.
13 Kenner, *The Counterfeiters*, p. 40.
14 Schaffer, 'Enlightened Automata', p. 144.
15 Schaffer, 'Enlightened Automata', p. 138.
16 Schaffer, 'Enlightened Automata', p. 138.

17 Mayr, *Authority, Liberty, and Automatic Machinery in Early Modern Europe*, p. 84.
18 Schaffer, 'Enlightened Automata', p. 134.

Chapter 12 Brain

1 See Langdon Winner, *The Whale and the Reactor: A Search for Limits in an Age of High Technology* ('Do Artifacts Have Politics?'), which also cites a series of sometimes controversial examples.
2 Mayr, *Authority, Liberty, and Automatic Machinery in Early Modern Europe*, p. 197.
3 Herbert Sussman, *Victorian Technology: Invention, Innovation, and the Rise of the Machine*, p. 50.
4 Kenner, *The Counterfeiters*, p. 37.
5 Kenner, *The Counterfeiters*, pp. 37 and 108.
6 Mirowski, *Machine Dreams*, pp. 34–5.
7 Alison Winter, *Mesmerized: Powers of Mind in Victorian Britain*, p. 285.
8 Winter, *Mesmerized*, p. 4.
9 Winter, *Mesmerized*, p. 57.
10 Winter, *Mesmerized*, p. 289.
11 Jackson Lears, *Fables of Abundance: A Cultural History of Advertising in America*, p. 224.
12 Kenner, *The Counterfeiters*, p. 114.
13 Kenner, *The Counterfeiters*, p. 40.

Chapter 13 Genes

1 See Bruce Clarke and Linda Dalrymple Henderson, eds, *From Energy to Information: Representation in Science and Technology, Art, and Literature*.
2 See Mirowski, *Machine Dreams*, pp. 235–6.
3 Stefan Klein, *Der Sinn des Gebens*, pos. 354.
4 Eric Michael Johnson, 'Survival of the Kindest'.
5 Richard Dawkins, *The Selfish Gene*, p. 52.

Chapter 14 Kinship

1 See Nasar, *A Beautiful Mind*, p. 110.

2 Binmore, *Game Theory and the Social Contract: Volume 1: Playing Fair*, p. 231.

3 Daniel C. Dennett, *Darwin's Dangerous Idea: Evolution and the Meanings of Life*, p. 59.

4 John Maynard Smith, 'Genes, Memes, & Minds'.

5 Binmore, *Game Theory and the Social Contract: Volume 1: Playing Fair*, p. 231.

6 Stephen Jay Gould, 'Darwinian Fundamentalism'.

7 Das, *Extreme Money*, p. 424.

Chapter 15 Schizophrenia

1 Manuel Castells, *The Rise of the Network Society: The Information Age: Economy, Society, and Culture, Volume 1*, p. 3.

2 Ken Binmore, *Game Theory and the Social Contract: Volume 2: Just Playing*, pp. 205–6.

3 Nir Vulkan, 'Economic Implications of Agent Technology and E-Commerce', p. 5.

4 Vulkan, 'Economic Implications of Agent Technology and E-Commerce', pp. 4–5.

Chapter 16 Lightning

1 Jerry Adler, 'Raging Bulls: How Wall Street Got Addicted to Light-Speed Trading'.

2 Scott Patterson, *Dark Pools: The Rise of AI Trading Machines and the Looming Threat to Wall Street*, p. 46.

3 Dyson, 'Conversation: Technology: A Universe of Self-Replicating Code'.

4 Patterson, *Dark Pools*, p. 62.

5 Patterson, *Dark Pools*, p. 315.

6 Patterson, *Dark Pools*, p. 6.

7 Patterson, *Dark Pools*, p. 40.

8 Neil Johnson et al., 'Financial Black Swans Driven by Ultrafast Machine Ecology', p. 1.

9 'Conversation: Technology: A Universe of Self-Replicating Code'.

10 Dave Cliff, 'Man Versus Machine, Part One'.

11 Patterson, *Dark Pools*, p. 307.

12 Stephen T. Asma, *On Monsters: An Unnatural History of Our Worst Fears*, p. 168.
13 Geoffrey M. Hodgson, *From Pleasure Machines to Moral Communities: An Evolutionary Economics without Homo Economicus*.
14 Gerd Gigerenzer et al., *Simple Heuristics That Make Us Smart*.

Chapter 17 Politics
1 Nicholas Negroponte, *Being Digital*, p. 7.
2 Zygmunt Bauman, *Wasted Lives: Modernity and Outcasts*, p. 132.
3 Lewis, *The Big Short*, p. 14.
4 John Perry Barlow, 'A Declaration of the Independence of Cyberspace'.
5 Matthew Lynn, 'Greek Crisis Isn't Economics, It's Game Theory'.
6 Brian D. Singer, 'Positioning Portfolios for Turbulent Times', p. 48.
7 Singer, 'Positioning Portfolios for Turbulent Times', p. 50.
8 Singer, 'Positioning Portfolios for Turbulent Times', p. 54.

Chapter 18 Matrix
1 Knorr Cetina, 'How Are Global Markets Global? The Architecture of a Flow World', p. 47.
2 Knorr Cetina, 'How Are Global Markets Global? The Architecture of a Flow World', p. 48.
3 Knorr Cetina, 'How Are Global Markets Global? The Architecture of a Flow World', p. 47.
4 Das, *Extreme Money*, p. 229.

Chapter 19 Mind's eye
1 Mark Buchanan, 'The Science of Subtle Signals', p. 8.
2 Buchanan, 'The Science of Subtle Signals', p. 8.
3 Andy Greenberg, 'Mining Human Behavior at MIT'.
4 Noah Shachtman, 'Exclusive: Darpa Director Bolts Pentagon for Google'.
5 Bobbitt, *Terror and Consent*, p. 87.
6 Robert T. Collins et al., 'A System for Video Surveillance and Monitoring'.

7 James Pita et al., 'Using Game Theory for Los Angeles Airport Security'.

Chapter 20 Coordination

1 Thomas Frank, *One Market under God: Extreme Capitalism, Market Populism and the End of Economic Democracy*, p. 55.
2 Frank, *One Market under God*.
3 Bobbitt, *Terror and Consent*, p. 90.
4 Mirowski, *Machine Dreams*, p. 505.
5 Bobbitt, *Terror and Consent*, p. 87.
6 Philip Bobbitt, 'Preface', p. ix.
7 Bobbitt, *Terror and Consent*, p. 390.
8 Bobbitt, *Terror and Consent*, p. 385.
9 Bobbitt, *Terror and Consent*, p. 390.

Chapter 21 Big data

1 James Manyika et al., 'Big Data: The Next Frontier for Innovation, Competition and Productivity'.
2 John Markoff, 'Government Aims to Build a "Data Eye in the Sky"'.
3 Nicholas A. Christakis, 'Conversation: Culture: A New Kind of Social Science for the 21st Century'.
4 Dirk Helbing, 'Conversation: Technology: A New Kind of Socio-Inspired Technology'.
5 Nate Silver, *The Signal and the Noise: Why So Many Predictions Fail – But Some Don't*, p. 218.
6 Silver, *The Signal and the Noise*, p. 197.
7 Silver, *The Signal and the Noise*, p. 11.
8 Silver, *The Signal and the Noise*, pp. 22–3.

Chapter 22 Subjugation

1 Ellen Ullman, *Close to the Machine: Technophilia and Its Discontents*, p. 188.
2 Ullman, *Close to the Machine*, p. 89.
3 Milonakis and Fine, *From Economics Imperialism to Freakonomics*, p. 21.
4 Milonakis and Fine, *From Economics Imperialism to Freakonomics*, p. 19.

5 Matt McGee, 'Google's Schmidt: "Next Great Stage" of Search Is Autonomous, Personal'.
6 Rebecca Greenfield, 'The Google Maps of the Future Sounds Useful but Creepy'.
7 Castells, *The Rise of the Network Society*, p. 13.

Chapter 23 The secret

1 Barbara Ehrenreich, *Bright-Sided: How the Relentless Promotion of Positive Thinking Has Undermined America*, p. 61.
2 Ehrenreich, *Bright-Sided*, p. 71.
3 Isaac Newton, *Optics*, p. 541.
4 Ronald Reagan, 'Address at Moscow State University' (31 May 1988).
5 Jeremy Rifkin, *The Age of Access: How the Shift from Ownership to Access is Transforming Modern Life*, p. 37.
6 Ronald Reagan, 'Frontiers of Progress' (2 May 1961).

Chapter 24 Success

1 George Gilder, 'The Soul of Silicon'.
2 Gilder, 'The Soul of Silicon'.
3 George Gilder, 'Happy Birthday Wired'.
4 Kevin Kelly, *New Rules for the New Economy: 10 Radical Strategies for a Connected World*, p. 2.

Chapter 25 Alchemists

1 Spencer R. Weart, *The Rise of Nuclear Fear*, p. 3.
2 Mark Morrisson, *Modern Alchemy: Occultism and the Emergence of Atomic Theory*, p. 12.
3 Morrisson, *Modern Alchemy*, pp. 163–4.
4 Morrisson, *Modern Alchemy*, p. 144.
5 Frederick Soddy, *Wealth, Virtual Wealth and Debt*.
6 George Gilder, *Wealth and Poverty*, p. 63.
7 Kevin Phillips, *Bad Money: Reckless Finance, Failed Politics, and the Global Crisis of American Capitalism*, p. xxiv.

Chapter 26 Transmutation of the soul

1 Frank, *One Market under God*, p. 57.

2 Kevin Kelly, *Out of Control: The New Biology of Machines, Social Systems, and the Economic World*, p. 85.
3 Kelly, *Out of Control*, p. 188.
4 Stiglitz, *Freefall*, p. 14.
5 Mark Gilbert, *Complicit: How Greed and Collusion Made the Credit Crisis Unstoppable*, p. 36.
6 All of the examples are taken from Lynn Thorndike's encyclopaedia *A History of Magic and Experimental Science*.
7 Theodore Roszak, *The Cult of Information: A Neo-Luddite Treatise on High-Tech, Artificial Intelligence, and the True Art of Thinking*.
8 Frank, *One Market under God*, pp. 10–11.
9 Mircea Eliade, *The Forge and the Crucible*, pp. 160–8.
10 Tara Nummedal, *Alchemy and Authority in the Holy Roman Empire*, pp. 44–5.
11 Hans Christoph Binswanger, *Money and Magic: A Critique of the Modern Economy in the Light of Goethe's Faust*.
12 Mirowski, *Machine Dreams*, p. 515.

Chapter 27 Death dating

1 Edward Bernays, *Propaganda*, pp. 37–8.
2 Giles Slade, *Made to Break: Technology and Obsolescence in America*, p. 73.
3 Vance Packard, *The Waste Makers*, p. 60.
4 Slade, *Made to Break*, p. 89.
5 Slade, *Made to Break*, p. 43.
6 Slade, *Made to Break*, p. 32.
7 Eli Pariser, *The Filter Bubble: What the Internet Is Hiding from You*, p. 98.
8 Pariser, *The Filter Bubble*, p. 121. See also the review by Evgeny Morozov in *The New York Times*, 'Your Own Facts', which explicitly points out that the book lacks a working definition of serendipity.
9 Neil Postman, *Amusing Ourselves to Death: Public Discourse in the Age of Show Business*.
10 Reid Hoffman and Ben Casnocha, *The Start-Up of You: Adapt to the Future, Invest in Yourself, and Transform Your Career*, p. 35.
11 Robert Cohen, *Freedom's Orator: Mario Savio and the Radical Legacy of the 1960s*, p. 190.

12 Clark Kerr, *The Uses of the University*, p. 93.
13 Hoffman and Casnocha, *The Start-Up of You*, p. 38.
14 Hoffman and Casnocha, *The Start-Up of You*, pp. 50–1.
15 Hoffman and Casnocha, *The Start-Up of You*, p. 186.
16 Hoffman and Casnocha, *The Start-Up of You*, p. 189.
17 Hoffman and Casnocha, *The Start-Up of You*, pp. 189–90.

Chapter 28 Re-engineering

 1 Earl Shorris, *A Nation of Salesmen: The Tyranny of the Market and the Subversion of Culture*, pos. 1749.
 2 Danah Boyd quoted in Quentin Hardy, 'Rethinking Privacy in an Era of Big Data'.
 3 Duncan J. Watts, *Six Degrees: The Science of a Connected Age*, p. 246.
 4 Quentin Hardy, 'How Big Data Gets Real'.
 5 Quentin Hardy, 'Big Data for the Rest of Us, in One Start-Up'.
 6 Shorris, *A Nation of Salesmen*, pos. 1796.
 7 George Gilder, *Microcosm: The Quantum Revolution in Economics and Technology*, p. 21.
 8 Hardy, 'Rethinking Privacy in an Era of Big Data'.
 9 Hoffman and Casnocha, *The Start-Up of You*, p. 22.
10 Hardy, 'Rethinking Privacy in an Era of Big Data'.
11 Sigfried Giedion, *Mechanization Takes Command: A Contribution to Anonymous History*.
12 L.R. Smith, 'We Build a Plant to Run without Men', *The Magazine of Business*, February 1929.
13 Kenner, *The Counterfeiters*, p. 25.
14 Shoshana Zuboff, *In the Age of the Smart Machine: The Future of Work and Power*.

Chapter 29 You

 1 Elizabeth Charnock, *E-Habits: What You Must Do To Optimize Your Professional Digital Presence*, p. 6.
 2 Charnock, *E-Habits*, p. 6.
 3 Charnock, *E-Habits*, p. 23.
 4 Charnock, *E-Habits*, p. 7.
 5 Charnock, *E-Habits*, pp. 4 and 3.
 6 Charnock, *E-Habits*, pp. 6–7.

7 Charnock, *E-Habits*, p. 16.
8 Charnock, *E-Habits*, p. 21.
9 Charnock, *E-Habits*, p. 6.

Chapter 30 Mass delusions
1 Peter H. Diamandis and Steven Kotler, *Abundance: The Future Is Better Than You Think*, p. 9.
2 Joseph A. Tainter, *The Collapse of Complex Societies*, p. 111.
3 Thomas L. Friedman, 'Time of the Turtles'.
4 Friedman, 'Time of the Turtles'.
5 Emanuel Derman, *Models. Behaving. Badly.: Why Confusing Illusion with Reality Can Lead to Disaster, on Wall Street and in Life*, p. 192.
6 Frank, *One Market under God*, p. 157.
7 Gilder, 'The Soul of Silicon'.
8 Diamandis and Kotler, *Abundance*, p. 13.
9 Gilder, *Microcosm*, p. 21.
10 Michael Lewis, *Boomerang*, p. 197.
11 Lewis, *Boomerang*, p. 199.
12 Castells, *The Rise of the Network Society*.
13 Tyler Cowen, *The Age of the Infovore: Succeeding in the Information Economy*, p. 13.

Chapter 31 Ego
1 Kenner, *The Counterfeiters*, p. 171.
2 Gabe Zichermann, 'Rethinking Elections with Gamification'.
3 Dyson, 'Conversation: Technology: A Universe of Self-Replicating Code'.
4 Mark Buchanan, 'This Economy Does Not Compute'.
5 Kenner, *The Counterfeiters*, p. 172.
6 Davis, *Individuals and Identity in Economics*, p. 216.
7 Evgeny Morozov, personal information.
8 Paul Valéry, *Monsieur Teste*, p. 10.
9 Valéry, *Monsieur Teste*, p. 6.

Appendix
1 W. Brian Arthur, 'Designing Economic Agents That Act Like Human Agents: A Behavioral Approach to Bounded Rationality'.

2 Dhananjay Gode and Shyam Sunder, 'Allocative Efficiency of Markets with Zero-Intelligence Traders: Markets as a Partial Substitute for Individual Rationality'.
3 Dave Cliff and Janet Bruten, 'Animat Market-Trading Interactions as Collective Social Adaptive Behavior', p. 393.
4 Cliff and Bruten, 'Animat Market-Trading Interactions as Collective Social Adaptive Behavior', p. 393.
5 Patterson, *Dark Pools*, p. 28.
6 Patterson, *Dark Pools*, p. 29.

REFERENCES

Adler, Jerry, 'Raging Bulls: How Wall Street Got Addicted to Light-Speed Trading', *Wired*, September 2012, accessed on *http://www.wired.com/2012/08/ff_wallstreet_trading/all/*

Amadae, S.M., *Rationalizing Capitalist Democracy: The Cold War Origins of Rational Choice Liberalism* (Chicago: University of Chicago Press, 2003)

Arthur, W. Brian, 'Designing Economic Agents That Act Like Human Agents: A Behavioral Approach to Bounded Rationality', *The American Economic Review*, Vol. 81, No. 2 (1991), 353–9

Asma, Stephen T., *On Monsters: An Unnatural History of Our Worst Fears* (New York: Oxford University Press, 2009)

Barlow, John Perry, 'A Declaration of the Independence of Cyberspace', accessed on *https://projects.eff.org/~barlow/Declaration-Final.html*

Bauman, Zygmunt, *Wasted Lives: Modernity and Its Outcasts* (Cambridge: Polity, 2004)

Belletto, Steven, *No Accident, Comrade: Chance and Design in Cold War American Narratives* (New York: Oxford University Press, 2012)

Berg, Nathan and Gerd Gigerenzer, 'As-If-Behavioural Economics: Neoclassical Economics in Disguise?', *History of Economic Ideas*, Vol. XVIII, No 1 (2010), 133–66

Bernays, Edward, *Propaganda* (Brooklyn, NY: Ig Publications, 2005)

Binmore, Ken, *Game Theory and the Social Contract: Volume 1: Playing Fair* (Cambridge, MA: MIT Press, 1994)

Binmore, Ken, *Game Theory and the Social Contract: Volume 2: Just Playing* (Cambridge, MA: MIT Press, 1998)

Binmore, Ken, *Game Theory: A Very Short Introduction* (Oxford: Oxford University Press, 2007)

Binswanger, Hans Christoph, *Money and Magic: A Critique of the Modern Economy in the Light of Goethe's Faust*, trans. J.E. Harrison (Chicago: University of Chicago Press, 1994)

Bobbitt, Philip, *Terror and Consent: The Wars for the Twenty-First Century* (London: Allen Lane, 2008)

Bobbitt, Philip, 'Preface', in Lenn Scott and R. Gerald Hughes, eds, *Intelligence, Crises and Security: Prospects and Retrospects* (Abingdon and New York: Routledge, 2008), pp. ix–x

Buchanan, Mark, 'The Science of Subtle Signals', *strategy + business*, Issue 48 (2007), accessed on *http://web.media.mit.edu/~sandy/Honest-Signals-sb48_07307.pdf*

Buchanan, Mark, 'This Economy Does Not Compute', *The New York Times*, 1 October 2008, accessed on *http://www.nytimes.com/2008/10/01/opinion/01buchanan.html*

Byrne, Rhonda, *The Secret* (New York: Atria Books, 2006)

Callon, Michel, 'Introduction: The Embeddedness of Economic Markets in Economics', in Michel Callon, ed., *The Laws of the Markets* (Oxford: Blackwell, 1988), pp. 1–58.

Callon, Michel, 'What Does It Mean to Say That Economics Is Performative?', in Donald MacKenzie, Fabian Muniesa and Lucia Siu, eds, *Do Economists Make Markets? On the Performativity of Economics* (Princeton: Princeton University Press, 2008), pp. 311–57

Cartwright, Nancy, *The Dappled World: A Study of the Boundaries of Science* (Cambridge: Cambridge University Press, 1999)

Castells, Manuel, *The Rise of the Network Society: The Information Age: Economy, Society, and Culture, Volume 1* (Malden, MA and Oxford: Blackwell, 1996)

Castells, Manuel, 'Information Technology and Global Capitalism', in Will Hutton and Anthony Giddens, eds, *On the Edge: Living with Global Capitalism* (London: Vintage, 2001), pp. 51–74

Charnock, Elizabeth, *E-Habits: What You Must Do To Optimize Your Professional Digital Presence* (Dubuque, IA and London: McGraw Hill, 2010)

Christakis, Nicholas A., 'Conversation: Culture: A New Kind of Social Science for the 21st Century', *Edge*, 21 August 2012, accessed on *http://edge.org/conversation/a-21st-century-change-to-social-science*

Clarke, Bruce and Linda Dalrymple Henderson, eds, *From Energy to Information: Representation in Science and Technology, Art, and Literature* (Stanford: Stanford University Press, 2002)

Cliff, Dave, 'Man Versus Machine, Part One', interview in *The Trading Mesh*, 1 December 2011, accessed on *http://www.thetradingmesh.com/pg/blog/mike/read/27568*

Cliff, Dave, and Janet Bruten, 'Animat Market-Trading Interactions as Collective Social Adaptive Behavior', in *Adaptive Behavior*, Vol. 7, No. 3–4 (1999), 385–414

Cohen, Robert, *Freedom's Orator: Mario Savio and the Radical Legacy of the 1960s* (New York: Oxford University Press, 2009)

Colander, David, Michael Goldberg, Armin Haas, Katarina Juselius, Alan Kirman, Thomas Lux and Brigitte Sloth, 'The Financial Crisis and the Systemic Failure of the Economics Profession', *Critical Review: A Journal of Politics and Society*, Vol. 21, No. 2–3 (2009), 249–67

Collins, Robert T., Alan J. Lipton, Takeo Kanade, Hironobu Fujiyoshi, David Duggins, Yanghai Tsin, David Tolliver, Nobuyoshi Enomoto, Osamu Hasegawa, Peter Burt and Lambert Wixson, 'A System of Video Surveillance and Monitoring', Robotics Institute, Carnegie Mellon University, 2000, accessed on *https://www.ri.cmu.edu/pub_files/pub2/collins_robert_2000_1/collins_robert_2000_1.pdf*

Cowen, Tyler, *The Age of the Infovore: Succeeding in the Information Economy* (London: Penguin, 2010)

Das, Satyajit, *Extreme Money: The Masters of the Universe and the Cult of Risk* (Harlow: Pearson Financial Times/Prentice Hall, 2011)

Davis, John. B., *The Theory of the Individual in Economics: Identity and Value* (London: Routledge, 2003)

Davis, John. B., *Individuals and Identity in Economics* (Cambridge: Cambridge University Press, 2011)

Dawkins, Richard, *The Selfish Gene*, 30th anniversary edition (New York: Oxford University Press, 2006)

De Grauwe, Paul, 'Economics Is in Crisis: It Is Time for a Profound Revamp', *Financial Times*, 22 July 2009, accessed on *http://www.ft.com/cms/s/0/478de136-762b-11de-9e59-00144feabdc0.html*

Defoe, Daniel, *Robinson Crusoe* (London: Penguin, 2012 [1719])

Dennett, Daniel, *Darwin's Dangerous Idea. Evolution and the Meanings of Life* (London: Allen Lane, 1995)

Derman, Emanuel, *Models. Behaving. Badly.: Why Confusing Illusion with Reality Can Lead to Disaster, on Wall Street and in Life* (Chichester: Wiley, 2011)

Diamandis, Peter H. and Steven Kotler, *Abundance: The Future Is Better Than You Think* (New York: Free Press, 2012)

Dick, Philip K., *Solar Lottery* (London: Legend, 1955)

Diderot, Denis, *Encyclopédie de Diderot et d'Alambert Tome III – A à E* (Paris: Éditions la Bibliothèque Digitale, 2012 [1751–72])

Diderot, Denis, *Encyclopédie de Diderot et d'Alambert Tome III – P à Z* (Paris: Éditions la Bibliothèque Digitale, 2012 [1751–72])

Dupuy, Jean-Pierre, 'Cybernetics Is an Antihumanism: Advanced Technologies and the Rebellion against the Human Condition', 1 September 2011, accessed on *http://www.metanexus.net/essay/h-cybernetics-antihumanism-advanced-technologies-and-rebellion-against-human-condition*

Dyson, George, *Darwin among the Machines* (London: Allen Lane, 1997)

Dyson, George, 'Conversation: Technology: A Universe of Self-Replicating Code', *Edge*, 26 March 2012, accessed on *http://edge.org/conversation/a-universe-of-self-replicating-code*

Edwards, Paul N., *The Closed World: Computers and the Politics of Discourse in Cold War America* (Cambridge, MA: MIT Press, 1997)

Ehrenreich, Barbara, *Bright-Sided: How the Relentless Promotion of Positive Thinking Has Undermined America* (New York: Picador USA, 2009)

Eliade, Mircea, *The Forge and the Crucible* (London: Rider & Company, 1962)

Fine, Ben, *Social Capital versus Social Theory: Political Economy and Social Science at the Turn of the Millennium* (London: Routledge, 2001)

Foucault, Michel, *Discipline and Punish: The Birth of the Prison*, trans. Alan Sheridan (New York: Vintage, 1995 [1975])

Foucault, Michel, *The Birth of Biopolitics: Lectures at the Collège de France,*

1978–79, ed. Michel Senellart, trans. Graham Burchell (Basingstoke and New York: Palgrave Macmillan, 2008)

Frank, Thomas, *One Market under God: Extreme Capitalism, Market Populism and the End of Economic Democracy* (London: Secker & Warburg, 2001)

Friedman, Thomas L., 'Time of the Turtles', *The New York Times*, 18 August 1998, accessed on *http://www.nytimes.com/1998/08/15/opinion/foreign-affairs-time-of-the-turtles.html*

Galison, Peter, 'The Ontology of the Enemy: Norbert Wiener and the Cybernetic Vision', *Critical Inquiry*, Vol. 21, No. 1 (1994), 228–66

Ghamari-Tabrizi, Sharon, 'Cognitive and Perceptual Training in the Cold War Man-Machine System', in Duncan Bell and Joel Isaac, eds, *Uncertain Empire: American History and the Idea of the Cold War* (New York: Oxford University Press, 2012), pp. 267–94

Giedon, Sigfried, *Mechanization Takes Command: A Contribution to Anonymous History* (Minneapolis: University of Minnesota Press, 2014)

Gigerenzer, Gerd, Peter M. Todd and the ABC Research Group, *Simple Heuristics That Make Us Smart* (New York and Oxford: Oxford University Press, 1999)

Gilbert, Mark, *Complicit: How Greed and Collusion Made the Credit Crisis Unstoppable* (New York: Bloomberg Press, 2010)

Gilder, George, *Wealth and Poverty* (New York: Basic Books, 1981)

Gilder, George, *Microcosm: The Quantum Revolution in Economics and Technology* (New York: Free Press, 1989)

Gilder, George, 'Happy Birthday Wired', *Wired*, January 1998, accessed on *http://archive.wired.com/wired/archive/6.01/gilder_pr.html*

Gilder, George, 'The Soul of Silicon', *Forbes*, 6 January 1998, accessed on *http://www.forbes.com/asap/1998/0601/110.html*

Gleick, James, *The Information: A History, a Theory, a Flood* (London: Fourth Estate, 2011)

Gode, Dhananjay and Shyam Sunder, 'Allocative Efficiency of Markets with Zero-Intelligence Traders: Markets as a Partial Substitute for Individual Rationality', *Journal of Political Economy*, Vol. 101, No. 1 (1993), 119–37.

Gordon, Deborah M., 'Twitter in the Ant Nest', *Natural History*, Vol. 119, No. 6 (2011), 10–41

Gould, Stephen Jay, 'Darwinian Fundamentalism', *The New York Review of Books*, 12 June 1997, accessed on *http://www.nybooks.com/articles/archives/1997/jun/12/darwinian-fundamentalism/*

Greenberg, Andy, 'Mining Human Behavior at MIT', *Forbes*, 8 December 2010, accessed on *http://www.forbes.com/forbes/2010/0830/e-gang-mit-sandy-pentland-darpa-sociometers-mining-reality.html*

Greenfield, Rebecca, 'The Google Maps of the Future Sounds Useful but Creepy', *The Wire*, 3 January 2013, accessed on *http://www.thewire.com/technology/2013/01/google-maps-future-sounds-useful-creepy/60542/*

Hardy, Quentin, 'Big Data for the Rest of Us, in One Start-Up', *The New York Times*, 19 March 2012, accessed on *http://bits.blogs.nytimes.com/2012/03/19/all-about-big-data-in-one-startup/*

Hardy, Quentin, 'How Big Data Gets Real', *The New York Times*, 4 June 2012, accessed on *http://bits.blogs.nytimes.com/2012/06/04/how-big-data-gets-real/*

Hardy, Quentin, 'Rethinking Privacy in an Era of Big Data', *The New York Times*, 4 June 2012, accessed on *http://bits.blogs.nytimes.com/2012/06/04/rethinking-privacy-in-an-era-of-big-data/*

Hassoun, Jean-Pierre, 'Emotions on the Trading Floor: Social and Symbolic Expressions', in Karin Knorr Cetina and Alex Preda, eds, *The Sociology of Financial Markets* (Oxford: Oxford University Press, 2005), pp. 102–20

Helbing, Dirk, 'Conversation: Technology: A New Kind of Socio-Inspired Technology', *Edge*, 19 June 2012, accessed on *http://edge.org/conversation/a-new-kind-of-social-inspired-technology*

Hertzberg, Hendrik, 'Comment: Tuesday, and After', *The New Yorker*, 24 September 2001, p. 27

Hobbes, Thomas, *Leviathan*, ed. J.C.A. Gaskin (Oxford: Oxford University Press, 1996 [1651])

Hodgson, Geoffrey M., *From Pleasure Machines to Moral Communities: An Evolutionary Economics without Homo Economicus* (Chicago and London: University of Chicago Press, 2013)

Hoffman, Reid and Ben Casnocha, *The Start-Up of You: Adapt to the Future, Invest in Yourself, and Transform Your Career* (London: Random House Business Books, 2012)

Honneth, Alex, *Freedom's Right: The Social Foundations of Democratic Life*, trans. Joseph Ganahl (Cambridge: Polity Press, 2014)

Houston, Gail Turley, *From Dickens to Dracula: Gothic, Economics, and Victorian Fiction* (Cambridge: Cambridge University Press, 2005)

Huxley, Aldous, *Brave New World* (New York: Harper & Row, 1969 [1932])

Johnson, Eric Michael, 'Survival of the Kindest', *Seed Magazine*, 24 September 2009, accessed on *http://seedmagazine.com/content/article/survival_of_the_kindest/P2/*

Johnson, Neil, Guannan Zhao, Eric Hunsader, Jing Meng, Amith Ravindar, Spencer Carran and Brian Tivnan, 'Financial Black Swans Driven by Ultrafast Machine Ecology', 7 February 2012, accessed on *http://arxiv.org/abs/1202.1448#*

Kahn, Herman, *On Thermonuclear War* (Princeton: Princeton University Press, 1960)

Kaiser, David, 'The Postwar Suburbanization of American Physics', *American Quarterly*, Vol. 56, No. 4 (2004), 851–8

Kang, Minsoo, *Sublime Dreams of Living Machines: The Automaton in the European Imagination* (Cambridge, MA and London: Harvard University Press, 2011)

Kaplan, Fred, *The Wizards of Armageddon* (New York: Simon & Schuster, 1983)

Kaplan, Fred, *1959: The Year Everything Changed* (Hoboken, NJ: Wiley, 2009)

Kelly, Kevin, *Out of Control: The New Biology of Machines, Social Systems, and the Economic World* (Reading, MA: Addison-Wesley, 1994)

Kelly, Kevin, *New Rules for the New Economy: 10 Radical Strategies for a Connected World* (New York: Viking, 1998)

Kenner, Hugh, *The Counterfeiters: An Historical Comedy* (Baltimore: Johns Hopkins University Press, 1985)

Kirchgässner, Gebhard, *Homo Oeconomicus: The Economic Model of Behaviour and Its Applications in Economics and Other Social Sciences* (New York: Springer, 2008)

Klein, Naomi, *No Logo*, 10th anniversary edition (New York: Picador, 2010)

Klein, Stefan, *Survival of the Nicest: How Altruism Made Us Human and Why It Pays to Get Along*, trans. David Dollenmayer (New York: The Experiment, 2014)

Kleist, Heinrich von, 'On the Marionette Theatre', *Animations*, Vol. 6, No. 3 (1972 [1810]), 22–6.

Knorr Cetina, Karin, 'How Are Global Markets Global? The Architecture of a Flow World', in Karin Knorr Cetina and Alex Preda, eds, *The Sociology of Financial Markets* (Oxford. Oxford University Press, 2005), pp. 38–61

Lears, Jackson, *Fables of Abundance: A Cultural History of Advertising in America* (New York: Basic Books, 1994)

Lerurth, Luc E. and Pierre J. Nicolas, *The Crisis and Miss Emily's Perceptions* (Washington, DC: International Monetary Fund, 2010)

Levy, Steven, 'Secret of Googlenomics: Data-Fueled Recipe Brews Profitability', *Wired*, 22 May 2009, accessed on *http://archive.wired. com/culture/culturereviews/magazine/17-06/nep_googlenomics?current Page=all*

Lewis, Michael, *The Big Short: Inside the Doomsday Machine* (London: Penguin, 2011)

Lewis, Michael, *Boomerang* (London: Allen Lane, 2011)

Light, Jennifer S., *From Warfare to Welfare: Defense Intellectuals and Urban Problems in Cold War America* (Baltimore: Johns Hopkins University Press, 2005)

Lynn, Matthew, 'Greek Crisis Isn't Economics, It's Game Theory', MarketWatch, 22 February 2012, accessed on *http://www.market-watch.com/story/greek-crisis-isnt-economics-its-game-theory-2012-02-22*

McGee, Matt, 'Google's Schmidt: "Next Great Stage" Of Search Is Autonomous, Personal', Search Engine Land, 7 September 2010, accessed on *http://searchengineland.com/schmidt-great-stage-search-is-autonomous-personal-50014*

Manyika, James, Michael Chui, Brad Brown, Jacques Bughin, Richard Dobbs, Charles Roxburgh and Angela Hung Byers, 'Big Data: The Next Frontier for Innovation, Competition, and Productivity', McKinsey Global Institute, May 2011, accessed on *http://www.mckinsey.com/ insights/business_technology/big_data_the_next_frontier_for_innovation*

Markoff, John, 'Government Aims to Build a "Data Eye in the Sky"', *The New York Times*, 10 October 2011, accessed on *http://www. nytimes.com/2011/10/11/science/11predict.html?pagewanted=all&modul e=Search&mabReward=relbias%3As&_r=0*

Mauss, Marcel, *The Gift: The Form and Reason for Exchange in Archaic Societies*, trans. W.D. Halls (London: Routledge, 2002 [1923–4])

Mayr, Otto, *Authority, Liberty, and Automatic Machinery in Early Modern Europe* (Baltimore: Johns Hopkins University Press, 1986)

Mendell, David, 'Obama Would Consider Missile Strikes on Iran', *Chicago Tribune*, 25 September 2004, accessed on http://articles.chicagotribune.com/2004-09-25/news/0409250111_1_nuclear-weapons-iran-missile-strikes

Milonakis, Dimitris and Ben Fine, *From Economics Imperialism to Freakonomics: The Shifting Boundaries between Economics and Other Social Sciences* (London: Routledge, 2009)

Mirowski, Philip, *Science-Mart: Privatizing American Science* (Cambridge, MA: Harvard University Press, 2001)

Mirowski, Philip, *Machine Dreams: Economics Becomes a Cyborg Science* (Cambridge: Cambridge University Press, 2002)

Mirowski, Philip, 'A Revisionist's View of the History of Economic Thought: Interview with Philip Mirowski', *Challenge*, Vol. 48, No. 5 (2005), 79–94

Mirowski, Philip, *Never Let a Serious Crisis Go to Waste: How Neoliberalism Survived the Financial Meltdown* (London and New York: Verso, 2013)

Mirowski, Philip and Edward Nok-Khah, 'Markets Made Flesh: Performativity, and a Problem in Science Studies, Augmented with Consideration of the FCC Auctions', in Donald MacKenzie, Fabian Muniesa and Lucia Siu, eds, *Do Economists Make Markets? On the Performativity of Economics* (Princeton: Princeton University Press, 2008), pp. 190–224

Morozov, Evgeny, 'Your Own Facts', *The New York Times*, 10 June 2011, accessed on http://www.nytimes.com/2011/06/12/books/review/book-review-the-filter-bubble-by-eli-pariser.html?pagewanted=all&_r=0

Morrisson, Mark, *Modern Alchemy: Occultism and the Emergence of Atomic Theory* (New York: Oxford University Press, 2007)

Nasar, Sylvia, *A Beautiful Mind* (London: Faber, 1998)

Negroponte, Nicholas, *Being Digital* (New York: Vintage, 2000)

Neumann, John von and Oskar Morgenstern, *Theory of Games and Economic Behavior* (Princeton: Princeton University Press, 1953)

Newton, Isaac, *Optics* (Chicago: Encylopedia Britannica, 1952 [1704])

Nummedal, Tara, *Alchemy and Authority in the Holy Roman Empire* (Chicago and London: University of Chicago Press, 2007)

Orwell, George, *Nineteen Eighty-Four* (London: Penguin, 2013 [1949])

Otis, Laura, *Networking: Communicating with Bodies and Machines in the Nineteenth Century* (Ann Arbor. University of Michigan Press, 2001)

Packard, Vance, *The Waste Makers* (London: Longmans, 1960)

Packard, Vance, *The Hidden Persuaders* (New York: Ig Publishing, 2007)

Pariser, Eli, *The Filter Bubble: What the Internet Is Hiding from You* (New York: Penguin, 2011)

Patterson, Scott, *The Quants: How a Small Band of Maths Wizards Took Over Wall Street and Nearly Destroyed It* (New York and London: Random House, 2010)

Patterson, Scott, *Dark Pools: The Rise of AI Trading Machines and the Looming Threat to Wall Street* (New York and London: Random House, 2012)

Philips, Matthew, 'The Monster that Ate Wall Street', *Newsweek*, 26 September 2008

Phillips, Kevin, *Bad Money: Reckless Finance, Failed Politics, and the Global Crisis of American Capitalism* (New York and London: Penguin, 2009)

Pimbley, Joseph, 'Physicists in Finance', *Physics Today*, January 1997, pp. 42–6

Pita, James, Manish Jain, Fernando Ordoñez, Christopher Portway, Milind Tambe, Craig Western, Praveen Paruchuri and Sarit Kraus, 'Using Game Theory for Los Angeles Airport Security', *AI* Magazine, Spring 2009, 43–57, accessed on *https://www.aaai.org/ojs/index.php/aimagazine/article/viewFile/2173/2067*

Postman, Neil, *Amusing Ourselves to Death: Public Discourse in the Age of Show Business* (London: Heinemann, 1986)

Reagan, Ronald, 'Frontiers of Progress' (2 May 1961), accessed on *http://www.smecc.org/frontiers_of_progress_-_1961_sales_meeting.htm#reagan*

Reagan, Ronald, 'Address at Moscow State University' (31 May 1988), accessed on *http://millercenter.org/president/speeches/speech-3416*

Riesman, David, *The Lonely Crowd: A Study of the Changing American Character* (New Haven: Yale University Press, 1950)

Rifkin, Jeremy, *The Age of Access: How the Shift from Ownership to Access is Transforming Modern Life* (London. Penguin, 2000)

Roszak, Theodore, *The Cult of Information: A Neo-Luddite Treatise on High-Tech, Artificial Intelligence, and the True Art of Thinking* (Berkeley: University of California Press, 1986)

Rubinstein, Ariel, *Economic Fables* (Cambridge: Open Book Publishers, 2012)

Rushkoff, Douglas, *Life Inc.: How the World Became a Corporation and How to Take It Back* (London: Vintage, 2010)

Sandel, Michael J., *What Money Can't Buy: The Moral Limits of Markets* (New York: Farrar, Straus and Giroux, 2012)

Schabas, Margaret, *The Natural Origins of Economics* (Chicago and London: University of Chicago Press, 2005)

Schaffer, Simon, 'Enlightened Automata', in Jon Golinski and Simon Schaffer, eds, *The Sciences in Enlightened Europe* (Chicago and London: University of Chicago Press, 1999), pp. 126–65

Shachtman, Noah, 'Exclusive: Darpa Director Bolts Pentagon for Google', *Wired*, March 2012, accessed on *http://www.wired.com/2012/03/dugan-darpa-google/*

Shelley, Mary W., *Frankenstein, or the Modern Prometheus* (London: Lackington, Hughes, Harding, Mavor & Jones, 1818)

Shorris, Earl, *A Nation of Salesmen: The Tyranny of the Market and the Subversion of Culture* (New York and London: W.W. Norton & Co., 1994)

Silver, Nate, *The Signal and the Noise: Why So Many Predictions Fail – but Some Don't* (New York: Penguin, 2012)

Singer, Brian D., 'Positioning Portfolios for Turbulent Times', June 2012, accessed on *http://www.williamblair.com/~/media/Downloads/Insights/DAS%20Assets/Positioning%20Portfolios%20for%20Turbulent%20Times%20-%20June%202012.pdf*

Slade, Giles, *Made to Break: Technology and Obsolescence in America* (Cambridge, MA: Harvard University Press, 2006)

Smith, John Maynard, 'Genes, Memes, & Minds', *The New York Review of Books*, 30 November 1995, accessed on *http://www.nybooks.com/articles/archives/1995/nov/30/genes-memes-minds/?pagination=false*

Smith, L.R., 'We Build a Plant to Run without Men', *The Magazine of Business*, February 1929

Soddy, Frederick, *The Interpretation of Radium* (London: John Murray, 1909)

Soddy, Frederick, *Wealth, Virtual Wealth and Debt* (New York: Dutton, 1926)

Sontag, Susan, 'The Imagination of Disaster', in *Against Interpretation* (London: Vintage, 1994), pp. 209–25

Stevenson, Robert Louis, *The Strange Case of Dr Jekyll & Mr Hyde* (London: Hand & Eye Editions, 2010 [1886])

Stiglitz, Joseph, *Freefall – America, Free Markets, and the Sinking of the World Economy* (New York: W.W. Norton & Co, 2010)

Stoker, Bram, *Dracula* (London: Penguin Books, 2003 [1897])

Stout, Lynn. A., 'Taking Conscience Seriously', in Paul J. Zak, ed., *Moral Markets: The Critical Role of Values in the Economy* (Princeton: Princeton University Press, 2008), pp. 157–72

Stout, Lynn A., *Cultivating Conscience: How Good Laws Make Good People* (Princeton: Princeton University Press, 2011)

Sussman, Herbert, *Victorian Technology: Invention, Innovation, and the Rise of the Machine* (Santa Barbara: Praeger Publishers, 2009)

Tainter, Joseph A., *The Collapse of Complex Societies* (Cambridge: Cambridge University Press, 1988)

Taleb, Nassim Nicholas, *The Black Swan: The Impact of the Highly Improbable Fragility*, 2nd edition (London: Allen Lane, 2011)

Thorndike, Lynn, *A History of Magic and Experimental Science* (New York: Columbia University Press, 1923ff.)

Ullman, Ellen, *Close to the Machine: Technophilia and Its Discontents* (London: Pushkin Press, 2013)

Valéry, Paul, *Monsieur Teste*, trans. Jackson Matthews (Princeton: Princeton University Press, 1989 [1896])

Varian, Hal R., 'Economic Scene: You've Seen the Movie. Now Just Exactly What Was It That John Nash Had on His Beautiful Mind?', *The New York Times*, 11 April 2002

Volkmann, Laurenz, *Homo Oeconomicus: Studien zur Modellierung eines neuen Menschenbilds in der englischen Literatur vom Mittelalter bis zum 18. Jahrhundert* (Heidelberg: Universitätsverlag Winter, 2003)

Vulkan, Nir, 'Economic Implications of Agent Technology and E-Commerce', July 1998, available at *http://else.econ.ucl.ac.uk/papers/ej4.pdf*

Watts, Duncan J., *Six Degrees: The Science of a Connected Age* (London: Heinemann, 2003)

Weart, Spencer R., *The Rise of Nuclear Fear* (Cambridge, MA and London: Harvard University Press, 2012)

Wells, H.G., *The World Set Free* (London: Macmillan, 1914)

Winner, Langdon, *The Whale and the Reactor: A Search for Limits in an Age of High Technology* (Chicago and London: University of Chicago Press, 1986)

Winter, Alison, *Mesmerized: Powers of Mind in Victorian Britain* (London: University of Chicago Press, 1998)

Zaloom, Caitlin, *Out of the Pits: Traders and Technology from Chicago to London* (Chicago and London: University of Chicago Press, 2006)

Zichermann, Gabe, 'Rethinking Elections with Gamification', *The Huffington Post*, 20 November 2012, accessed on *http://www.huffing tonpost.com/gabe-zichermann/improve-voter-turn-out_b_2127459.html*

Zuboff, Shoshana, *In the Age of the Smart Machine: The Future of Work and Power* (New York: Basic Books, 1988)

INDEX OF NAMES